W9-CZI-820

Hartshorne and Brightman
on God, Process, and Persons

Other titles in the series include

Dewey's Empirical Theory of Knowledge and Reality
John R. Shook

Thinking in the Ruins: Wittgenstein and Santayana on Contingency
Michael P. Hodges and John Lachs

Pragmatic Bioethics
Edited by Glenn McGee

Transforming Experience: John Dewey's Cultural Instrumentalism
Michael Eldridge

Hartshorne
and
Brightman
on God, Process, and Persons

THE CORRESPONDENCE
1922–1945

Edited by

Randall E. Auxier

and

Mark Y. A. Davies

Vanderbilt University Press

Nashville

© 2001 Vanderbilt University Press

05 04 03 02 01   5 4 3 2 1

Library of Congress Cataloging-in-Publication Data
Hartshorne and Brightman on God, process, and persons : the
correspondence, 1922-1945 / edited by Randall E. Auxier and Mark Y. A.
Davies.— 1st ed.
p. cm. — (The Vanderbilt library of American philosophy)
Includes bibliographical references and index.
ISBN 0-8265-1376-X (alk. paper)

1. Hartshorne, Charles, 1897–   —Correspondence. 2. Brightman, Edgar
Sheffield, 1884–1953 —Correspondence. I. Auxier, Randall E., 1961–
II. Davies, Mark Y. A., 1966–   III. Series.
B945.H354 A4 2000
191—dc21   00-010467

Permission to use material from the correspondence between Charles Hartshorne
and Edgar Sheffield Brightman, held in the Brightman Papers Collection, Mugar
Memorial Library, granted by Boston University, as well as by Charles Hartshorne
and by Robert S. Brightman.

Contents

Acknowledgments

This project has occupied us for nearly five years, and during that time we have incurred heavy debts to seemingly numberless people. The story of the correspondence is given in the Introduction, but here we must thank, in particular, Charles Hartshorne, Robert S. Brightman, Walter G. Muelder, Charles I. Richey, Robert Fowler, and Bill Myers for facilitating our research in various ways in Austin and New England. We must also thank the Dulaney-Browne Library of Oklahoma City University and Margaret Goosetray, now retired from the special collections department of the Mugar Memorial Library at Boston University. A number of Prof. Auxier's graduate assistants also did much of the dreaded work of entering the letters into the computer, and they are Staci Gerlitz Ross, Stacy McNeiland, Jeannette Fekke, Douglas M. Coulson, and Eric D. Reiss. Thanks are due also to Travis W. Smith for his help with the index; to the Center for Process Studies, especially Randy Ramal for assistance at several points along the way; to our colleague Toby J. Sarrge for helpful mediation; and particularly to Emily Hartshorne Schwartz for legal and other advice and for her help all along the way. In addition, we would like to thank Charles Backus, former director of Vanderbilt University Press, and Bill Adams, former managing editor of Vanderbilt University Press, for their efforts to bring this book into print.

Introduction

How the Correspondence Came to Be Published

It is worth giving a brief account of how these letters came to be published. Professor Charles Hartshorne, then in his ninety-seventh year, responded in the affirmative to an invitation to come and speak to Auxier's seminar on God and process at Oklahoma City University in the fall of 1993. During his visit he mentioned that he had carried out a long and fruitful correspondence with Edgar Sheffield Brightman. Since both of the editors were interested in Brightman's and Hartshorne's thought, they were intrigued by the possibility of examining the correspondence to see whether it would be of any interest to the wider philosophical community. Inferring that Hartshorne's letters were probably preserved among the Brightman papers at the Mugar Library of Boston University, we wondered whether Brightman's letters still existed. Auxier inquired of Hartshorne whether he had them, and Hartshorne looked but could find none immediately. At that time we abandoned the idea.

But by chance Davies, then a graduate student at Boston University, struck up a conversation about Brightman with Robert Fowler, a retired United Methodist minister, an alumnus of Boston University, and the proprietor of Bob's Books in Portsmouth, New Hampshire. From his own research at Boston University, Fowler knew that Brightman had kept carbon copies of many of his own letters and that they were preserved at the Mugar Library. Through him Davies and Auxier learned that both sides of the correspondence had been preserved.

Davies and Auxier visited the Mugar Library on several occasions and were given permission to make copies of the correspondence. It was determined that it was adequately complete and was indeed of significant philosophical and historical value. At this time Davies and Auxier arranged to meet with both Professor Hartshorne and Robert S. Brightman, the youngest son of E. S. Brightman. All were satisfied that the prospect of editing the correspondence into book form was promising and acceptable.

As work commenced on the project, it also became plain that the correspondence alone did not represent the complete intellectual conversation between the two thinkers. As a result the task of collecting and documenting everything the two thinkers had said about one another's ideas in their many publications began. This forms an important part of the context for understanding their letters. The most important items and exchanges have been included either within the correspondence or as appendices in this book, as well as an edited transcript of an interview Auxier did with Professor Hartshorne at the television station at Oklahoma City University during a 1993 visit, largely because it offers some closure on the discussion and also because many who follow Hartshorne's work may be surprised to learn the extent to which he was still committed to the personalistic ideas that were much more prevalent in his early work than in his middle and later work.

The Critical and Interpretive Essays

At the invitation of Professor Thomas O. Buford, Davies and Auxier presented their critical and interpretive essays (which constitute Appendices 4 and 5 of this book) before the Personalist Discussion Group at the American Philosophical Association's annual Eastern Division meeting in New York City in December 1995. At that time the editing of the correspondence was in midstream, and the key issues were beginning to become clear. The two major philosophical issues discussed in the letters were divided between Auxier and Davies according to the specialties of each, who then summarized, contextualized and interpreted the debate. The appendices presented here are expanded from those presentations, and versions of these essays have also appeared in *Process Studies,* the editors having given their kind permission to reprint them here. However, it became clear in the course of Auxier's investigations that a more complete treatment of the issue of "purpose" in Brightman's philosophy was quite important to a full understanding of the correspondence. Accordingly Auxier's essay "Immediacy and Purpose in Brightman's Philosophy" was prepared for the semiannual Personalism Seminar held at Western Carolina University, June 9–13, 1998, and was also presented before the Society for the Study of Process Philosophy, in Washington, D.C., December 28, 1998, at the Eastern Division meeting of the American Philosophical Association.

It seemed fitting that some effort should be made not only to survey— with the benefit of historical distance—the meaning and philosophical import of this correspondence, but also to resituate the thought of Brightman and Hartshorne in the philosophic present and to orient it toward contemporary readers. It seems clear that process philosophy and theology have an important role to play in near future. Whether personalism as a philosophical perspective has a significant role to play is an open question. That it played an important role in the early and middle twentieth century is beyond question, but its present is admittedly precarious. The three interpretive essays attempt to bring these perspectives together by means of an "effective history," or Nietzsche's term "*Wirkungsgeschichte.*" By holding philosophical fidelity to the present and the future to be the most important kind of fidelity to history itself, one may put history to work without mindlessly or unconsciously distorting it. That is goal of these essays.

The State of the Letters

In the event that at some later date the Hartshorne-Brightman letters come to have greater historical value than would be placed upon them today, some effort should be made to explain briefly how their authenticity was verified and how they have been edited. The correspondence as presented here reflects, for the most part, the state of the file of Hartshorne's originals and Brightman's carbons held by the Mugar Library, as carefully disentangled by Auxier and Davies. Once it had been decided that publication of the letters would be a desirable goal, the entire file was photocopied and taken by Auxier to Austin, Texas, in February 1995 to be examined by Hartshorne. He read the entire file, offered editing suggestions in the margins, and helped to interpret some difficult-to-discern places in the manuscripts. Somewhat later Hartshorne also searched through his own papers for originals of the Brightman letters and carbon copies of his own—he sometimes made carbons and sometimes did not—and he was able to find a few samples of each that he generously donated to the project. Auxier went again to Austin in June 1996 to search for other original letters from Brightman and carbon copies Hartshorne might have kept of his own letters. It was then that Auxier found, among other things, Brightman's letter of July 25, 1935, which was not in the Mugar Library's collection. It is the only handwritten letter by Brightman in the correspondence, which is why Brightman had not retained a carbon copy of it. This completed the correspondence, with the exception of one possible letter by Brightman on August 12, 1937, and perhaps two from 1944. An effort was made to find these letters among Hartshorne's papers, but without success.

The recovered originals and carbons from Hartshorne's papers were helpful as a way of contrasting the file at the Mugar Library with some outside documents. They showed, for example, that Hartshorne had a habit in proofreading of making significant additions and corrections to his original letters, that is, the ones Brightman actually received, both by hand and by reinserting letters into his typewriter. These corrections and changes do not, however, show up on the carbons Hartshorne kept of his own letters to Brightman. Looking at the letters Hartshorne received from Brightman, on the other hand, indicates that Brightman does not seem to have done the same with his originals. Hence it is fortunate that it was the Brightman file that survived mostly intact, for otherwise we would have lost a great number of corrections, amplifications, and second thoughts that Hartshorne placed in the margins of his letters and occasionally on the back or below his own signature. Also Brightman had a habit of annotating Hartshorne's letters to remind himself of how he intended to respond, and these marginal notes—easily distinguished from Hartshorne's marginalia, since the handwriting of the latter is quite identifiable—are also of philosophical interest sometimes. They are indicated as they occur in the editors' notes. Brightman also sometimes noted on Hartshorne's original the date of a letter's arrival and the date it was answered. The surviving originals from Brightman to Hartshorne indicate that Hartshorne was not in the habit of annotating the letters that he received from Brightman. Again it is fortunate that the Brightman file is the one that survived substantially intact.

In presenting these letters to the public, every effort has been made to remain faithful to the most plausible or authoritative interpretation of difficult spots, of which there are not terribly many. In cases where no date was written on the letters, they have been inserted wherever the internal clues in their content suggest they belong. In one case an important letter was misdated but has now been correctly dated and placed in its proper position in the sequence of letters. In general potentially controversial decisions have been indicated in the editors' notes, along with alternatives. In terms of typography, words are underlined where the two philosophers underlined them for emphasis, but titles of books and foreign terms are put in italic type, even when they had been underlined in the letters.

It is not out of place to address briefly here the only other major study of this correspondence that has appeared in print. This was done by Robert A. Gillies under the title "The Brightman-Hartshorne Correspondence, 1934–1944," in *Process Studies*, 17 (Spring 1988): 9–18. This study is quite good, especially regarding the arguments about pantheism between Hartshorne and Brightman, but here a few corrections need to be offered.

A. On page 9 Gillies states that "the correspondence began . . . with a now lost or uncopied note and some articles from Brightman."

There are several problems here. First, Brightman's letter mentioned above has indeed been preserved and is in the same packet of letters in the Mugar Library of Boston University from which Gillies took all his information on the correspondence. He must have overlooked it. The letter is dated September 16, 1934. Second, the correspondence actually began in 1922, although it is sparse and spotty, and consists mostly of short notes and postcards from Hartshorne in which he is trying to arrange a talk by Brightman before the Harvard Philosophical Club. Third, it is not accurate to identify Brightman's sending of his articles as the proper beginning of the correspondence, even with the unimportant notes and postcards set aside. The correspondence began in earnest when Hartshorne had dinner with Brightman in Boston in November 1933. They evidently discussed matters relevant to their recent writings, and, upon returning to Chicago, Hartshorne sent Brightman some offprints of recent articles. Brightman acknowledged receiving these materials in a letter dated December 3, 1933, also in the Mugar Library but overlooked by Gillies. However, this exchange did not begin the written philosophical discussion. Nearly a year later,

Hartshorne sent Brightman more of his recent offprints, and Brightman acknowledged receiving these in the letter of September 16, 1934, which Gillies identifies as "lost or uncopied."

An important point in understanding this correspondence is that through the 1930s Brightman was the well-known philosopher and Hartshorne was unestablished. Brightman had known Hartshorne when the latter was only a graduate student at Harvard, and he tends to adopt the role of teacher in the early years. The burden of proof in argumentation is always upon Hartshorne during these years, which is one reason why, as Gillies rightly notes (9), Hartshorne invariably wrote the longer letters. This is also why it was up to Hartshorne to pique Brightman's interest in the correspondence. Brightman was by no means an unwilling participant in the exchange, and his respect for Hartshorne's ideas is abundantly clear, but it took Hartshorne quite a number of attempts to get the correspondence going in the first place, and when it lapsed somewhat in the years 1935–1938, it took Hartshorne three tries (long letters) to get Brightman interested again.

B. On page 14, Gillies says that the correspondence lapses for "three years," between May 1939 and January 1942.

Aside from the fact that this is not three full years, it is also not the whole story. During that time Brightman and Hartshorne went public with their differences. First, Hartshorne published a criticism of Brightman's view of God in *Man's Vision of God* (New York: Harper and Row, 1941), 73 f. (reprinted below), which draws directly from what he learned in their correspondence. Second, Brightman reviewed this book in the *Journal of Religion,* 22 (January 1942): 96–99 (also reprinted below). Third, in response to this review, Hartshorne wrote to Brightman on January 22, 1942, perhaps only days after the review appeared, answering by the numbers the four major criticisms that the review contained. Gillies misidentifies the book reviewed by Brightman as *Moral Values and the Idea of God* (14), for which he gives no author or publication information. It is clear that he did not look up the review to see to what Hartshorne was alluding in the answering letter of January 22, 1942.

C. On page 11 Gillies quotes a letter from Hartshorne dated January 30, 1938.

This error is not Gillies's but Hartshorne's. Close scrutiny of the correspondence reveals that it is misdated. It should have read 1939 instead. Given the scope of Gillies's study, there was no reason for him to discover this error.

D. At two points Gillies's leaves his readers with the impression that there was some measure of ill will between Hartshorne and Brightman during letters of the 1940s.

He says that their "earnest goodwill" of the 1930s "was not to last" (15) and later that "Brightman is angered" (16). Had he wanted to, Gillies could have made this conflict sound much more intense than he did, especially by quoting some excerpts regarding their heated discussion of pacifism during World War II. Gillies was not sensationalizing the conflict by any means, but it is a bit misleading to use even these less strident words out of their context. Mutual respect and admiration are the prevailing dispositions of the two thinkers throughout the entire correspondence, and it is clear that both are motivated foremost by a philosophical desire to seek the truth. Any stridency of tone in the letters derives clearly from this desire, and not from ill will or personal dislike of any kind. So there is in the correspondence an occasional sense of philosophical frustration from both thinkers, but nothing to indicate a loss of respect or goodwill.

E. On page 18, and in his title, Gillies says that the correspondence ended May 19, 1944.

That is indeed the last of Brightman's *preserved* letters. In a pattern which is by now well established, it appears that Hartshorne answered this letter three times with substantive arguments on postcards to try to get the correspondence started again: May 25, 1944; July 1, 1944; and March 15, 1945. Sometime between August 9, 1944, and March 15, 1945, Brightman sent Hartshorne a critical analysis of Hartshorne's article "The Formal Validity and Real Significance of the Ontological Argument," in *Philosophical Review,* 53 (May 1944): 225–245, but this letter does not survive. Still Hartshorne's response on March 15 has been preserved.

The postcard of March 15, 1945 may point to further missing letters, but Brightman's health was failing at the time, and this was the reason he stopped answering. This still does not finish the correspondence, however, since Hartshorne also sent letters on July 17 and August 20, 1945. These dealt mostly with professional matters and not philosophical issues. That is the end of the letters preserved in Brightman's papers in the Mugar Library. In spite of poor health Brightman wrote and published a great deal during those years and was quite capable of writing letters. Among the many things Brightman published between 1945 and 1953 is his review of Hartshorne's important book *The Divine Relativity* (reprinted here in Appendix 1). But the exchange between Hartshorne and Brightman continued even after Brightman's death. Brightman's magnum opus, *Person and Reality,* appeared posthumously in 1958 and reflects many things Brightman had learned from his correspondence with Hartshorne. Hartshorne promptly wrote an article on the book (reprinted here in Appendix 2). This is the true end of the correspondence.

We should note that if indeed there are more letters, Brightman's half of them may be extant among Hartshorne's massive (and uncataloged) accumulation of personal papers, although a thorough search has not uncovered them. It is likely to be many years before future researchers can conclude that probably there are no more letters. Hence Gillies is overly hasty in his conclusion.

Returning to our editorial decisions regarding this correspondence, we have also tried to assist the reader's understanding of the conversation wherever persons, places, or ideas have been mentioned that are not commonly known to the philosophically trained reader, at least in cases where the information could be uncovered by a reasonable amount of investigation. So, for example, we include a note explaining who Durant Drake was, but not William Ernest Hocking; where Garrett Theological Seminary is but not Harvard University; what Brightman means by the phrase "the Given," but not what is meant by Hegel's notion of "the Absolute." Appendix 4 of this volume clarifies why the phrase "the Given" is sometimes capitalized and sometimes lowercased. Regarding ideas, the three interpretive essays will explain much to readers who are less familiar with the thought of one figure or the other.

We have provided in the editors's notes bibliographical information regarding all published writings mentioned in the correspondence, whenever it was at all clear what was being talked about, and we have made educated guesses where clarity was lacking. There are adequate bibliographies available that cover what both thinkers published. While numerous books and articles have been published that treat the thought of both thinkers, the main secondary sources that will lead the reader to further helpful material are the festschrifts for each. In Brightman's case the most important is the memorial issue of the journal he founded, *Philosophical Forum*, 12 (1954). This publication is also the main source of biographical information about Brightman, since it contains a biographical essay by Jannette E. Newhall, who was for years Brightman's personal secretary and who later, in 1949, joined the faculty of Boston University School of Theology. Her biographical essay contains references to other published biographical materials. Another important bibliographical source for Brightman's writings, along with those of other Boston personalists, is Bogumil Gacka's *Bibliography of American Personalism* (Lublin: Oficyna Wydawnicza "Czas," 1994), 41–57.

Hartshorne probably had more festschrifts dedicated to him than any other philosopher in history. This is partly owing to his importance as a philosopher, partly because of the fact that he had an unusually high number of successful and professionally active students, and partly resulting from his amazingly long teaching career and life. By far the most important of the several festschrifts is *The Philosophy of Charles Hartshorne*, ed. Lewis E. Hahn, which is volume 20 of the Library of Living Philosophers Series (LaSalle, Ill.: Open Court Publishing, 1991) and which contains an extensive bibliography through 1986 (735–765); after that time Dorothy Cooper Hartshorne was unable to maintain the bibliography, and Hartshorne's fairly extensive publication activity between 1986 and his death in October 2000 has not been as well documented. The main sources of biographical information about Hartshorne are the numerous short and long autobiographical writings that have appeared since the 1960s. The reader should consult the autobiographical essay "Some Causes of My Intellectual Growth" (3–45) in the above-named festschrift for something fairly up to date as well as *The Darkness and the Light: A Philosopher Reflects upon His Fortunate Career and Those Who Made It Possible* (Albany: State University of New York Press, 1990) for something more exhaustive.

The editors have taken the liberty of standardizing the forms of dates, spelling, and punctuation in the letters. In a small handful of cases, punctuation has been added to make the sentences in question clearer, but this has been done only when really necessary. They have occasionally corrected grammar and filled out abbreviations, with interpolations being indicated by brackets. The fairly common expressions in French, Latin, and German the two thinkers employ rather freely have not been translated, since these enhance the style of the letters and indicate a vocabulary common to learned people of that generation. In most cases the context makes the meaning clear, and in the few cases where it does not, we have provided the necessary explanations in the notes.

One further matter: Professor Hartshorne specifically requested the inclusion of a disclaimer regarding his own use of gender exclusive language in referring to God and to the human race in general. In these letters Hartshorne does use gender exclusive language, and it would be historically questionable to alter that language now. Nevertheless Professor Hartshorne was in no way philosophically committed to that idiom or to anything it may imply about the gender of God. He did not himself understand why he ever used it, except that everyone did at that time. Further, Professor Hartshorne was committed to the end to the more inclusive idiom regarding both the deity and the human race in general.

The Correspondence

Charles Hartshorne
32 Conant Hall
Harvard University
Cambridge

November 30, 1922

Dear Dr. Brightman,

It was very kind of you to give me some of your scanty time and I didn't sufficiently thank you for it.

I hope you can talk to us (The Philosophical Club) on Friday, Feb. 2, or, if not then, a week later, Feb. 9. If there is a better day than a Friday in the early part of February, please let me know. As I remember it the topic was to be: the Personalist position in epistemology, but it can be what you like, and need not be settled until two weeks before the time. The time itself need not be settled until January, but perhaps we could reach at least an approximation now?

Your Value Bibliography has been of great assistance—value—to me.[1]

I hope you are finding some time for work on your two books![2]

Sincerely,
C. Hartshorne

C. Hartshorne
32 Conant Hall
Harvard University
Cambridge

[no date]

Dear Dr. Brightman,

I seem to be a poor arranger of dates. The fellows suggest that Feb. 9th is the time people may be taking an after-exam holiday. I hate to trouble you again, but hope you will perhaps be glad of another week or so—although I believe you said the last time or implied that "the sooner the better!" Would Feb. 16th be a possible date for you? If not, the 23rd?

Sincerely,
C. Hartshorne.

[no date]

Dear Dr. Brightman,

I meant to write at least to express my sympathy long before now. I felt sorry that your engagement with us should be one more thing you had to think about during your troublous time. I hope of course that you are comfortable now.[3]

I don't know whether to think that you will now be so busy as a result of your lost time that you would be glad not to have us trouble you with an attempt to make new arrangements. But our desire to have you come has not been diminished by the postponement, so it is at your discretion. Thinking you may be so busy that it would require a greater sacrifice than you could afford to make, or than we could ask, still I thought you might have already largely prepared your mind on the subject you proposed, and so <u>would</u> perhaps care to talk on it yet. If so, we should be glad.

The time would be some Thursday or Friday night in the Latter half of March or in April or May—*[quand] vous voulez.*

Sincerely yours,
C. Hartshorne

[postcard]

Cambridge, Mass

March 13, 1923

Dear Prof. Brightman,
    Your news is excellent. We choose the 27th of April, if it remains conven-
ient for you.

    Sincerely,
    C. Hartshorne
    32 Conant Hall
    Harvard Phil. Club

[Brightman contacted Hartshorne and moved his talk to May 7, 1923.]

[postcard]

Cambridge, Mass

April 25, 1923

Dear Prof. Brightman,
    Allan, with whom I conferred, on my problem, mixed his dates. Apparent-
ly the 7th is the week of "Prelims." We thought it was the week before. Did you
not say the 14th was a possibility? It would be very well, because the shouting
even will be over then about the exams.

    Sincerely,
    C. Hartshorne

*[Brightman did give his talk on the personalist position in epistemology to the Har-
vard Philosophical Club, May 14, 1923. Between 1923 and 1925 Hartshorne went
to Germany to do postdoctoral work while Brightman remained in Boston.
Brightman and Hartshorne had some limited contact between 1925 and 1928
while both were in Boston, and they became more familiar. In 1928 Hartshorne
left to take a permanent position at the University of Chicago. Brightman spent*

most of 1930–1931 in Germany and traveling in Europe, during which time he
*wrote two of his most influential books—*The Problem of God *(New York: Abing-*
don, 1930), and The Finding of God *(New York: Abingdon, 1931). In particu-*
lar these books articulate Brightman's view that God is both infinite and finite,
which provides the framework for much of the discussion in the correspondence.
There seems to have been no appreciable contact between the two men until
Hartshorne returned to Boston for a visit in 1933. It is likely that Hartshorne
spoke at a meeting of Brightman's seminar during this visit, since Brightman
refers to it some years later (letter of January 1, 1939). At that time, in 1933,
Hartshorne was working on his first book, The Philosophy and Psychology of
Sensation *(Chicago: University of Chicago Press, 1934). He discussed it at a din-*
ner with Brightman, which led to the true beginning of their correspondence.]

November 26, 1933

Dear Mr. Brightman,

I must thank you for the Bibliography etc., and again for the dinner.

Since you go in so strongly for German bibliography you might be somewhat interested in the enclosed reviews, written 5 years ago, as you note.

We are packing of[f], having had an interesting visit.

Cordially,
Charles Hartshorne

December 3, 1933

Dear Hartshorne,

Many thanks for your letter with the offprint of your valuable review of
Husserl-Heidegger.[4]

I am sorry you g[o]t away without my seeing you again, but I greatly enjoyed the brief contact we had. You sowed seed of some discord and perhaps
promise in my mind when you urged the case of panpsychism. I can see its advantages better than I can see the evidence for it; but you have set me thinking,
which is no small service.

Our small band of American philosophers has met with a real loss in the
passing of Durant Drake,[5] who was perhaps my best friend in the Association,[6]
although I disagreed with most of his characteristic theories. I hardly think his

kind of panpsychism would satisfy you any better than it did me. But he was a real man, a loyal friend, and an earnest exponent of moral idealism in his social thinking. I shall miss him. E. W. Burch of Garrett,[7] the New Testament man, was also a life-long friend of mine. Did you know him? He was quiet, but solid and genuine.

Come again. Faithfully yours,

[Brightman]

September 16, 1934

My Dear Professor Hartshorne,

On my return from vacation I am pleasantly surprised to find your reprint on Ethics and the Assumption of Purely Private Pleasures,[8] and *The New Humanist* containing your "Redefining God."[9] Both articles have interested me very much, but I must confess that the argument in the latter is so compact that I am somewhat baffled. You may, however, be interested to know that in my Lowell Lectures, just published as *Personality and Religion*,[10] I discuss God as "finite-infinite," in harmony, I believe, with your view as far as I can grasp it, but independent of both Hocking and Whitehead.

I am looking forward to reading your new book in the not distant future.[11]

Under separate cover I am sending you a few of my ephemera. Will you be good enough to consider ordering the *Idealismus*[12] for the University Library? It bids fair to be a real event in international philosophy.

Sincerely yours,
[Brightman]

October 18, 1934

Dear Professor Brightman,

Thanks for your note and articles. I have been aware for some time that we are not far apart in theology, since reading *The Problem of God*, in fact. I am not sure just how well I like the concept of the Given in God as you expound it, but I do not at present feel much more than a verbal question between us there.[13] The only thing that seriously worries me about your philosophy, as it used to be at any rate, is the idea that other selves are merely inferred but never given. This is the windowlessness of Leibniz's monads.[14] Literal participation in each other's being is about my strongest belief, though I grant that other human selves are, for practical purposes known in-directly. But there are the low-grade psyches of the bodily cells and also God, and these are, I cannot but think, directly intuited, with appreciable vividness (even human fellows being intuited with some degree of vividness, however slight). Unless souls literally overlap, some cement is needed to bind them to-gether, and if not a self (God, for Leibniz) then personalism is not really made the basic principle.

Of course nothing is given that is not a part of the self, but the question is, are we not parts of each other, members of one another? This would, I grant, be a contradiction if it were not possible to distinguish between specifically dif-ferent senses of part and whole, with a generically common meaning. If I am the whole of which you are only a part then I cannot in just the same sense be the part of which you are the whole. But even Leibniz had the clue to this dif-ference in his theory of perspectives.[15] I see how one could object to the theory. But the immanence of God has to be construed somehow.

Maybe it's mostly verbal. Personalists say that other persons are necessary to my existence. But necessary to my being and part of my being are the same, on my definitions.

Another angle is that such terms as "part of" must be interpreted spiritual-ly or in terms of love, if one really believes deus est caritas. I am not sure that a single philosopher has ever really made that the basis of his system. I intend to have that much originality that I will make all concepts get their meaning from that axiom.

Another aspect is that spiritualism seems to me identical with the acceptance of the principle of relativity or continuity. Materialisms are never really monisms, but always posit an absolute gap somewhere. If we say that the difference in qual-ity between one individual and another is always a matter of degree, hence that all individuals could be regarded as personal in some degree, it simplifies matters at least to say that difference in substance is also only a matter of degree, that the boundaries of individuality are no more absolute than distinctions of kind.

I must order *Idealismus.* Will the English and American contributors write in German or English? I should like to try a hand.

I liked your American Scholar article especially.[16]

Have you happened to see *The New Frontier,* September issue, graced by G. Santayana and Robert Frost and me?[17] (Old Corner Bookstore and Smith and McCance). It is a magazine developing a new brand of socialism, which ap-peals to me.

My favorite among your articles is still the Temporalistic View of God.[18] I wonder if investigation would not show that in India the notion of a timeless absolute was much less central than in medieval thought. This would help to dispel the idea that this notion has universal tradition behind it. Nor could the answer be that the notion is specifically Christian, for as you point out it has no special fitness to express the Christian message.

I feel very much encouraged to find so many protestant theologians converging toward about the same set of ideas. Whitehead does well, it seems to me, to speak of the New Reformation. Only he does not know to what extent it is a *fait accompli*. How do you like Montague's *Belief Unbound*?[19] Except for the title I like it very much. I wish it were more widely read.

The length of this letter suggests an apology. Still I must add one more remark. Your point about the behaviorist's neglect of facts is what I refer to as his dualism. He pretends to deny colors, feelings, images; but since we all experience these facts the practical effect is only the separation of reality into appearance and physical substrate with radical discontinuity of nature between. Synechism gives spiritualism a logic.[20]

Enough laryngeation!
Charles Hartshorne

December 10, 1934

Dear Professor Hartshorne,

Your good letter of October 18 is too long unanswered. Practical problems have piled up so high in my pathway that everything I really want to do is postponed in honor of what I have to do. This morning I'm taking the bull by the horns and reversing the process.

Your worry about my philosophy is the idea that other selves are merely inferred but never given, you say. It is also my worry, a worry such as one experiences when one has a debt far larger than one can possibly pay. I'd like to be able to make sense out of the idea of a literal participation in other selves. But I have not yet been able to do so. Whenever I try, I find myself landed in contradiction, in epistemological chaos, and in unfaithfulness to experience—all of which is hopelessly unenlightening, I know. Let me get at it in another way. It seems to me that there are two fundamental categories which need both to be related to each other. They are the categories of part-whole and of purposer-purposed. It seems to me that your contention about a cement needed to bind souls together has force if the fundamental category is purposer-purposed. I have never been able to perceive logical force in Bosanquet's footnote against a creator of creators.[21] It seems to me that the category of purpose is equally compatible with metaphysical singularism and metaphysical pluralism, provided there are, as I believe, sufficient grounds for accepting epistemological dualism. I do not see that an experience which might be called direct intuition would in any way refute this, for the intuition itself is exclusively a member of me, whereas its object is always problematic and distinct from the conscious experience which refers to it. When God intuits me, I am not a part of him, but he wills that I should be other than himself, yet known by him. May not his immanence be construed as reasonably in his purpose to maintain my otherness as in the theory that I am included within him?

Your statement that "necessary to my being and part of my being are the same" seems to me to surrender the empirical and psychological to the logical too completely. It seems to me too short and easy a way of becoming an absolutist. I make a sharp distinction between my actual self and its causes, just as I make a distinction between a flower and the soil which nourishes it. I cannot say that the flower is the same as the soil or that the soil is part of the flower simply because the soil is necessary to the flower. Particularly if I take, as you and I do, real stock in the idea of love, it seems to me that I have to combine the sharing of purpose with [the] windowlessness of being. My love for another is totally different in kind from any love that I could ever have for a part of myself. Perhaps the word "totally" is to be taken *cum grano salis;* but there is at least an important difference which I am unable to disregard. Although it is true that the beloved is necessary to my being, at least to the achievement of the highest value by me, it is also true that love presupposes otherness as well as relation. It is possible to love only when there are two persons involved who trust each other and their mutual devotion to a common purpose. If there were a point at which the two streams of consciousness were actually confluent, at that point love and trust would be superfluous, if not wholly meaningless. Love would then be changed to self-respect or self-ratification. Suppose I abandon the attempt to define myself in terms of whatever is necessary to being, namely, the entire universe; then I might define myself in terms of whatever my conscious being (my specious present, my datum self) is, has been, and will be or may be, and my basis would then be a combination of the empirical and the logical rather than the abstractly logical alone. Is there any solid objection to this view? Is the *lex continui* sufficiently certain and specific to warrant concrete metaphysical inference?

As you see from my reprint that I sent the other day, the rule of *Idealismus* is "Each in his own tongue." If you are interested in writing for it, as I hope you are, write directly to the editor, Dr. Ernst Harms, Limmatquai 50, Zürich 1, Switzerland.

The New Frontier has eluded me. I must get hold of it.

Montague's *Belief Unbound* I regard as decidedly on the right track. There are some annoying paradoxes, like "that in God which is not God,"[22] and I take exception to his militant anti-prohibitionism. Nevertheless I admire the book as a remarkably sound fruit on an unsound neo-realistic tree.

With best wishes for a pleasant Christmas and happy New Year, and with regret that a minor operation is going to prevent my attending the Association,[23] I remain

Most cordially yours,
[Brightman]

February 10, 1935

Dear Professor Brightman,

I was glad to see a disciple of Hegel taking his effect upon social philosophy seriously. It seems to me that aspect of Hegel is many times more important than all other aspects put together. Even from that point of view I find more help from other approaches, but the fact of vital influence upon social thought to this day is patent.

By the way, did I ask you if you had seen H. C. Simons *Positive Program for Laissez Faire* (U[niversity] of C[hicago] Press, 25 c[ents]).[24] It states the economic side of the present social problem beautifully. Economists seem to agree it is excellent.[25]

Your letter brings out some of the subtle difficulties involved in the problem of relating individuals together in the world, including the Maximum individual.

In part you seem to presuppose the logic of absolute differences even while arguing for a particular application of that logic. To say the self is given but other-selves are not, i.e., absolutely not, is to assert such an absolute difference. You defend this by assuming that its denial would mean that other-selves are given just as much and in the same way as the self. My and Whitehead's position is that the self is given under a limitation, and that other selves are under different limitations, that the difference is relative, not universal. This involves a very complex picture, as complex as physics and physiology and psychology and sociology make necessary. It will be a generation before the view can be profoundly criticized. First it must be grasped. One aspect is that self-love is not so simple as it sounds. The lover is the present self, the beloved is partly potential and imaginatively constructed. No one loves himself completely or as much as he ought. Hence we are told first to love God, since that implies complete love of all his creatures including us. It follows that a point of identity of self with others does not annul love any more than self-identity does. It is in both cases no complete identity. Plurality is real and unity transcending the plurality is real. Relativism is equally incompatible with absolute singularism and absolute pluralism. Immanence can be literal and yet a matter of degree, permitting also of transcendence.[26]

I agree that part-whole is to be subordinated to another category, but purpose[r]-purposed would not be my first choice for that other category. Rather sociality, *sharing of creative experience*. Of course I believe with you in a creator of creators.

As to the distinction between a thing and its causes, I do indeed believe that this distinction is to be explained and not taken as ultimate. The only explanation the wit of man appears to have devised is Whitehead's notion of causality as identical with memory plus the essentially structural character of the unity of consciousness. This means that the cause is a part of its effect via memory construed as real preservation of the past itself into the present. This perhaps makes part-whole more fundamental than cause; but I should rather say it makes directly experienced facts of memory and the aesthetic unity of awareness more fundamental than either. "Part" itself must be defined in terms of aesthetic-social relationships. To say my neighbor is a part of me means that I love him sometimes and to some extent as myself, for I take the language of love to be the language of languages. I find in your account an apparent oscillation between this point of view and another, according to which part has an independent non-agapistic meaning. Of course I also do not love my neighbor as myself, and in so far he is different from me. Nor does God love each of us as himself and only as himself.

I certainly think the notion that self-love is metaphysically and totally different from altruism is a socially harmful one, and therefore am glad you propose it only cum grano salis. It is the great Aristotelian anti-Christian doctrine which has almost ruined Christendom theoretically and practically—not [the] notion of merely distinct "substances" (e.g., "Subject-predicate logic").

If I could get an unambiguous meaning from Hegel I would say his position was mine on this point, but I get no such meaning. But at least I seem to see the impossibility of getting yours unambiguously from him.

I must point out that the other self most completely intuited on the Whiteheadian view is not the human neighbor but the bodily cells or molecules, taken panpsychically. Human neighbors are mostly imagined and inferred, but then so is my own self, very little of which is distinctly intuited at any moment. Degrees of vagueness in intuition are vital to the doctrine. Obviously our difference is partly verbal. And obviously no set of words will be perfect.

Cordially,
Charles Hartshorne

P.S. I think my best statement of Relativism (Theistic Relativism) is still the articles in Sept. and Nov. *New Frontier* (3335 Main St., Buffalo, N.Y.) I mention these because they contain important articles on social philosophy, besides my stuff.

Box 35, Newton Center,
Massachusetts

May 30, 1935

Dear Professor Hartshorne,
Your letter of February 10 has remained much too long unanswered. Circumstances beyond my control have prevented me from keeping up with my

correspondence this semester, but I have finally come to and hope that it is not too late to comment on your letter.

There are three terms which arouse my interest and I should like to comment briefly on each, hoping that you will help me understand them better. They are given, love, and intuition. In your treatment of the given, it seems to me that you and Whitehead are more Hegelian than I am by a good deal. I regard givenness as a unique, irreducible, brute fact. I think that there is an absolute difference (as regards givenness-to-me) between what is given as myself (namely, the datum-*Gestalt* of the specious present) and all other selves. The fact that my own past and future have to be inferred does not place them in the same category as other selves, for they are inferred as what has been or will be given to a self which experiences itself as the same as the self of the specious present. No sooner have you started treating the given than you begin to talk about love. Now I cannot see exactly what you mean by love. Is it *amor intellectualis dei,* or love of persons, or mere curiosity? The third concept which troubles me is intuition. Probably this is too large a question to do much with in correspondence, but I wonder whether any objects other than our own conscious experience can be asserted to be on the ground of intuition alone. You say that bodily cells or molecules are the other self most completely intuited on the Whiteheadian view, while human neighbors are mostly imagined or inferred. But must not the bodily cells also be imagined and inferred? If everyone intuited them as Whitehead thinks, why would not everyone accept his theory? Can I strictly intuit anything except the content of the specious present, which then becomes a basis for imagination and inference about the world?

You are doing magnificent work and I expect to learn much from you.

Sincerely yours,
[Brightman]

July 19, 1935

Dear Professor Brightman,

I too have scarcely been able to correspond lately. By the way, I heard you were not very well. This reminded me of how much you have accomplished in recent years and made me wonder if you hadn't worked a bit too hard. I certainly did this last winter, and intend to have more sense in the future.

I can't pretend to give much of an answer in a letter to your three questions concerning my notions of the given, love, and intuition, but here goes! "Love" is more general than any of the kinds you mention. It means "feeling of feeling," direct participation in other-feeling, sharing (literal) of feeling by two or more feelers. We have a Hindu student here, an Indian monk, very religious and a keen metaphysician. He said his basic concept was love. And what is that? I asked. "Consciousness of consciousness, or feeling of feeling," was his reply. So East and West can meet. (He was not borrowing from Whitehead. And this view is in many details like Whitehead's, except where science has taught the West more accuracy.)

It is obvious that "love" implies my position about the given, namely that the own-self is not the only existent that is given. I agree with you that the "datum-*Gestalt* of the specious present" is the whole of the given, and that this whole is one's self. But not exclusively that self (see *Sensation*, paragraph on pp. 100–101).[27] The self is this whole in one aspect, other aspects of the same whole are other selves (or sub-selves, e.g., cells, molecules, etc.). This leads to your third topic, how, if other individuals are directly "intuited" anyone can fail to know this and agree with Whitehead. I could have but one answer; givenness is more or less vague. In this sense I can accept Donald Williams' "Innocence of the Given."[28] This is the Leibnizian doctrine of gradations of awareness.[29] To feel something is not, vastly not, the same as to be able to say that [we feel] and what we feel. Introspection is not identical with primary feeling, but is a secondary feeling-complex. It involves judgment, propositions, language. It is what Whitehead calls consciousness, or one phase of this, and acc[ording] to him not all feeling or most feeling is conscious.

I agree that when we imagine or infer our future selves we imagine them as what will be given to a self "identical" with the present self. But also different from that self. Identity is not mere identity. Furthermore, it is essential to the Whiteheadian position to hold that one's past self is not merely inferred but is given, and that this givenness of past in present is an essential aspect of what is meant by the endurance of the "identical" self. This is Whitehead's new view of substantial identity (see Chapter on "The grouping of occasions" in *Adventures*),[30] his crowning achievement acc[ording] to yours truly. The specious present includes all preceding presents of the self, but the succeeding only in the vague or outline form constitutive of futurity. (This vagueness is not merely in the givenness but in its object, though subjective and objective sides coincide only for God since our foresight is much less definite than the laws of nature, which themselves are, however, not absolutely definite.) Though past specious presents are still given they are nevertheless past, because they are the less definite parts of the present. Thus my youthful aspirations and plans are less definite than my actual accomplishments since, even to absolute (divine) memory.

Now the other selves again. They too are integral to my present in that their pasts enter into it (for Whitehead only after a finite lapse of time, measured by relativity physics). Thus I am identical not only with my past self but with other past selves. But not in the same degree and pattern. Empirical facts easily distinguish my past from yours consistently with this metaphysics. My past selves are still distinct or definite for me, but your past is so only as I earlier distinctly inferred or imagined it. The own-self is the only individual <u>distinctly</u> given. All our difference of opinion concerns <u>vague</u> givens. But the pains and pleasures of my cells are given and remembered with some vividness, only without distinct separation between one cell and another, i.e., with blurring of outlines but preservation of quality (as painful, intense, etc.).

Thus all individuals are given and all are made much more distinct than as given by inference and imagination, but other selves require more of this supplementary definition than the self (hence egotism). And thus all selves are identical as well as different, and thus the cosmic identity of God (and of being) is accounted for. All real questions, as Peirce said, are questions of degree, on this view.

I wish I could find a department of philosophy which had a modest place for a favorite student of mine about to get his degree. Vincent Evaud.[31] He is well versed in Whitehead and Peirce, but specializes in aesthetics, in which his thesis is excellent. He is a fine teacher (I have tried him in my classes), a superfine character, genuinely spiritual without bigotry of any kind. He can teach all the usual philosophical subjects.

It is heartbreaking having graduates with so few openings.

I am greatly encouraged by your interest in my philosophical development.

I see you are included in the *Christian Century*'s 40 best religious books of recent times, as you should be.[32]

I think D. Williams is one of those worth debating with; [there are] not so many of them either.

Cordially,
Charles Hartshorne

Edgar S. Brightman
Box 1053
Oak Bluffs, Massachusetts

July 25, 1935

Dear Hartshorne,

The summer seems to agree with you and me—and to be much needed for us both, too. We have both overworked, as you intimate. This is the first summer for some time that I have not taught. The Island of Martha's Vineyard and the salt water and air are doing me a great deal of good.

It seems to me that the whole point in Whitehead-Hartshorne that perplexes me is due to my bondage in the fallacy of exclusive particularity bezw. simple location.[33] Of course I see that Perry is right in holding that a point in one line may also be in any number of other lines.[34] But I cannot see that this is true of psychic "points." Partly because there are no psychic points, and partly because the very experience of love would lose its <u>very</u> meaning the moment there ceased to be two lovers (insofar as they <u>become</u> one, the experience is not love), and partly because of my deep-rooted epistemological dualism.

My consciousness, as I see it,—i.e., my whole datum self—is wholly and nothing but <u>myself.</u> It includes knowledge of, feeling of, purpose toward, and interaction with other beings. But it is exclusively itself.

What I now want to get at is the ground and the importance of the difference between your view and mine. My view is based on: (1) the empirical givenness of consciousness, (2) the fact that I can remember only my own past from within, (3) the uniqueness and value of the individual. It emphasizes interaction and communication. What truth or value do I lose that you have? Am I wrong in saying that there is a difference in ultimate categories? For me, the category purposer-purposed is ultimate. Rational purpose <u>explains</u> interaction, separateness of persons, etc. Is it true that you make the category includer-included equally ultimate? In love, part of each lover's very being must, you think, be included in the very being of the other. Whereas I think that the purpose to love and to share, entertained in a world in which purposes are communicated by the cosmic purpose, is a truer account of the essence of love. Yet I do not reduce feeling to will; I mean only that feeling without purpose is not love. Is my pluralism really missing something? What?

Faithfully yours,
Edgar S. Brightman

[Hartshorne indicates in the following letter that he did not answer Brightman's "last letter," which was likely the one above of July 25, 1935. In any case, the correspondence picks up again in 1937.]

July 31, 1937

Dear Professor Brightman,
We are expecting soon to give the Ph.D. to Mr. M. Brahmachari.[35] He is a Hindu monk, a very fine scholar in Indian philosophy, particularly those branches of it which are clearly theistic. He would like to teach a year or so before going back to India. I have had him lecture to my class, to its great delight, and know he can teach. The question is, where in America would there be a modest salary available for him, for a term or two. This would be once when

there would really be no obligation beyond the first year. I thought possibly you might have some idea. Of course it is late for next year.

Your and our student Gilmore is here, and looks promising.[36] He is impressing me again with how much Ward anticipated later doctrine, of Whitehead, for instance.[37] Whitehead does not limit self-activity to attention, but the theory of "rapport" seems the same.[38] I remember how we debated that. I did not answer your last letter. The answer I had in mind was that either you use the conception of social feeling to explain how one mind can act on another, or physical things, so-called, on mind, or you have some alleged distinct conception of causality or influence through which you explain social feeling, love. The former I take to be the religious way, and also the only one that really dips its meanings up out of experience. Personalism apparently accepts a conception of causality not illustrated in experience in order to transcend experience.[39] If only the self is given then no causality is given except self-control. This form of control cannot guarantee an order extending beyond the self, or explain it, if you make the relation of the self to itself quite incomparable to its relations to other selves, as is surely done if you say that in the latter case the terms of the relation are not in the same immediacy. And how then are we data for God? It's exactly Leibniz's difficulty over again isn't it? Whereas if you say that self-control is between two selves which are both the same and different, e.g., selves of different moments, then one can say control of one mind by another is a more radical case of the same principle of identity in difference. In any case unless God is given I do not see how he could be inferred, for the foundation of inference beyond immediacy seems to me necessarily the reality of God as the ground of world order. If God were not given could he be constructed? Is the idea of God the expression of what is directly apprehended, though vaguely, or is it a pure hypothesis to explain data in an experience which has no immanent transcendence, which experiences only its experience?

The temporalistic view of God which we share is more important to me than the foregoing question, which I incline to see as more purely verbal. Concerning the relation to other human minds we hold, apparently, the same view. The "rapport" is with cell and molecule minds below us and God above us, in both cases vague but distinct enough to yield certain important results.

Perhaps we will see you at Princeton this December?[40]

Sincerely
Charles Hartshorne

[Brightman indicates that he answered this letter on August 12, 1937. It may have been by postcard or only a short note from Martha's Vineyard, while he was away from his typewriter. Brightman did not retain a copy of this answer, and it was not to be found among Hartshorne's papers. This makes little difference in the

overall correspondence, however, since Hartshorne did not answer it. Hartshorne resumes the correspondence by referring back to Brightman's letters of 1935.]

Dec. 22, 1938

Dear Professor Brightman,

To answer your letter of three years ago![41] I am not able to see what the issue is as to the given as unique, irreducible, brute fact, between me, or Whitehead, and you, unless it is that we think most of what is given is given more or less faintly and beyond the reach of clear introspection. Clearly given is not only no other than our own selves but only a slight aspect of that. But faintly given is the whole past, including the past of other individuals, particularly those composing the body. These form part of the datum-*Gestalt* of my present self, and this participation of the present self in other selves is love in one aspect, feeling by one feeler of the feelings of others. That everyone does not accept this mutual immanence[42] is due for us of course to the faintness spoken of. It is explicable why the faintness should be, for in it lies on the one hand our lack of omniscience as compared to God, and on the other, our freedom from tyrannous spying by others, or too great dependence on the feeling of any one of them. They are merged in the background, the fringe, and the foreground is mostly taken up with our own memories and anticipations, or with sensory patterns which are distinct only in outlines not in individual parts. The sense of the retinal cells is a fusion of the individual cell-feelings so that their separateness is beyond our introspection ("transmutation"). This is not an easy doctrine, but it does offer an explanation of the body-mind relation and of causality. Your view must take as a postulate, it seems to me, the idea of one self influencing another. Such influence cannot be a datum, for if a relation is given are not its terms given?[43] But Whitehead's theory of thought, and any I can grasp, make it impossible to think a principle of explanation incapable of illustration in the given.

The basic metaphysical love is neither intellectual nor necessarily love of person nor mere curiosity, but mutuality, feeling of feeling, thinking of thinking, awareness of awareness, or willing of willing. It involves some activity and some passivity on both sides, and the duplication of states with differences of distinctness, between individuals. It is intellectual with beings that are intellectual, but always it is the relation whereby things are, under a limitation, each other's being. It is the denial of the absolute individual substance, the assertion that to be is to be related, that to act is to interact, that to be for another, to be for oneself, and for the other to be for oneself, are all inseparable aspects of one thing.

Relatively, your statements are all acceptable, if one denies only their absoluteness. And how do you find evidence in the half-light of human insight for such absolutes? Even God according to you and me is not sheerly absolute.

This may start the ball rolling again. Thanks for your letter.

Yours,
Charles Hartshorne

January 1, 1939

Dear Professor Hartshorne,

It just happens that your letter reached me as I was returning from the meeting at Wesleyan,[44] and so all full of desire for discussion. Hence I am keeping the ball rolling at once.

Distinctions of clarity and faintness in the given I grant to the limit. In fact, I have a man now working on clarity and vagueness for his dissertation, starting from Whitehead. However, it does not seem to me that my knowledge of the past corresponds to the vague areas of consciousness.[45] When I know the past at all it seems to me that there are the same distinctions of clarity and faintness in it as in my knowledge of the present. But when you say that the whole past is faintly given, it seems to me that the word given is experiencing so complete a change in meaning as to be unwarranted. Not even faintly do I remember even some of yesterday's deeds; or if I do remember faintly in spite of having not the faintest consciousness of so doing, then faint givenness is really an ungivenness. And I am not able to persuade myself that my participation in the life of another self is literally immanence in that other self. My view must indeed take as a postulate that there is a faint givenness, so faint that it is for the most part totally absent from the given—a given that is not given. I see no contradiction in my postulate; yours seems to play on the term given in such a way as to assert that the very faint is both given and not given. I wish you would pull this criticism to pieces, for I am deeply interested in the problem and in your ideas.

In your second paragraph you state the formula that "to act is to interact." This I quite agree with, but I hold that interaction is meaningless unless two beings are involved. The entire sentence in which that formula occurs is more Hegelian, however, than I am prepared to be (in spite of your unfavorable comment on Hegel when you visited my seminar). Yet I do hold that one must deny the absolute individual substance; still, a monad may be genuinely private without being absolutely independent. It may be in constant interaction with other monads and dependent for its very being on the monad of monads without being a part of any other monad in any respect whatever.

Your sentence about Whitehead's theory of thought goes to the root of matters: "impossible to think a principle of explanation incapable of illustration in the given." This is a very fundamental postulate. Just what does it mean, literally? "The given" surely does not mean <u>my</u> given, does it? If so, it sounds solipsistic, in spite of mutual immanence; it would have to be at least "our given." Yet the belief that any aspect of my given is also ours would be an additional postulate, akin to the postulate that what is totally absent from consciousness is really faintly given. If I were to grant that all principles of explanation are capable of illustration in someone's given sometime, and were allowed to locate the principle of interaction in the given of God, I could follow this principle. Otherwise, not. It seems to me that my postulates are less arbitrary than the ungiven given, my absolute less absolute than yours!

Faithfully yours (and expectantly),

[Brightman]

Jan. 30, 1939[46]

Box 754, Menlo Park, Calif.

Dear Professor Brightman,

That was a swell letter. It goes so deep that maybe we are not likely to get much deeper by correspondence. Your first point I agree with, that knowledge of the past does not correspond to the vague areas of consciousness, and that within the past there are distinctions of clarity and faintness. Pastness of course is not faintness, and in God's past all is clear, except as the past itself, when present, was unclear, and that is, as it had an indeterminate future. The faintness of our memory is subjective, is our limitation. So far I see no disagreement between us. But you object to making more than a part of the past even faintly given to us, on the strong ground that if we have not the faintest consciousness of remembering, then this is the same as not remembering. You would not perhaps say that to know is, with equal distinctness, to know that we know, but apparently you hold that if we know at all, then, even if more faintly, we must be able to know that we do. Or, do you hold that to be aware of, and to be aware of this awareness, is just the same, and allows of no difference even in degree? Now there seems to be a problem of regress here. If we know that we know, less clearly than we know the object known, then we know that we know that we know, less clearly than we know that we know. Now you claim to know that you do not know certain parts of the past (directly), to which I say that you do know it, but don't know that you know it. God sees you faintly feeling the past and still more faintly feeling your feeling of it.[47]

On second thought, the above is perhaps not to the point. Granting that if you faintly remember the past, you are faintly, but no more so, aware that you remember it, but both so faintly that you cannot <u>pick out</u> separate items, which is what you mean when you say you are not conscious of the business. If the items are already conscious one can make them more so by attention, but how can direct attention upon what one feels only as part of a larger feeling which, only as a whole, is known to be felt? In short, only what is felt to be felt as one item, an "it," can be made clearer by effort; not all that is merely felt. Still we do remember by <u>effort</u> what is not consciously remembered before the effort. The matter is complex and subtle. Effort <u>may</u> help to bring out an item not previously there as an item, as one object of attention. But if it doesn't, that proves nothing.[48]

Consider it this way. Your experience at each moment is a unique individual whole. True you can consciously note things which are perhaps, in combination, peculiar to this whole in fact, but do these clear items exhaust the individual flavor of the experience? To me the background of feeling quality is given as something elusive, in which I could hardly know certainly that any item you mention is not essentially involved (except items belonging to the future, which therefore do not exist). At this point our difference seems to reduce to a verbal one. You agree that other individuals which I do not consciously remember are necessary to my experience, that the latter simply could not have existed without the others just as they are. Or do you rather hold that influence of one self on another is arbitrary, put over by God (by a non-arbitrary influence to be sure) between monads whose quality does not involve the quality of the other monads? (If you agree that the quality of the one could not have existed without the quality of the other, then you seem to me to be saying what I wish to say.) For I know of no difference between "part" in the broadest sense, and "necessary to."[49] That without which a thing would *ipso facto* or necessarily be something else is a part of that thing, in my language. If you take the arbitrary view I feel you are presupposing something else to explain at least God's influence.

I might add that those who say the future is necessitated by the present say, to my ears, that it is a part of the present, and therefore (I object) not really future but present. But the past can be a part of the total present reality and yet be distinguished from the new part we ordinarily call the present by virtue of the one-way relations between the indeterminate anticipations and the determinate realization so that we can abstract from the new part (and this abstractability is its newness) and see the old just as they were, but we cannot abstract from the old without altering the new in our thought. If I had not had a certain plan I could not have experienced the fulfillment or frustration of the plan, but if I had not experienced just the fulfillment or frustration I did I could still have had the same plan (earlier) and experienced some other form of realization or frustration of it.

But an other than merely verbal question seems at least nearer at hand in your wanting influence to be a postulate not a datum (<u>to me</u>, the speaker or listener—I hope I can do both!). I do not really know how anything can be postulated except through some <u>analogy</u> at least with the given, so I would have to know what the analogous case to influence <u>in the given</u> is. I really have, I think, no "faintest" notion of interaction between experiences neither of which experiences the other. To me the disadvantage of having to agree with Hume and the positivists that influence is not directly known overweighs almost an infinity of other difficulties, unless one is to give up metaphysics. But, without further explanation, that is a subjective consideration, if you will.

Of course any given is both <u>my</u> given and <u>our</u> given, on my view. As given there is a difference, but <u>what</u> is given is the same, and also the way of being given to you is itself, with some grade of relevance, or vividness, given to me.

Of course I hold that the experience of God as the principle of interaction is useless as explanation unless we can reach God on the basis of what we experience, and on this basis must rest also the knowledge of interaction between us and God which enables us to conceive Him.

Regarding clearness, there seem to be two views. Clearness in its degrees means the number of parts of the object that are given compared to those not given. Objection: the object is a unity, and totally without any part it just isn't the object. Thus to have any item with absolute clearness would be to be God, omniscient. This leads to the other view, according to which all parts of the object, which is the universe as actual, one individual whole, the consequent nature of God, the objective side of God's experience as one experience, are given but not to the same degree. Degree of givenness then is an irreducible category. Now a degree may be awfully slight and still not be zero. How easy to confuse the two! To know certainly or even probably that I do not feel x would be to know <u>all</u> that is in my momentary self. I have a sense that this I do not know, though God knows it.

Of course my view makes a continuity between ordinary and mystical experience, which, taken literally, seems excluded on yours.

It seems to me that our differences are of a pretty technical order, not so substantial as, for example, those between either of us and a neo-thomist.

Your notion of the "given" to God seems close to what I think of as the dependence of God upon the past as the sum of acts of more or less free beings, to whose activity God is passive, since otherwise it would not be real activity. Since the past never began, as I take it, God never at any moment, or in any act, for all his acts were at a moment, had a clean slate to just make a world out of the realm of logical possibilities, but always had to make the best of a world that could have been better. Is this your notion, or anywhere near it?

We met your student Wiederholt (?). Seems very bright, and told me in glowing terms about your teaching.[50]

Sincerely yours,
Charles Hartshorne

[Hartshorne continues to type under his signature]

You know the case of perceiving that a is different from c while unable to perceive that a is different from b or b from c. This is variously interpreted, but suggests that we feel without being able to know it, all the more as "guesses" on the difference from a to b would give a statistical superiority to the judgment agreeing with the relation implied by the difference between a and c.

In religious terms I would say that all human functions are imperfect, such as the quality as well as the scope of givenness and of knowing that we know. We are a mystery to ourselves, even in our momentary reality (in which, after all, our personality must be immanent somehow). Still, you could reply that the scope of our givenness is the same as God's, on my view. So I must rephrase the matter: clearness and scope in us vary inversely, so that we lose on one dimension while we gain on the other, not to the same extent always, but enough to guarantee our essential inferiority to God. We know all in the poorest possible way (the way the animals even know all), but only a little in a good way and nothing in the best way, since to see anything quite clearly one must see also clearly all things which are even slightly important for the anything, though, since they are slightly important (that is, the thing would be but a little different without them) we can see the object pretty clearly while seeing some other things with nearly zero clearness. This scheme seems to provide fully for error, and also for the never to be too much wondered at possibility of our knowing the omniscient while not being omniscient. The advantage too of making the scope of our knowledge, if quality be left unspecified, equal to that of God is that then we know how it is that we can refer to the universe, the objective correlate of omniscience. For it is also the correlate of our awareness, what we are aware of, though poorly, as God's perfection of love is the ideal we directly sense though weakly and confusedly (distracted by more clear but superficial perceptions) in our aspirations.

(We could not reach omniscience as such by starting with the universe, for the universe is constituted by omniscience, and could not be its independently knowable measure.)

In short we know the omniscient because in one way we are omniscient, the knower is the image of the known. This dispenses with the need to infer God from the merely imperfect, involving the difficulty, as this would, that the perfect would be presupposed as the measure of the imperfect. We immediately know the perfect and the imperfect, but both in deficient ways, with knowledge poor in quality. Then we can clarify both data of our knowledge together.

I also can avoid having to say that there are some things we absolutely do not know, that the universe, which I know, since I speak of it as the measure of my ignorance, includes things I wholly fail to know. There is no paradox if we say that the universe, which I know as a whole, though inaccurately, not <u>both</u> clearly and truly, includes in this wholeness factors which of course I know, since without them there would be a different whole, but which I know almost completely, many of them, without accuracy, if that means clearly and truly. I can make distinct ideas which are not true, or fall back on my indistinct awareness which is true but useless for purposes of discrimination, though not useless in its contribution to the flavor of my experience and in its generic or metaphysical import as uniting me to God and the world.

February 18, 1939

Dear Hartshorne,

Your very interesting letter leaves me a little dazed with all its subtleties, and I shall need to re-read it often in order to digest it.

Meanwhile one point stands out. I mean, among a great deal that seems true and profound, I find one point of real disagreement. You say you know of "no difference between 'part' in the broadest logical sense, and 'necessary.'" If you are talking about logic only, this proposition may be valid, although it sounds to me dangerously like a doctrine of internal relations that would lead to a logical absolutism which neither you nor I would welcome. But it seems to me that there is a world-wide difference between the logical and ontological use of the word "part." The sun, moon, and stars, yea the entire firmament, are all necessary to me as I am; but I can make no sense of saying that they are ontologically part of me. Is this assertion of mine a statement of what you call "the arbitrary view"?

Since this is a very important point with me, I should like to have your view of it.

Most cordially yours,
[Brightman]

The Quadrangle Club
Chicago

May 8, 1939

Dear Brightman,

I have been looking at Bertocci's book, of which I should think you'd be proud.[51] I understand better now why you are interested in maintaining a distinction between what is necessary to and what is part of a thing. In my essay in *Essays for A. N. Whitehead*,[52] I distinguish between internal and external parts,[53] giving definitions that seem to me to be free from the apparent contradiction. You personalists I see are defending the most extreme side of Leibniz—only you go further. For Leibniz admitted a part of the monad corresponding to each item in the universe.[54] Thus he had on his hands the chief difficulty of internal relations, the necessity for holding that we are aware of many things we cannot introspectively detect as definite items—in short, an immense, literally infinite realm of subconscious or undetectably faint intuitions. This staggers the imagination, but perhaps offers no logical difficulty?

But in so far as you and Leibniz deny windows,[55] except toward God, you make a distinction that I find meaningless, especially so (if there be degrees of meaninglessness, or rather of obviousness of meaninglessness) if one conceives God as temporal. For, granted that monads can interact only thanks to the mediation of God, they also exist at all only thanks to Him, hence there is no difference between their being and their relations in this respect. The being they enjoy through God is a being of mutuality, a social being, a participation in each other. The unity of God's being embraces them all and this can only mean, I must think, that the difference between them is relative not absolute, they overlap in varying ways and degrees. Put it thus: we include God, for he is genuinely immanent in us. But God includes all the monads; hence, by the transitivity of "includes," every monad includes every other, so far as coactual with it. God is more inclusive in two senses: more vividly aware of his parts; and second, he will survive to be aware of all that ever comes to be (perhaps we will too, but not all creatures, anyway, will). Under the first sense is included that God was there as an individual through all the past, whereas we "prehend" the past only as what mostly preceded us.[56]

I hold that if we are directly aware of the sun it is a part of us. That is, relations of minds define all relations. ("Part" is no meaning fixed independently of direct awareness.) But nothing I am wholly unaware of (directly) can be necessary to me. For I <u>am</u> just an awareness and its contents. Indirect awareness? That is a way of making direct awareness yield the one thing it lacks, distinctness. "What I mean" must be a factor in this meaning state.

Anyhow you have to unify the whole in God's direct awareness, and I give up trying to have unity unless the diversity is relative, a matter of degree somehow, such as degree of vividness.

On external relations, I accept them for the relation of particulars to generals, and of details of moments of "time" to earlier moments; otherwise I want to defend internal relations. But the divine that makes all actual (present and past) things one is <u>passive</u> as well as <u>active.</u> God doesn't decide everything, though he <u>is</u> everything, <u>suffers</u> all experiences as content of his experience which in its way of integrating the contents into one whole is active also. Thus there is no tyranny of the one.

The sun seems not a part of me because it is such a faint part, the vivid sense datum here being mostly my awareness of the state of the eye and brain. And my friends are not obviously parts of me because my vivid awarenesses of them are really awarenesses of the state of my brain in acts of perception and imagination. The direct relations are very faint. But I include my bodily parts rather vividly, and they include light rays, etc., and these include in their meager way the quality of their source. So I include the whole chain. But only low grade monads can directly and vividly include their neighbors, have social relations primarily direct rather than imaginative, with equals. This enslaves them, they have little individual independence. God has the model social relations, wholly direct and yet not enslaving, simply because he is always so superior in power to the relata. Our weakness makes it necessary for us to have vivid awareness only of such things as our own cells, which, as radically inferior to us (their deity, almost) cannot (wholly) enslave us. I think personalism is in danger of over (or under really) generalizing the specifically human type of social relation.

Does your given in its generic traits add any limitations any God could conceivably lack—or does your empirical method balk at such a question? If you say any God must confront a given, then we are agreed on the main point. If not, I am more traditional than you. I want to say God has the greatest power possible as the power of any single agent and to define omnipotence thus, for why define something inconceivable—and "more than the greatest possible power" is naturally inconceivable or nonsense. Why set up nonsense and then limit it?

I think careful explorations of moderate, more or less minimal ideas of God are valuable contributions to balance Thomism et al., but I see three main positions here, not two. God may be perfect in all conceivable ways yet not perfect in all mentionable ones. If perfect happiness is mentionable though not conceivable, or if "all the power there is"—wielded by a single agent—is not conceivable, then God is not in such ways perfect but because the word loses its meaning in such application.

Or do you go to other extreme and hold that God is not even perfect in the ways in which this has real meaning?

I shall value and probably use your answer, but may not be able to reply, as I am deep in my next and racing against a time limit (unfortunately).

Charles Hartshorne

[Hartshorne continues under his signature.]

I discussed internal rel[ation]s in *Phil[osophy] and Psych[ology] of Sensation,* Ch. I, and in "Four Principles of Method," *Monist,* about 1931.[57] I go beyond Whitehead (who makes contemporaries mutually external, following

physics[58]) but in conversation he said, "I have not made the nec[essary] qualifications."

May 12, 1939

Dear Hartshorne,

Your very interesting letter was brought to me while I was conducting a
class on Bowne's Metaphysics. I read them the unusual message on the flap,[59]
and only rigid self-control prevented me from reading the letter aloud to the
class and making it the subject for the hour's discussion. I am especially pleased
at what you say about Bertocci's book.

It almost seems to me as though our difference were more verbal than real.
I rebel heartily against your use of the word "parts," but I quite understand
and agree with the concept of mutual immanence and service relation which
you speak of in the Whitehead volume in connection with internal and external
parts. It seems to me that you are talking about types and degrees of interaction. But the empiricist in me finds it necessary to distinguish between actual
experience and the (epistemologically) hypothetical entities to which my actual
experience refers, which it implies, or with which it interacts. Starting with my
actual experience, which is the datum self, I am led to distinguish between
those hypothetical entities which were once or which may become my actual
experience (and which as a whole history are my total self) and those other hypothetical entities which constitute the environing universe, interacting with
me yet never a part of me. Among such entities I should count my body, my
subconscious, society, the natural order, and God. My fundamental category is
not "in-ness" but rather purpose. I can understand my universe only in terms
of the purpose that there shall be otherness, which at the same time is a purpo-
sively cooperating otherness. Hence I deny windows through which parts of
anything else can come in or go out, but not windows through which purposes
may interact. Your difficulty regarding the distinction between the power of
God which establishes the interaction of monads and his power by means of
which monads exist can arise only because you view God's purpose (it seems to
me) purely abstractly, without regard to the possibility of there being different
purposes for different ends. There seems to me to be no meaninglessness at all
in saying that God purposes interaction while at the same time purposing that
the individuals who interact shall receive from God a power of self-determination which God does not himself exercise. The meaninglessness that you find is
the same as that in Bosanquet's argument against the creation of creators.[60] It is
an argument at once against creation and against freedom. Waiving creation
for a moment, I do not see how you can conceive mutuality or social being
without a certain amount of freedom or self-determination in each of the

participants. It seems to me that we are fairer to all the facts if we describe mutuality as cooperation rather than as identity of parts.

"If we are directly aware of the sun it is a part of us," you say. This is at the heart of epistemology. My heart is dualistic, yours monistic. For me, I am directly aware only of my own experience. What we (confusedly) call direct awareness of the sun is really a direct awareness of myself-as-believing-in-sun, or as referring-to-sun. No part of me is any part either of the sun or of God. I thoroughly accept your dictum that "'Part' is no meaning fixed independently of direct awareness," but regard direct awareness as always and only of myself, when it is purely direct. Usually it (or what passes for it) is a judgment that there is an object, one of whose properties is to produce a recognizable effect in my consciousness; but I do not judge this effect to be any part of the object. Your further thesis, that "nothing I am wholly unaware of directly can be necessary to me," seems to me to need many qualifications. I'd say that nothing that I have never been and never shall be aware of is a part of me; yet I must add that much that I cannot in any meaningful sense be said to be aware of directly (the past, other minds, not to mention numbers larger than the largest number I shall even think) is still necessary to a coherent interpretation of the world with which I interact. A direct awareness that is so lacking in distinctness as to be entirely absent from my consciousness so far as I am aware seems to me no longer to deserve the name "direct awareness." It might be called implication or potentiality, but not directness.

To say, in any sense, that God "is everything" seems to me to declare that he is, *inter alias,* inconsistency and incoherence. Of course you escape this by saying that he suffers everything; but suffering (the effects of, a perception of, or knowledge of) is not the same as being identical with. Here you are really more Hegelian than I am. Again, your admission that the vivid sense datum is not a part of the sun leaves the sense in which the sun is a part of me so very obscure and Pickwickian that I can't see the empirical ground for it.

My empirical mind finds reason to be an empirically verifiable property of minds, and so it does not balk at generalizations. I quite agree that any God must confront a given. However, the nature of such a given must always be deduced from experience. In general, any God (as creative will) must confront within the total unity of his consciousness a twofold Given, consisting of Form (logic, mathematics, Platonic ideas) and Matter (brute fact content, a "receptacle"). What amazes me about the traditional view of God is that it admits the eternal nature of form, but will not admit this as a given limit; and (except for Aristotle) denies that matter is given (you understand I mean content, not some extra-personal entity). I do not "set up nonsense and then limit it"; but I find nonsense in the traditional view and then redefine God so as to make clear that any possible eternal activity must act under limits.

Your distinction between the conceivable and the mentionable is useful in this connection. If under conceivable you include what can be conceived in the present of all the empirical evidence, then I hold that God has every conceivable perfection. But this statement is rather anemic until interpreted in detail.

I am also deep in "my next" as you in yours.[61] It's a Philosophy of Religion, and just now it's "got me down." I passed my time limit some months ago!

Your letters are always a challenge. Let there be more of them.

Faithfully yours,
[Brightman]

[True to his word, Hartshorne did not have time to answer this letter, and went to New York City to teach at the New School for Social Research for the 1941–1942 academic year. The direct correspondence broke off for more than a year. However, the exchange did not break off; rather, it went public. In 1941 Hartshorne published Man's Vision of God, *in which he included a critical treatment of Brightman's view. Brightman in turn reviewed the book. Relevant excerpts from* Man's Vision of God *are included below, followed by Brightman's review, in its entirety, of Hartshorne's book. The correspondence then continued this discussion privately. In the excerpt below, we have included Hartshorne's remarks about pacifism because they will figure prominently in the correspondence hereafter. For a fuller discussion of this issue, consult the interpretive essay by Mark Y. A. Davies in Appendix 5.]*

Charles Hartshorne, Man's Vision of God,[62] *pp. 73–74, 166–173.*

. . . Professor Brightman says God's will is perfect, though his ability to carry it out is not. But on empirical grounds (unless religious experience be made the decisive datum) how can we decide between this view and the notion that God's ability is perfect, although his intentions are not wholly benevolent? Either way we explain the facts of evil which Professor Brightman has in mind. Further, his notion of the Given as an intrinsic limitation of God's power, a passive element in his activity, analogous to sensation and emotion in us, can be defined and defended only in the context of an adequate analysis of what is or can be meant by "passivity," "sensation," etc.; and the exploration of such concepts taken in their most fundamental or general senses, as they here must be, can only amount to a metaphysical system whose defense is not merely empirical, since the very meaning of "experience," "facts," etc., will have to be grounded in this system. (In such a system it might, I suggest, appear that "passive" only means "acted upon by another," so that the Given can only be a relation to some activity other than the divine, and therefore cannot be explained merely by a limitation, or anything else, in God alone.) . . .

. . . Which has caused the fearful catastrophes of the past decade—excess of social awareness and of the striving for it, or deficiency of these attitudes? Let us see. The German republic collapsed, students agree, partly because of its adherence to a theory of freedom which says, in effect, grant civil rights even to those who will use them to deprive others of these same rights. Is adherence to this theory an expression of social awareness or is it not rather just bad thinking? Of course one should appreciate, be socially aware of, the desire of some to deny to others the rights they claim for themselves, but since this desire conflicts with other desires of men with which one should also sympathize, one has to make an adjustment in which in some sense there results the least sacrifice of the desires sympathized with. Any other course shows a net deficiency, not a net excess, of social awareness. It shows a failure in so far to imitate the divine awareness, which feels all desires for what they are, and seeks the lesser sacrifice, the most valuable adjustment. To veto a desire is not necessarily to fail literally to sympathize with it; for sympathy only makes the desire in a manner one's own, and even one's own desire one may veto, because of other more valuable desires. Love makes all control of others also self-control, all denial self-denial, it does not abolish control or denial.

Again, the German republic fell partly because of the theory of proportional representation which says, in effect, that the minority is to be ruled by the majority, but in such a way that any minority is always to be free to put such obstacles in the way of the will of the majority that that will is bound to come to naught, although the will of the minority will not come to anything either. This theory may seem to careless inspection like a corollary from the principle of social awareness, but really it contradicts it.

Why were the Germans first hindered by other peoples from succeeding in their democratic venture and then ineffectually opposed after they had given it up and made themselves into a self-announced threat to mankind? Clearly the reparation and guilt-admission sections of the Versailles treaty showed a lack not an excess of social awareness or even-handed sympathy. So did American tariff policy combined with a lending program that made unpayable debts inevitable. As to the ineffectual opposition to the subsequent tyranny, it does indeed seem clear that those pacifists who deduced absolute renunciation of military means from their conception of love were in effect staunch allies of Hitler rather than of his victims. But is this doctrinaire pacifism the expression of too much will to or achievement of social awareness? The saintly English pacifist who held that Hitler was not beyond the reach of kindly impulses because Hitler had been courteous to him personally seems to have shown in this argument the dominance of blind sentiment or of fanatical doctrinaire bias, rather than the reality of social appreciation. It is not love to deny what men are, rather it is love to get out of oneself sufficiently to see what they are. To try to keep life on a pleasant level by suggesting that tyrants are not so very bad, nor so very powerful or dangerous, may be preferring one's own sentiment or theory to the achievement of social realization.

But there is the argument that love is not only a motive and goal, it is also a method, the only valid method, of influencing others. Yet to try to base one's own action solely upon social awareness, and to wish that others might do so also, seems not necessarily to imply the exclusive use of direct appeal to this attitude in others as a *means* of expressing it in oneself and of promoting its growth in the world. Social realism—and unless that is what love is it is pernicious, and is besides unworthy to be used as the defining trait of deity—may enable us to see that to hand over the use of force to those inferior in love is to guarantee that there will be less and less social awareness in the end. To oppose by force is not necessarily to fail in social appreciation; one may be sorrowfully aware of what the force means to its victims, innocent or guilty. To deny this is merely to bear false witness against many noble soldiers, whose departures from love can be matched by those of any other class of men. There is evidence enough that dogmatic pacifism is often the expression of a preference for a certain enjoyable sentiment as against facing the tragedy of existence, which even God does not escape, and which we must all share together. To decide to shorten a man's life (we all die) is not *ipso facto* to lack sympathy with his life as it really is, that is, to lack love for him. It may not be to love him less but someone else more, in comparison with the pacifist. Where lives come into fundamental conflict, sacrifice of life there will be, even if only by slow starvation. To fight without hate or indifference may be hard, but so is it hard to do business or compete for honors in art, or to live at all, without envy, callousness, willful blindness to others. Love, being in its literalness the unique privilege of deity, is infinitely difficult. Many a pacifist is clearly no model of love. The few really noble ones can be matched by the noble warriors, so far as my observations go at least. And theoretically I do not see why we should expect otherwise.

From all this it does not follow that war is not a tremendous evil, but only that there are even worse ones, just as liberty for others is sometimes better than life for oneself. Nor does it follow that most of those who take to the sword have a justification in love for doing so. Nothing is more horrible than the lightness with which men have been slaughtered, even on the merest whim. Indeed a just objection to sheer pacifism is that by making war as such the greatest possible evil it puts discrimination as to wars and their causes to sleep even more effectively than does extreme militarism. If to fight is *ipso facto* to give up love, then it is vain to ask, Does this *particular* cause rightfully demand military support from the loving or does it not? All such discrimination between causes is left to others by pacifists, who naturally enough like to point out the virtues of the bad causes and the vices of the good ones until all comparative judgments, the only ones by which men can live, are discouraged and action ceases to have meaning. The field is then open to those who know too well what they prefer and also know how to get it—which the pacifists alas do not, whatever services they may perform in counteracting irresponsible militarism or in other ways. Undoubtedly, pacifists can remain more aware of *some* of the social realities than can those engaged in the military struggle. They can specialize in their sympathies. The soldier cannot dwell too much on the sufferings of the enemy, any more than a lawyer can be as aware of the interests of his client's opponent as of those of his client. Only God can entirely avoid specialization of sympathy without falling into utter superficiality. What we have all to do is to try to see in abstract principle what the interests we have not concretely attended to require of us. As to this the pacifist has no monopoly.

As to the argument that the greatest exponents of love have been pacifists, that one cannot imagine Jesus leading men into battle, etc., I wish to venture a word or two. Can one imagine Jesus as a corporation lawyer or a policeman? After all, founding a religion is one thing, winning battles or law cases or arresting criminals another, but it does not follow that the principles of that religion condemn the other mentioned activities. Also it is not clear that the Jewish nation, had it fought the Romans, had a very valid cause of battle, including a reasonable chance of gaining the victory. The Roman Empire was probably the best organization of affairs available at the time. (Should anyone say this of the nazi empire today, he would, I think, be radically mistaken. Germany is strong enough to organize Europe by brute force and to enslave the whole to twenty million ruling-class Germans, and for this reason alone it would be better for Britain, which *cannot* control Europe except by getting it to control itself more or less cooperatively, to have the leading part in the beginning. The advantages would be not for a decade; they might be for a thousand years. Those who speak of the rebelling of the conquered do not tell us, even vaguely, how it is to be done.) Had Jesus a definite stand on military ethics it is strange that his only references to military affairs state nothing any militarist need deny, except as incontrovertible facts compel denial of one statement in its literal unqualified meaning. (Not all who take up the sword do perish by the sword.) And if the injunctions to love enemies and turn the other cheek have absolute scope and the meaning strict pacifism requires, then the pacifist must be ready to cooperate with anyone who sets out to take advantage of him. Who supposes that he will be ready actually to do this, to rely exclusively upon "heaping coals of fire" upon all men who are ready to infringe upon his rights? There is plenty of meaning left to these words, indeed all the real consistent meaning they ever can have, without any such literal absolutism being involved. The tendency to think revenge its own justification, resentment its own excuse for being, to meet injury with injury whether or not there is another, superior method for achieving important adjustments, is one of the greatest evils in life. No man ever threw such a bright light upon the possibilities for avoiding this evil as did Jesus. It is quite another matter to exclude the use of force even where no superior method can be found. And there are such occasions, as can be seen perfectly well today, when those who are not in favor of stopping aggression by force offer no alternative likely to stop it at all until the world is in the hands of the aggressors and pacifists will not even be allowed to argue any longer.

The career of Gandhi is another possible case from which to argue for pacifism. It is to be noted that Gandhi is admittedly a partisan, not just a lover of humanity. His cause is first of all India's. Now there may be a method superior to military resistance to wring freedom from the British. The British have the weapons, on the one hand, and they have a considerable willingness to extend justice on the other. On the contrary, if the United States tries to deal with aggression by appeasement it will merely be despised for neglecting its huge potential capacity for armament, and will meet with an inability to understand even what we mean by the liberties we wish to preserve, and ought for mankind's sake to preserve. With no little justice it will be said that we valued the comforts of peace, our automobiles and other material advantages, more than the defense of immaterial and priceless right to religious, educational, and other forms of freedom. We will seem to care more about wealth or the immediate ease of following our habits of life and thought than about the long-run development of American life in accordance with American ideals.

The true role for pacifism lies in keeping in mind a goal for the nations, to be pursued by all means, including force, likely to lead to it, in which a place for all the peoples will be found. Now those who want to stop aggressor peoples as such are the enemies of humanity, but those who want to do it by the unscrupulous method of killing off troublesome populations, dismembering troublesome nations, and the like. The right combination of firmness and generosity which alone can really give lasting peace will require all the social awareness, all the love, that can be mustered. But mere generosity to the aggressor without regard to the need for freeing his victims will only be generosity coming to the rescue of ungenerosity as such, that is it will be self-refuting. To argue that any victors are bound to impose a vindictive, bad peace is relevant only if it be shown that there is a better alternative than to have another set of even less scrupulous victors impose a worse peace. A "peace without victory" might be the thing, but that is no help until it is shown how it can be achieved as other than a thin disguise for the victory of the wrong side, the side that doesn't even want or profess to do justice.

In a heroic time dedicated to the salvation of freedom and the minimal conditions of human brotherhood, it is of service to recall a being to whom suffering is never alien, and who is the individual of all others the most tolerant of the variety of wills, the most ready to cooperate with their efforts, and the most free from the vain or stupid desire to have nothing to gain from the results of their initiative. Proud, willful, uncooperative men will never understand the gentle passivity of God, as weak and flabby men will never understand the energy of his resistance to the excesses of creaturely will at the point where these excesses threaten the destruction of creaturely vitality. The best expression of belief in God is an attitude of social awareness which treats all problems in the spirit of mutuality except where others insist upon treating them in another spirit, at which point we must in our local way, like God in his cosmic way, set limits by constraint to the destruction of mutuality. "Violence" and the constraints it imposes are surely not in the world merely through the fault of good men. It is better that many should die prematurely than that nearly all men should live in a permanent state of hostility or slavery.

The divine love is social awareness and action from social awareness. Such action seems clearly to include the refusal to provide the unsocial with a monopoly upon the use of coercion. Coercion to prevent the use of coercion to destroy freedom generally is in no way action without social awareness but one of its crucial expressions. Freedom must not be free to destroy freedom. The logic of love is not the logic of pacifism or of the unheroic life. . . .

E. S. Brightman's Review of *Man's Vision of God*

Man's Vision of God. *By Charles Hartshorne. Chicago: Willett, Clark & Co., 1941. xxi+360 pages. $3.00.*[63]

Many contemporary philosophers practice the art of evading thought about God while not denying themselves the luxury of intense negative convictions. Charles Hartshorne is not of that ilk. His rugged originality and penetrating insights merit serious attention. Perhaps his often obscure and uneven style repels some readers; but the enigmatic Preface to *Man's Vision of God* should not deter anyone from reading the book, which is Hartshorne's most adequate work up to the present.

Hartshorne is engaged, along with numerous other philosophers, in an attempt to revise the traditional idea of God which has prevailed in Jewish and Christian philosophy and theology from the time of Philo Judaeus, through Maimonides, Aquinas, and Spinoza down to contemporary Neo-Scholastics and many Protestants. "Theologians," he declares," would be no more justified in denying offhand that they can have misled religious thought for centuries than doctors were in their indignant denial that it was they themselves who consistently infected mothers with puerperal fever." Progress is possible. Atheism has no better friend than the theologian who confines the reality of God within one particular definition.

In undertaking his contribution to revisionism, Hartshorne aims to be rigidly logical. Since the idea of God is the idea of a perfect being, the logical possibilities may be grouped under three types. Type I: There is a being in *all* respects perfect (absolutism, Thomism, the Philonian type). Type II: There is a being in *some* respects absolutely perfect and in some not (a finite-infinite, perfect-perfectible God). Type III: There is a being in *no* respects absolutely perfect (a merely finite God). These might be called the Parmenidean, the Heraclitean and the Epicurean types, although Hartshorne does not name them thus. Hartshorne contends that traditional Type I theology has been able to maintain its hold largely because it succeeded in creating the impression that Type III (a manifestly inadequate view) was its only rival. Only since about 1880 has Type II been brought to general attention, chiefly by Protestant philosophers and theologians.

In his numerous arguments against Type I, Hartshorne seems to the present reviewer to be in the right at every important point. This doctrine, he says, quoting Peirce, serves to "block the path of inquiry" into more qualified formulations. He points out that the traditional view contains many nonreligious tenets, such as God's nontemporality, his pure activity (denying him any personality), his creation of the world out of nothing, his absolute simplicity, even his lack of will and emotions (p. 95). The perfection of God, even for such liberal Neo-Scholastics as Gilson and Maritain, implies that "be we saint or sinner, no matter what we choose to do, it is all one to God, for his glory has the identical absolute perfection in either case" (pp. 117–118). Such a God is "incapable of responding to our noblest need" (p. 118); he is too perfect. Hartshorne's treatment would have been strengthened had he gone back of Philo to Aristotle and Parmenides and had he considered the thought of A. C. Knudson, the ablest living exponent of Type I. Be that as it may, Hartshorne of Chicago has dealt the old view shrewd blows in one of its modern citadels.[64]

This book is worthy of commendation for its criticism of Type III, which rests on purely empirical arguments (as Type I rests on purely a priori grounds). However, it must be said that Hartshorne's treatment of religious naturalism is too cursory; that he does not sufficiently analyze the thought of a representative naturalist like H. N. Wieman (pp. 209–210); and that he does not consider critically the precise nature of empiricism. Historically, empiricism meant Hume's analytic sensationalism, James's doctrine that relations as well as terms are given, as well as Dewey's identification of experience with nature. Hume and James make experience mean less than the whole of any man's consciousness; Dewey makes it mean far more than any human consciousness could ever include. Should we not rather equate experience with actual consciousness and thus become "empiricists of consciousness" (like Hegel as Haering sees him)?[65]

In the main, Hartshorne's case for Type II theology is well grounded. He defends anthropomorphism as inevitable (p. 88); holds that God is "individual and personal" (pp. 249–250); rejects *creatio ex nihilo* in favor of a temporalistic view of God (pp. 230, 255; Bergson, Whitehead); and interprets foreknowledge, according to "the principle of Gersonides,"[66] as meaning that "the true way to know the future is as undetermined" (p. 98); and favors panentheism instead of pantheism (p. 347; cf. p. 208, n.5 and pp. 289–290).

There are at least four points at which questions arise:

1. Is Hartshorne too fully committed to the a priori? "The a priori method, not the empirical, . . . is capable of adjudicating the claims of the two methods" (p. 64); this statement is true in a sense, false in a sense, and needs analysis. It is, however, less misleading than the constant assumption that arguments for a necessary being must "involve necessity" (p. 251) and that all metaphysical knowledge is a priori (p. 60). In harmony with this excess of rationalism is the omission of the teleological arguments (preferred by Gifford lecturers, as well as by Hume and Kant) in favor of the cosmological and ontological. But the rejection of Type I theology, the emphasis on "the religious strand" in theology (chap. iii), which is called "more than formal" (p. 137), and the clear statement that "we are always talking about experience if we talk significantly at all" (p. 79) betray an empirical conscience in revolt against a priorism. Perhaps the worst effect of a priori thinking in the book is the rejection of pacifism on the grounds derived from the abstract nature of social awareness (pp. 166–168), without concrete consideration of actual long-run consequences.

2. Does not Hartshorne's logical method suffer from a neglect of the criterion of coherence and of the principle of probability? This criticism is closely related to the first. Hartshorne thinks in terms of the logic of consistency and necessary implication, overlooking the fact that coherence, which is the mark of concrete, empirical truth, is far more than noncontradiction; and also overlooking the fact that all our knowledge of existential propositions is empirical and probable. Paul Weiss, it is true, has argued that it is a priori and metaphysically necessary that I shall not meet myself walking down the street; but he omitted to add that the proposition is empty unless we add "if there be myself," a protasis that can be established only empirically. Hartshorne's criticism of the present reviewer's conception of God is due to his failure to consider empirical coherence (p. 73). However, he dimly recognizes the probability underlying the claims of logical certainty when he says: "Faith in God means trust in the value of choice. . . . The very 'ground of induction' . . . is some sort of faith" (p. 81). But the principle of coherent faith is not made fundamental, as it should be in a critical philosophy of religion.

3. Is panpsychism necessary to Type II theology? Hartshorne is strongly convinced of the truth of panpsychism. He develops the view in one of his most original and stimulating chapters, the one on "Theological Analogies," in which, after criticizing the mind-idea relation,

the artisan analogy, and the social analogy, he finds the analogy of God as cosmic poet, cosmic father, and "monarch or world boss" (pp. 202–205) to be far less satisfactory than the analogy of God as cosmic mind, whose body is the universe. Here, at least, Hartshorne is plainly using the method of empirical coherence rather than his usual a priorism. However, he is on insecure ground when against all epistemological dualism he speaks of "the surely immediate mind-body relation" (p. 187). Although Hartshorne is right in holding that in some sense man controls his body more directly than anything else (p. 183), he fails to explain in detail why he infers panpsychism from this fact. Still worse, he fails to make his panpsychism coherent. A "cell" of the body is "too light and weak a thing for its feeling to have any predominant influence" (p. 189). "These creatures [the cells] are too limited in knowledge to co-operate to any concerted end such as might interfere with the human being" (p. 189). Here is the crux of panpsychism: How can cells be foolish and wise at once? How can they be so knowing as to co-operate in harmony with physico-chemical and biological laws, and yet not knowing enough to co-operate in a common revolt against the human mind of which they are the body? In fact, when disease and death come, their rebellion becomes a revolution. Then, are not the cells much wiser and more powerful than the original definition supposed? Does not this indicate that their real function is simply to be agents of cosmic law—that is, expressions of God's will? Why, then, nick Occam's razor with a dense population of superfluous sub-electrons, when God suffices to do the work of matter? Panpsychism is a possible but hardly probable view. Type II is better off without it.

4. Does Hartshorne meet the case against pantheism? Although rejecting pantheism, he is too sympathetic with it. He notes that the argument against pantheism is that an omniscient mind could not contain lesser minds as parts of itself without entertaining their partly erroneous beliefs (p. 289). He then goes on to a subtly meant refutation to the effect that this assures that "the only way to contain a belief is actively to believe it. But perhaps one can passively suffer it." In thus arguing, Hartshorne omits the main point, which is that if one mind is part of another, then the former must be included *as it is,* with all its actively erroneous beliefs. If active error is not God's, then something is not God, and pantheism is refuted.[67]

These criticisms are not intended to detract from the importance of a weighty and suggestive book.

Edgar Sheffield Brightman
Boston University

January 22, 1942
270 Riverside Dr., N.Y.C.[68]

Dear Professor Brightman,

I have just received my copy of your meaty review. I should think it fair enough, no doubt fairer than I was to you in the book. I certainly did no sort of justice to either you or Wieman.[69]

I shall give my impressions on your four criticism[s].

1) The a priori. I left out a long chapter in which I tried to give the "analysis" which you rightly say is called for. The book had become pretty long. I think it is partly a verbal question. The criterion of coherence is certainly more than non-contradiction, and I think I say so now and then. I accept the criterion. The only problem is as to the kind[s] of data that are decisive as materials for the coherence. Of course all data must cohere with the true idea of God, but contingent data cohere only so well as their contingent alternatives, and so decide nothing as to the necessary aspect of God. They do, however, decide as to the accidents of God, and this I too seldom stress, I imagine. The teleological argument is of course sound if used to show what good works are being done now, but without a necessary essence of God they cannot, so far as I see, show the existence of an everlasting, primordial, or omniscient being, for the reasons that Hume and Kant gave.[70] The decisive data are what I call the generic aspects of experience, the absolutely basic traits of existence and awareness. To these there is no alternative, probable or improbable, but only words without coherent meaning. The improbable is not, on my view, the incoherent as to meaning, but the incoherent as to its agreement with the whole of the data. Now not all the data are required to furnish meaning; if it were, we could never test hypotheses, for we should have to know how the test will come out in order to plan the test. But in metaphysics, the data that suffice to furnish meaning also suffice to verify the meaning, for in the meaning itself is involved the impossibility of alternatives. Only God, for instance, is meant as the ground of possibility of existence and non-existence of all things. Now the non-being of the ground of possibility cannot be a possibility. This proves God's being only if we are sure that the status of "ground of possibility" is involved in ideas which define God without incoherence. I do not "forget" myself when I say, we are always talking about experience, since I hold that everything metaphysical, including God, is always experienced. It is a question of contingent or variable and necessary or invariable aspects of experience. I assert a duality in experience, and you and Wieman seem, though I am never sure about this, to assert a monistic view from the standpoint of modality, of contingency and necessity.

As to pacifism, I thought I pointed to the concrete consequences of pacifism. Do we differ there as to the conclusion? If so, in the Conference on

Science, Religion and Philosophy you will find my empirical discussion.[71] I was primarily trying to combat the a priori argument <u>for</u> pacifism, in the book. I never yet met a pacifist with much interest, as distinct from profession of interest, in the consequences, short or long, of his doctrine. I mean this and I know of no exception. I am plenty interested in the empirical aspects of this issue I assure you. I am writing a pamphlet chiefly concerned with them.[72]

2) "Probability" I admit applies to arguments for God, but in somewhat the manner in which it applies to mathematical calculations. Nothing can <u>insure</u> human thought against error, not even the mathematical method in its own field. But I see only a stark contradiction in making the existence of a necessary being probable <u>in an objective sense</u>. Certainly frequency wouldn't do. Of course, probability is one of the deepest mysteries of logic, and we are in danger of arguing about an undefined word. I do not think I am recognizing "dimly" that God's existence is <u>probable only</u>, in saying that faith in God is trust in the value of choice. Of course faith in God is faith in whatever God implies, such as that our choices have value. But faith here is left undefined, and I should think it wrongly defined as, "I assert that God is probable." I should say rather, I <u>think it probable</u> that I am not mistaken in asserting that God is necessary, or in asserting that, to the belief in his existence there is no genuine alternative (but only various forms of confusion or pseudo-belief) just as to his existence (as necessary being) there is no such alternative as his merely possible being.

To state as a "fact" that all our knowledge of existential propositions is empirical means, I take it, the double assertion: (a) all our knowledge of existential propositions about contingent beings, that is those other than God, is empirical and probable; and (b) our knowledge of existential propositions about God is also empirical and probable. Now in what sense does this joint statement represent a "fact" which I overlook? I explicitly deny the alleged fact and see no evidence for it, except so far as "empirical" means, <u>based on some form of experience</u>, which I always insist a priori knowledge is, and in so far as all human reasoning is fallible and so its conclusion cannot be asserted as certain, this applying also to pure mathematics and to knowledge of propositions not existential. As someone said, a priori does not mean <u>before</u> all experience but <u>in</u> all experience.

I will make one concession, the scope of which is not as clear to me as I should like. If under induction and empirical reasoning one includes the performance of <u>ideal experiments</u> as the decisive test of truth, then induction can reach God. That is, if the data are the contents of imagination, not just as giving possibilities, but as giving in outline the <u>whole field</u> of the possible, then inductive generalization from this whole field, showing that even in any possible state of affairs God is involved, will exhibit the necessary being as such. This seems a "probably" misleading use of "induction." It is the only way I see to make a bridge from you and Wieman to me and Whitehead (as I interpret him at least, say in the opening passages of *Process [and Reality]*[73]).

3) The cells must, after all, cooperate to dissolve the body in death. Why then can't they do so at any time, if they are so "wise," so cooperative in the ultimate case[?] Of course my answer is largely furnished by your own excellent phrases. The cells' "real function is to be agents of cosmic law—that is, expressions of God's will." You may feel I have distorted the quotation. I have, by omitting "simply." God does not suffice to do the work of matter without the cells as real individuals because the work of matter is just to be such individuals and thus furnish higher individuals with one form of social relationship, enjoyment-of-enjoyment. To fulfill this function they must obey God's will and law, except for slight deviations which add the spice of variety and the unexpected (for both God and man and for themselves). This spice is gone if you put mere law or mere God in place of the cells. As for "expressions" this, as you no doubt have reflected, is a pretty vague metaphor. My notion of the only possible meaning of it is that individuals respond to other individuals in such way as to enrich the first individuals, and also to various individuals to symbolize other individuals.

As to why I infer panpsychism from the directness of the mind-body control, I made a mistake in not saying plainly that the argument for panpsychism was largely omitted from the book. Also in not making more clear that panpsychism is supported by the argument in that chapter chiefly in this way, that if the mind-body relation is to be taken as social, and if, when generalized to cover God as the extreme special case, it is still social, then God's relation to his body requires that all his "cells" be beings capable of serving as socii, and this, I take it, is panpsychism. Indeed, I should incline to use this as a definition.

4) I still think that it is untenable to infer from, x includes y and all its properties, that x has as its own all the properties of y. You see you say, if the error in a man's mind is not God's, then something is not God and pantheism is refuted. I note with gratitude that this is preceded by the statement that I reject pantheism. And surely I do not say that there is nothing which is not (in every sense) God. I only say there is nothing which is not in some sense God. Now a small part can, with its smallness, belong to a large whole without the large whole being simpliciter small. I think there would certainly be a sense, a sensible sense, in which the whole would be small, but not in wholly the sense as that in which the part is so. Now what I say is not that God has no errors but that he commits none, that he suffers rather than does the doings of his parts. When I think a simple thought am I as simple as the thought? Why then must God be as ignorant as our thoughts when he also has them in a certain sense as his thoughts?[74] You have yet to face the qualifications which any treatment of whole and part must put upon identity of properties as between whole and part. Or? So, once more, the actively erroneous beliefs are "included in" God but are God's only in the sense of beliefs he includes, not those he believes. You are saying, to include a belief is to have it in the sense of believing it. But then, to include a small thing is to have it in the sense of being no bigger than the

thing? And to include an ignorant belief is to have it in the sense of being no wiser. The ground?

Isn't it a verbal issue? I see no pragmatic, no real difference here between us.

If God knows all the universe, then God-and-the-universe contains no more items than God (as omniscient). Omniscience means immediacy, indirect knowledge cannot, I should suppose, be perfect. Hence in God's immediacy is everything, everything actual as such, everything potential also as such.[75]

Sincerely yours,
[Hartshorne]

Box 35, Newton Center
Massachusetts

September 18, 1942

Dear Professor Hartshorne,

Your good letter of March 29, commenting on my review of your book, should have been answered long ago. I'll take up your four points briefly.

1. The *a priori*. Your discussion turns on the distinction between the contingent and the necessary; and you identify the contingent with the variable and the necessary with the invariable aspects of experience. I believe you were wrong in thinking that I intend to assert a monism of contingency and necessity. What I do, rather, is to assert that the variable and the invariable, change and identity, are inseparably connected with each other. Furthermore I do not attach eulogistic meanings to the invariant and the necessary. Activity and contingency are more important in the sense of value-producing than is the necessary. However, the concept of necessity needs analysis: there is empirical necessity and logical necessity, and the former seems to lap over on the contingent. At any rate, arguments from necessity do not get me very far toward a God that I am interested in.

Note on pacifism. You include in your treatment of the *a priori* in the letter a remark on pacifism. If all you were trying to do in the book was to combat the *a priori* argument for pacifism, I am with you. The only valid argument is, I think, empirical. But when you write the following sentence, I am astounded: "I never yet met a pacifist with much interest, as distinct from profession of interest, in the consequences, short or long, of his doctrine. I mean this and I know of no exception." It happened that your statement came to me about the same time as the copy of *Fellowship* with Nels Ferré's article in it, pleading for pacifism precisely on the basis of consequences.[76] All the Quakers I know base their action and their faith largely on the successful consequences of peaceful behavior. Although not an absolutist, I call myself a pacifist, and argue solely from concern about consequences. The failure of the last war, the terrible revenge that the defeated country has taken, has seemed to me to be good evidence of the failure of victory in war to secure desired consequences. At present there is less hope for victory and less desire for decent consequences than in the other war. If you are going to say that any pacifist who professes interest in the consequences of the method of love has profession but not interest, I do not see what you are basing that on. I know dozens of pacifists who are far more concerned about the consequences of their views and of this war than are most supporters of the war. As for your statement, I deny the allegation and defy the allegator in so far as it is proper for a pacifist to assume such attitudes.

2. Probability. Your remarks on this subject I quite agree with. If God is at all as an eternal being, there is a sense in which it is always necessary that he be. Your formula: "I think it probable that I am not mistaken in asserting that God is necessary" is entirely acceptable to me. From your book, however, I gathered that you imputed necessity to your proof and not to God's being alone. I am glad to see your concession that induction can reach God provided one includes ideal experiments. Yet I should want to add that every experiment must be in part ideal. I'd like to see you work out this important suggestion further. I have always admired Kant's phrase *Gedankenexperimente*.[77]

3. The cells. Your argument that since they must co-operate to dissolve the body at death that therefore they can do so at any time seems to me circular. The problem is how they can co-operate at any time, being so ignorant. On the other hand, if you accept my view that their real function is to be expressions of God's will, why is not the assumption of their will as distinct from God's an unnecessary hypothesis?

4. On pantheism. You say that my argument is that "if the error in a man's mind is not God's, then something is not God and pantheism is refuted." That is a very backhanded and inadequate way of putting my argument, which is positive and not negative. My argument is that if pantheism is true, then errors belong to God, and God entertains contradictory opinions about the subject matter of the error, namely, the erroneous opinion and his omniscient knowledge that the error is error. If he does not believe the error to be true, as I in my error do, then my belief is not a part of him and pantheism is false, as you say. But the main point is that the truth of pantheism involves God's thoughts in a flat contradiction, for he has to assert and deny the truth of every proposition about which anyone errs. Your statement that "if God knows all the universe, then God-and-the-universe contains no more items than God (as omniscient)," is interpreted by your statement that omniscience means immediacy. This in turn I can take only in the sense of an epistemologically monistic identification of knowledge with its object. But I am an incurable epistemological dualist. I cannot believe that God's knowledge of me is ontologically identical with my actual being for myself.

Since your Riverside Drive address was back in March, I am assuming that you have returned to Chicago and am addressing the letter there. Please return good for evil and answer this more promptly than I answered yours.

Most cordially yours,
[Brightman]

Sept. 23, 1942

Dear Professor Brightman,

We seem to be making some progress in understanding, at least so far as the *a priori* and probability-and-necessity are concerned. Of course the variable and the invariable are inseparable for me too, in the sense that some variations or other are required by the invariant, necessary factor. And I agree of course that the necessary is no better than the contingent, in the sense that the contingent as aspect of the necessary is required for any value (or being). The necessary individual, God, is better than the non-necessary individuals, but God is of course not exclusively necessary and would be empty of value if *(per impossibile)* he were.

I do not grant that necessity is only in being but not in the proof. The proofs are necessary in the sense that mathematical proofs are, namely provided no mistake has been made. One thinks one is seeing that self-evident truths,[78] truths that could not be false, lead to conclusions which accordingly also could not be false. But one does not know for certain that the truths are necessary or that the deduction is valid. As to whether necessary proofs lead to the interesting kind of God, for me they lead to second type theism, which I hold to be the religious idea of God, so far as it goes. And they lead even further, though with further chances of error, to the assignment of attribute[s] to the status of A-perfect or R-perfect,[79] that is, to the sense in which God is perfect in knowledge, power, and goodness. I am rewriting the ontological argument to make more explicit than the book did what the argument is and what it proves.[80] Of course every argument is empirical, if that means experiential, drawing meanings as premises from concrete intuition. But intuitions are of two classes, intuition of variable, contingent details, and of invariant necessary things as such.

Ideal experiment is involved in ordinary induction, it seems to me, only as exploration of the possible and its interconnections. All decision as to which possibilities are actualized is made by perception of contingent details—induction in the ordinary sense. But in philosophy it is the non-existence of certain things that is seen to be impossible, or in other words here there are not alternative possibilities in all cases, and this discovery (not at all by perception in the usual sense), that the non-existence of something is not a possibility is not, without terrible danger of confusion, to be called inductive.

On pantheism we seem to make no progress whatever, and I still do not know at all what your argument is. For it cannot be what it seems to be, and yet be an argument against me. You say over and over that if there is belief—say some erroneous belief of mine—in God, then he believes an erroneous belief. I say, over and over, that I do not admit that to have a belief as part of oneself is necessarily to believe the belief.[81] Where do we go from there? I may not have proved my point by asserting it but neither have you by asserting the contrary. And I have developed a theory of two modes of inherence of belief, and of many other things, in a mind. Either you say it is self-evident that there can be but one mode, that of believing, or you deduce this monistic view of inherence from some more general proposition. You have yet to say which path you are taking, and, if the second, what the more general proposition may be. It cannot be, I have remarked, that "every adjective of a part applies in the same mode to the whole," for then to have small parts and to be a small whole would be the same thing. To embrace false beliefs within one's being and to believe falsely are, I say, no more the same than to embrace smallness as property of a part and to be small as a whole. What is your answer? I do not say you have none; but I am fairly confident that you have not stated it to me. Until you do, and I hope you will, we will just go round and round. I add that I hold, with Fechner, who knew a good many empirical facts about mind, that to include volition is not necessarily in all cases to will in the ways in question.[82] One may suffer the volitions of others as parts of one's being, but not one's own volitions, except in the sense in which the smallness of a part belongs to a large whole. Not merely is the volition not all of the whole's volition, it is not its at all in the same sense or mode as it is the volition of the part. God feels our volitions directly, and they are parts of him, as that to which one is passive is a part of the passive state, logically inseparable from its being as a whole. This doctrine may seem self-contradictory or meaningless but in any case it cannot be criticized by deducing consequences from its assumed impossibility. Thus you argue that if God has my false beliefs, and also all true beliefs, then he has self-contradictory beliefs; which contradiction follows only if it be admitted, which I shall not easily admit, that to include a belief is to have it as something which one believes oneself. Even we can consider incompatible beliefs, and my theory is that something further is possible, namely to have the beliefs as belonging to one's parts without their being beliefs of oneself. And I argue that the general principle of this is necessary if there are to be any real wholes with real parts at all, since obviously parts must have properties in some sense unique to them and not, in the same mode, properties of the whole. You continue to ignore all this and to re-assert its assumed falsity, from which you derive consequences that can only be used against me after I know the basis of the assumption.

On one point I admit what may seem the principle of your argument. I admit that the sufferings of the parts belong as sufferings of its own to the whole. But even here there is a change of mode. What is overwhelming suffering, nearly the whole content, of the part, is in the whole only as a very different proportion of its total value-state. The reason that the whole nevertheless does suffer in the sufferings of the parts is that suffering remains that, whether it is active or passive. To feel the suffering of others is to suffer, whereas to feel the volitions of others is not to will them, for willing as such is active not passive. All this is based on experiential, though not merely empirical or contingent, distinctions which you seem to abstract from. Altogether your procedure here seems to me *a priori* in, if I may say so, a purely bad sense. I have, so far, had only logic chopping from you, not traits of experience (except such as my theory accounts for).

My point may be summed as follows: the properties of parts belong to the whole as follows: properties-of-its-parts; in this special sense they are "its." They become "its" in the usual sense only with a change of mode, and in the case of volition and belief (which involves belief as an essential, I think) this means that the parts can will and believe what the whole merely suffers and does not believe. And I affirm that some such doctrine is required, theology apart, to give the idea of part and whole any sense.

It may be you have answered all this, but it seems unlikely this could be done in the brief remarks you have made on the subject. Anyhow I have wholly missed any answer.

Your point about cells is somewhat unclear to me partly because I forget where we were. I should say that there is no meaning in the idea that cells are merely parts of the will of God, for I do not believe will can have parts in the required sense. Will acts on something, and the cells give it something to act on in this case. There are many advantages also in not cutting off the series of sentient individuals below man at what must, it seems, be a purely arbitrary point short of cells, molecules and the like. Some of the best scientists here or anywhere agree with me in this, which shows at least that the matter has some empirical significance or application. The cells have very little freedom of action, and the limits of this freedom have been set by God in his double aspect of activity and passivity, the latter making all other past creatures to some extent responsible for the limits. In other words, I hold that a will can individuate parts only by producing individual wills within itself. This is what I and Whitehead call the social aspect of being (also D. H. Parker).[83] Mere things result from social transactions being grouped and lumped together. Of course one might say with Berkeley, in a possible interpretation of him, that physical things are mere knots in the social transactions between man and God, but while this view seems to me less clearly false than materialism or dualism, it seems to me an arbitrary and probably impossible truncation of the scale of beings.

Pacifism. This issue is much harder to discuss on the same intellectual level, it being a practical and emotionally charged one so obviously and directly. One can only try. Of course my sentence about pacifists not being much interested in consequences is at best elliptical. All of us have a tendency to make facts and real probabilities fit our views (or get out of our sight) rather than to make the views adjust to the facts and the knowable probabilities. Now my impression has decidedly been that pacifists do this even worse and much worse than other people, especially other people who are articulate and educated. Of course there are pacifists and pacifists. I should not compare you or Ferré with A. W. Palmer.[84] The latter seems to me just not to think at all, but just to talk and feel and fuss. I have read Ferré's article, also a long letter on the subject, and also talked with him. Interest in concrete knowable realities seems to me in the background even with him. He says, for example, that the only way for Europe to get along is to have the German people united and strong. Yet every known fact about Europe and the Prussian tradition and many other aspects of the matter, including the elementary geographical facts, imply that such an arrangement would mean that only by a lucky miracle could the other peoples in Europe get their minimal rights, unless the other peoples had first been made strong in independence of German influence. Germans have every military advantage, and this one-sidedness is the great problem, made much worse by many facts about Europe's traditions and structure. Ferré is too far in the clouds to consider such matters. He talks vaguely about the deep underlying forces, so loosely conceived that no empirical check is possible. He is a fine mind, but even he seem[s] to illustrate what I mean. So does J. H. Holmes[85] and numerous others. Hartman is ghastly![86]

Your own remarks are too brief to be fairly criticized. I am not sure though that it is wholly unfair to point out that you do not state what the question, realistically regarded, comes to. To call the last war a failure has to mean, for your argument, that a German victory might have been as well or better, unless you think we might somehow have gambled for a draw. The latter could only be a pretty wild gamble, for unless one tries to win one is very apt to lose, perhaps almost certain to. Now I see no good reason to think that a victorious Germany would have done less harm than a defeated one has done. On the contrary. We might now have not even a choice but to give in to the Germans. But further. The results of the last war were not fatalistically determined by the war itself, or there is no freedom. Winning gives us an opportunity, but opportunities are not guarantees. Now why was the opportunity not better used (it was not wholly wasted, in my view, far from it)? Well, are pacifists honestly surveying the mass of evidence for the conclusion that, as one of the best German students of the problem, a very religious man, has said, the greatest help of all to Hitler in his catastrophic career was given by "international pacifism." (E. Heiman[n][87]) This seems to me a plain fact. Hitler need not have been successful in his villainous plans, had enough people believed in the wisdom of stopping him by force. Surely the failure to stop him had something to do with the widely diffused notion that fighting never accomplishes anything. Thus this very belief that fighting is useless is one of the chief reasons why the fighting of the last war was not more useful. A wise discriminating use of force is one thing, a panicky resort to force at the last gasp, followed again by a wave of vague pacifism, is another. I shall fight this vicious cycle all my life. We must see this problem as steadily as we can. Pacifists do not achieve as [a] "consequence" of their activities or inactivities any such steadying, since their chief influence is in the treacherously peaceful times when few want to bother about armies and munitions anyway. I fail to see the slightest reason to think that pacifist argument or belief is going to help to get rid of war or to do anything but make it more terrible when it comes, by weakening the wrong side. It is just in the countries in which (and when) pacifism might do the world some good that pacificism has least chance of spreading, say in Japan now, or in the last decades.

So there we are and no doubt there we stay. I was a pacifist once, a very convinced one, rather long ago. One seldom reverts, so I am probably fixed in the other position.

Is the argument *a priori*? Absolute pacifism must be *a priori,* like all absolutes. Relative pacifism can appeal to contingent facts. However, in evaluating a principle of action rather than a description of facts there is in a sense necessarily an *a priori* element. That is, one must ask what the principle implies, should it be adopted, and this adoption is largely a possibility not a fact. In short, ideal experiment comes in to show what <u>would</u> happen. Still, that is not *a priori* in the strict sense. My argument was, that if all good men adopt the principle—or all wise men—that they will never use force, then force will be left as the monopoly of any men not good enough or wise enough to abstain from it. That there will be such seems sure enough on an empirical basis, and it follows almost *a priori* from the notion that there is at least some plausible case for fighting, and this again follows pretty certainly from the fact that most men[88] believe there is. Ferré says, and you I presume, that police force is justifiable if kept to a minimum or wisely economized.[89] But the distinction between police force, as in the interest of the whole community, and fighting among nations as only in their own several interests, can be shown, I hold, to be a highly relative one in view of the actualities. I have made this point against Ferré.[90] The United Nations are striving to bring the world closer to the state in which there shall be international policing.[91] The British and American navies constituted in some real though highly limited degree an approach to such a state, compared to anything to be hoped for from Germany and Japan.[92] If to use a police force is all right then to fight to achieve one should be also. And the irony is that if soldiers do in the end bring about an international police then many pacifists will say, now we are for the use of force against aggression. This seems to me behavior in which regard for consequences is not uppermost, but regard for words and over-absolute distinctions of concepts.

In any case, the primary consequences to be considered are those likely to follow from an Axis victory compared to those likely to follow from an Axis defeat. Each historical situation is in [a] profound sense and degree unique and must be judged without mechanical application of analogies. The Axis is not the Kaiser's Germany but something even more evil and dangerous. What they propose to do if they can is fairly well known. You say there is even less chance of a good outcome if we win than last time. I see many facts on the other side, but anyway that's not the question, which is, is not the danger from defeat much greater than the danger from victory? This is not purely a question of your values or mine, there is a democratic principle involved. The United Nations are certainly much closer to being representative of mankind than the Axis, by any standard almost you choose, including the numerical. India is in a peculiar way close to being on the fence, but the roughly equally numerous Chinese, and the third greatest group, the Russians, are very plainly and violently partisan against the Axis. You pacifists are at most representing the judgment of a minority, most of whom are either very ignorant and illiterate or are professed deniers of all basic human rights and decencies, when you say that an Axis victory would not be worse or much worse than an Axis defeat.

I quit. Thanks for your letter.

[Hartshorne adds the following handwritten paragraph at the end of the typescript.]

I add one thing out of unpleasant sense of duty, perhaps perverted. The more you argue that there is nothing to fight for now and little hope of victory the more you in effect fight—on Hitler's side. He'd pay you to do it, and wisely.

Sorry we have to argue this awful business.

Sincerely,
Charles Hartshorne

Box 35, Newton Center
Massachusetts

September 25, 1942

Dear Professor Hartshorne,

You are evidently blessed with more academic leisure, *otium cum dig.*, and the like, than we laboring Bostonians enjoy. Would that I had the time to answer your letter as fully as it deserves.

Taking up your first important proposition, that in philosophy the non-existence of certain things is seen to be impossible, I am not sure that this is the essence of philosophy. It is perfectly true that the proposition is valid and yet it is so formal and abstract that it is not, in my opinion, an important advance in philosophy. It becomes important only when applied to existing particulars which are inductively known.

About pantheism, I might have recourse to the carbon of my previous letter and point to the words that I am sure are there which express the vital point that you assiduously omit from your exposition. However, I'll not do it. The words may not be there, anyway. I'll start afresh. I agree entirely with all that you say about parts and wholes. I also grant that there are the different modes of inherence to which you hold, although that form of expression is to me offensively scholastic; it seems to me to imply that a belief is something distinct from a mind, which may or may not inhere in that mind, and which enjoys its own being as a "floating adjective" when not in that mind. But that is not the vital point. The v.p. now emerges. If a belief inheres in God without his believing it and the same belief inheres in me while believing it, everything is hunky-dory. This is exactly my view. It seems to me to be also the disproof of pantheism; for there is something in the universe not in God, namely, the belief that that false belief is true. Whether you call that belief a mode of inherence matters not a whit to me; whatever you call it, it is something that could not be in God as it is in me without making him utterly self-contradictory. If there is anything that is not in God and could not be in him without contradiction, pantheism is refuted. *Theos* is less than *pan*. I do not see that any truth about the relation of wholes and parts can make a contradiction less than a contradiction. There is no contradiction in saying that parts are small and the whole is great, or even that parts are bad and the whole good. But there is contradiction in declaring that a perfect mind entertains contradictory beliefs about the same belief, namely, the belief that it is true (which I in my ignorance do entertain with full conviction) and the belief that it is false (which the Omniscient One entertains). Have I made my point clearer? You can see that I do not maintain that there is only one mode of inherence. I maintain rather that if pantheism is true all possible modes of inherence must be part of God.

Now about cells. My remarks all aim at trying to find the evidence for believing in such beings. From your brief paragraph I can deduce three lines of evidence. (1) There are signs of freedom in nature, which may be accounted for by cells. (2) Cells are a necessary inference from the theory that a will can individuate parts only by producing individual wills within itself. Either I do not know what you mean by individual or else this seems to me an unempirical theory, surely not empirical evidence. (3) The scale of beings must not be truncated. Hence there must be cells all the way from the maximum cell, God, down to the minimum sub-electronic cell.—None of these arguments strikes me as convincing. As to the first, you admit that the degree of freedom is so small as to be hardly noticeable. God's freedom suffices, as Berkeley thought.[93] As to the second, I do not comprehend it at all; it seems to me utterly remote from anything that I have ever experienced except dream creatures, and I do not re-gard them as genuine individuals. The third argument is a very risky one. It proves Spinoza's infinite attributes;[94] it proves the wildest kind of pluralism; it proves magical materialism; in short, it proves a complete series of everything you want to start with. It seems to me an arbitrary supposition.

Just a word on pacifism. I believe that Russia was right in calling on the League of Nations to keep the pledge of Versailles for a general disarmament. If England, France, Germany (Weimar), and America had kept the treaty, this war would have been averted. Nations pledged themselves to a pacifist policy and broke the pledge. The number of sincere and intelligent individual pacifists is very small. I believe that it is their important function to work now and in the peace[time] for a reconciliation of humanity, to which they can make a unique contribution. This is not the whole story, but is part of it.

Time's up.

Most cordially yours,
[Brightman]

October 17, 1942

Dear Professor Brightman,

I too have become busy, terribly so. Too bad, but I still can't see your vital point as a point. You don't, I think, deduce the contradiction from my prem-ises, but from something you substitute for them. It is precisely my belief in my belief, or rather, in a certain proposition or state of affairs, that is in God without for all that being God's believing. My real believing is a property of his part but not a property or state of himself as a whole, analogously to the smallness of the part belonging to the whole only as its <u>parts'</u> property not as <u>its</u> property, state, or act. I find no argument, once more. God has the activity of my belief as an activity of his part, but as passivity of himself, as a whole, to the part, and thus the belief is felt and enjoyed but not believed, except by the part. In aesthetic experience of the beliefs of others we do something rather similar, only here because we are not omniscient we do not directly intuit the beliefs of others, to any great extent at least, but rather build up our own image of the belief, still without believing what the believer believes. God's immediacy is so far superior to ours that only a faint analogy can hold here, ex-cept as to the relation of mind to bodily members, and even then with severe limitations, and that relates us to individuals so humble as to scarcely "believe" at all.

Somebody, perhaps I am it, must translate Fechner's great chapter on this problem.[95] It's the berries.

Thanks for your letter, I may have time to do more justice to it later,

Sincerely
Charles Hartshorne

[Hartshorne continues to type under his signature]

If belief is potential readiness to act upon a certain fact or truth, then God finds his parts ready to act in ways in which he is not ready to act as a whole, and with regard to propositions upon which he would not act. Where is the contradiction?

Box 35, Newton Center
Massachusetts

October 31, 1942

Dear Professor Hartshorne,
    If I have not discussed the question of pantheism from your premises, it is because I cannot see the intelligibility of your premise.
    If I get the point, it is that you think that a small line can be part of a large surface, without any contradiction between the smallness of the line and the largeness of the surface. From that analogy you argue that a false belief of a small mind may be in a large mind without the large mind's accepting the false belief. The analogy does not make sense to me. It is what Bowne used to call picture thinking.[96] What is true of space relations is not true of a thinking mind. If from your premise I grant that you are right, then the only inference I can make is (a) that a false belief is part of a true one in the same sense in which a short line is part of a long one (which seems to me nonsense) and (b) that if the belief is not entertained as true by the mind of God as it is by my erring mind, then there is something in the universe which is not in the mind of God. On your premise, the false belief is in his mind, true enough, but my belief in its falseness is not in his mind as it is in mine. If not, then it is in my mind and not in his. Then there is something not in his mind, and pantheism is done for. It seems to me that your entire argument about whole and part is picture thinking, as you urge it, omitting the problems that arise from the nature of a mind.
    Belief cannot be reduced to potential readiness to act. It is at least an assertion of correspondence to reality; which usually is accompanied by readiness to act, but not always. There can, of course, be no contradictions among acts or readinesses to act, as such; only propositions can contradict.

I am not at all satisfied with the state of our discussion!

Cordially yours,
[Brightman]

Nov. 9, 1942.

Dear Professor Brightman,
    Another try.
    The exact point in dispute seems this: can my really <u>believing</u> P be within God without his really believing P? In other words, does "within" necessarily imply "of" or "by" God? Can my act of "assertion" be part of God though he <u>makes</u> no such act himself? Must one perform an act oneself to have it as part of one's being. Of course to contain the act <u>as something one acts oneself</u> one must perform it. But the question is not whether God contains my believing <u>as his act</u> but whether he can contain it <u>as mine,</u> and as "his" only in the sense in which what belongs to a part, in a different sense belongs to the whole?
    Now for God to have my believing, it cannot be necessary for him to believe as I do, merely by virtue of some <u>general proposition about part and whole.</u> For you have admitted that <u>in some cases</u> at least wholes have parts with properties which the wholes do not themselves have except <u>as</u> properties of their parts.[97] <u>So far,</u> it should be possible for God to have my belief <u>as</u> mine, but not as his except as I am his, and as in that limited sense what is mine is his. The point of my spatial example was not to argue by analogy but to find out whether or not you had <u>any</u> analogy to support your view. It cannot be an analogy with a spatial whole. A part can move, while its whole does not; a part might shrink while the whole expanded, etc. So your insistence that human believing <u>within</u> God must mean human believing <u>by</u> God, must rest on some <u>special</u> law of mind as whole, not on a general law of wholes.[98] Even this is in no way clearly stated, if you allow me to say so, in any of your discussions,[99] though I may easily have forgotten something here.
    Do you agree that a part can perform an act which the whole does not perform?
    If yes, what is peculiar about <u>believing</u> that exempts it from this possibility? Or "asserting"[?] Why cannot God find his part asserting something without his asserting it? Is there a carefully conceived reason against this?[100]
    <u>Of course my</u> asserting is not within God as <u>his</u> asserting, just as the fading out of one of my sensations is not <u>my</u> fading out. This example seems to prove that I need not stick to spatial examples (picture thinking). Now what examples do <u>you</u> offer? Is asserting absolutely unique as act in this matter? Or are all psychic acts equally and in the same sense done by whole and part?[101] Certainly not

all psychic properties are possessed in a univocal sense by whole and part as I just showed above.

Of course you can go on saying that believing <u>within</u> must be believing <u>by</u> God, but if you really go on with such contextless repetition you are not philosophizing, as I define that.[102]

To say that any other view than your own here is unintelligible is about the same thing. Only the truth is intelligible in philosophy. Besides, as Peirce said, he who says something is inconceivable or unintelligible should, if he expects this to look like an argument (and it is what your refutation has boiled down to), give a careful account of the variety of approaches he has taken to try to conceive it.[103] Now note that Fechner thought it eminently intelligible, and Fechner was expert in just such matters as lie between philosophy and psychology, and about nothing had he thought more carefully.[104] Wm. James spent a lifetime worrying about the problem and finally decided that Fechner was right in thinking a higher mind could include a lower, and God include us. (He only objected to the idea that God had <u>nothing</u> outside him, but his reasons can be met by showing that an internal environment does what he demanded.)[105] Then there is Varisco,[106] Montague, Whitehead, etc. You can't offer as argument that you just see that these men have been talking unintelligibly. That is only a sign that something is wrong, but whether in them or in you is all to seek.

To me nothing, and really nothing, could be less intelligible than that one could know a state of mind perfectly, as God is said to know ours, and have it not within but without one's own being, <u>not as factor in that being.</u>[107] It is my very believing of my belief that God knows, and therefore must have as factor in his own being—without, for all you show, necessarily <u>believing thus</u> himself.

I am not claiming, so far, to have proved your view wrong. I am <u>claiming to have proved,</u> and I appeal to your candor to admit it, that you have <u>not proved mine wrong</u> in any degree by your favorite method of refutation of pantheism, a refutation which does not even consider the distinction between pantheism and panentheism, though logically the two differ as much from each other as either from your view. The three together exhaust the possibilities between them.

Now I say a denial requires context in philosophy. I have only begun to indicate the rich context surrounding the Fechnerian view (Ch. II, *Zend Avesta,* for some of it). James gives some of it in *Pluralistic Universe.* You might well ask me for an example of one mind including the belief of another without believing similarly.[108] I answer: my mind now remembering my belief of yesterday with primary of true memory (Bergson) includes that belief in itself now but does not necessarily believe as in its former belief it believed.[109] You may have another theory of memory, but memory of not now accepted beliefs is a fact, and there might just possibly be difficulties in the view you might have to adopt to avoid my contention. As I said before, for an empiricist you rely strangely upon juggling words to prove your point. Or are you appealing to some self-enclosed, self-evident unique aspect of experience which just can't be further articulated? Then I deny philosophy can recognize any such without giving up any method for distinguishing rational from irrational assertion.[110]

I have pointed to aesthetic experience as giving something like having another's belief as part of oneself without accepting the belief as true. I believe that there is enough basis for the something like to carry weight, but I refrain from elaborating.

I hold also that we experience the experiences of our cells, and I hold this as an empirical description which alone is adequate to the way we feel ourselves to share feelings with the body. I know there are other descriptions but they seem to me to differ precisely by failing to describe as many aspects of the given truly, recognizably. This, though, is a subtle point, and subtle description of the given is not everybody's forte. Admittedly the previous sentence is open not only to the charge of conceit or arrogance but also to the charge of attempting to shut off criticism. But I only make it knowing it will not shut off criticism, and by itself ought not.

Further. The properties of parts do not belong to wholes so far as these properties are negative or privational, unless all the parts share in some privation, and not even then unrestrictedly. Now believing, in itself, has a positive aspect, but so far as erroneous it must have a negative one. Belief confronted with complete evidence is bound to be right. Only where assertion takes a chance beyond the evidence can there be error or contradiction among beliefs. Now just as a whole need not be faint because an element in it is faint, so it need not be ignorant because an element in it is ignorant. God feels the evidence confronting us, and he also yields to it so far as it goes. Where evidence as present to me stops he feels my act of assertion as going further, but he also feels all sorts of other things which make him "assert" otherwise.

But can one feel, endure an act and not enact it? I not only see no reason why not, but to me it seems that only so can we understand action and passion, whole and part. I feel activity as exerted upon me in the sudden burst of thunder, I feel it as activity I endure by my own passivity, not as my activity. But it is one with my feeling as its immanent datum. You may well hold another view about the unity of the mind with its data. Still, there surely is a lot of ground for discussion here which can never rightly be short-circuited by talking about contradiction.

If wholes can never be passive to the acts of the parts, I fail to see how in dynamic terms there can be whole and parts. The unity of the whole would be just the sum of the acts of the parts or it would be something which contradicted the possibility of these acts. Suppose the "plus" of being in the whole is purely active.[111] How is this activity which is the whole's as such related to the acts of the parts? Only by destroying all their independence, so far as I can see, <u>unless</u> the activity of the whole includes passivity toward the acts of the parts. To relate one activity to another is to yield in some degree to the other activity, to take form from it. Otherwise all one has is a single act with many facets, a single force with many merely logical distinctions, no real ones. So I feel that you are implicitly assuming a dynamics of whole and part which is impossible; or you are making a peculiar exception of believing as an act the ground for which—beyond that it fits the requirements of our debate (as debate and not as discussion)—I am still seeking.

The large whole is the small parts plus; the strong whole is the weak parts plus; the knowing whole is the ignorant parts plus; the whole which affirms only so far as the evidence goes may have parts which affirm beyond the evidence, because what is positive in this affirmation is felt passively as act of the part, and that only, by the whole, and what is negative is also felt but not, naturally, as limiting the whole in the same way—just as feeling a part to be faint does not make one feel faint as a whole.

No doubt you are quite unable to see any of this as intelligible. But I ask you if that amounts to your showing that I either talk nonsense or contradict myself, along with many first rate minds in many schools of thought with every intellectual asset, pretty much? We all get to thinking if we can silence pupils' objections we have practically proved something. Alas how we all fool ourselves!

If memory cannot include past experience of believing what we no longer believe, what is the unity of personality for personalism? Whatever it is, you cannot refute me merely by referring to it.

On a pleasanter note I add that most philosophers can't even be got to debate, not to mention discuss, very much. I honestly believe that we all fear the light. This may be a hard saying and you may reply, "speak for yourself." I only say, that's what I think of man and original sin, nowhere more evident than just here in philosophy, respectable a pursuit as it is.

One more thing. In a sense I admit my view is not intelligible, if that means that I don't understand it as clearly and vividly as God does. No facetiousness is intended, for it follows that I can sympathize somewhat with your difficulties, and can realize that you may be as anxious for the truth as I (however much that be!), but just balked by those difficulties. But what I feel is that you have not even begun to compare these difficulties,[112] objectively (in such degree and manner as this is possible for mortal man) with those which others have only to seek to find in your own view. That's where students are so deceptive. Only to a very limited extent can they compel such comparison. It takes mature persons trained largely in other traditions to do it. And difficulties in clearly imagining something are really to be expected in philosophy and are no argument; whereas the total impossibility of providing any context at all for assertions is fatal. And I see none whatever for the idea of a knowledge not immediate but exhaustive and infallible; or a knowledge immediate but of which, as a unity of being, the object is not a factor. This seems to me not much like a limitation of human intuition but like an error of human thinking.

That we can have only rather obscure direct intuitions of the structure of mind-within-mind can be deduced—or so I tried to show in [the] chapter on mind-body in the book[113]—from the status of the human mind as between the lower and the highest types of mind, deduced at least as a possibility whose actuality should not surprise us, even though we believe in the structure in question.

If you don't write me down as impossible on all counts for this letter, you must be at least as good a man as I take you to be. I feel somewhat bitter often because philosophers do so little honest facing of each others' criticisms, or if that is too unkind, because they are so stupid about it assuming they are honest. Is philosophy a rational discipline, or is it self-defense of one's own castle of ideas? You must have had trouble with this question too. And in the very act of feeling that the other fellow is guilty, one is apt to become unusually guilty oneself. The charge of pride is usually made proudly, of self-indulgence self-indulgently, etc. My house has glass bricks—and so would have any house I ever built, incidentally!

Rereading your letter makes me all the more certain that you don't argue with me, or with what I say. On my premises, say you, our belief in our beliefs is "not in God's mind as it is in ours. Therefore there is something that is not in God." A perfect non-sequitur. Of course what belongs to the part does not belong to the whole "as it belongs to the part." How ever should or could it? The part's part is "part" of the whole in a more of less different fashion. "Important" in the part, it may not be so in the whole, etc. But it does not in the least follow that something in the part is not in the whole. The part's having its part, or its act, certainly is "in" the whole, but naturally the act is not straightway [an] "act-of" the whole. I'll gladly submit the issue so stated to any logician in good standing.

Of course there has to be a generic sense of "belonging to" which applies to the part of the part in relation both to the inclusive part and to the whole; but there may also be a specific sense unique to the first relation. This is all my argument demands. The specific relation is that of a believing to its believer; the generic one that of a believing to a mind that in any way has the believing as [an] item in itself.

As to arguing from picture thinking without reference to the special nature of mind, what I in fact do is to take the idea of sympathy as literal "feeling of feeling," the "immediately social nature of mind" or the "social nature of immediacy" or the idea of the person as a society of experiences with a certain type of order or integration, as[114] explanatory of space along with everything else. It seems no apt way to describe this to speak as though it depended on an abuse of space metaphors.

To me your letter is fencing not discussion. Maybe that's all you can do on this issue. Probably it's all I can do on some issue, but not this one.

Remember I haven't chiefly attacked your position but protested against your speaking as though you had a refutation of my position. If you have it you

have not stated it, and I'll be glad to be judged by the correctness of that assertion, or denial.

[Hartshorne]

Box 35, Newton Center
Massachusetts

January 31, 1943

Dear Professor Hartshorne,

My long silence since receipt of your letter of November 9 does not mean
that I am silenced. It means only that an unreasonable amount of work has
confronted me, both by way of writing and of extra university duties. Also the
cancellation of the meetings of the learned societies caused me extra work.
Now I am somewhat nearer to normal, although I face two lecture trips this
week—one to Springfield, and one to the air base at Quonset Point.

Starting where you start, I reply that believing P cannot be within God unless God believes P. Believing is an act, as you grant; and every act in a mind is
an act of that mind. If this be not true, then I cannot imagine what it is an act
of; a mind is a unity of consciousness, and when it acts, the whole mind acts. If
God contains my act as mine, but not as his, then my act is not his act in any
personal sense, and the verb "contain" is being used in an impersonal or abstract sense. If God is a person, he performs all the acts within his personality; if
he is a collection of persons, a society, then your view would be possible, but I
should see no good reason for calling a society "God."

You can see that I derive my ideas, not from some general proposition
about possible relations of wholes and parts, but from a very specific proposition about the unique kind of whole which personality is empirically observed
to be. I see no reason for any analogy to support an empirical fact. In fact, any
analogy, spatial or otherwise, would be picture thinking and would be depart-
ing from the fact. No analogy is so strong or clear as the actual experience itself.
You rightly state that my view rests on some special law of mind as whole. If I
had not clearly stated this, it is because I do not like to harp too much on personalistic first principles.

I do not agree that a part of a mind can perform an act which the whole
mind does not perform, for the simple reason that I experience mind and its action as an indivisible, although complex, whole. To define other centers of activity within a mind is to deny its unity as a mind; to go against all personal
experience and arbitrarily to identify the individual with the social. Social interaction, co-operation, communication are, indeed, basic; but they are not found

within one mind. Your analogy that asserts the fading of one of your sensations is not your fading I reject on two grounds: (1) a sensation (pure) is not an act; and (2) its fading is your fading, to a certain extent. For you consist of conscious experience, and you change as it changes; you fade as it fades; you grow as it grows. All psychic acts are done by the whole, and all properties are properties of the whole. If they are not, then a mind is a mere assemblage, not a real unity, as I experience it to be.

I should like an exact definition from you of your definition of pantheism and panentheism before I comment further on the latter.

When I now remember my belief of yesterday, I do not literally experience yesterday's belief; I experience knowledge of it, which is what God has of my beliefs. I must stop here. Write!

Ever thine,
Edgar S. Brightman

June 5, 1943[115]

5642 Drexel Ave. or
The Univ. of Chicago

Dear Professor Brightman,
Maybe it is time to list some of the things we <u>do</u> agree upon. They are considerable.

1) God knows all things perfectly, including all our acts.[116]

2) What we do, our acts, are done by us not by God.

3) Would you also say that in so far as we are active God is passive, that he suffers what we do?

However, it seems you do not want to say God experiences our acts, but only "experiences knowledge" of them. His knowledge then is not by acquaintance, but by inference?[117] If the latter, I find no meaning to saying his knowledge is perfect, for inferential knowledge can be adequate only to abstract objects. Or, you draw a distinction between acquaintance and experience that strikes me as my idea of psychic parts (that are active but to which the whole is passive) strikes you; that is, as unjustified by anything in experience.

Your argument then might be that we know the past without experiencing it, and also without inferring it either? Here I assert as a fact of experience what you deny as such a fact, namely experience of the past.[118] I admit it is an obscure, subtle experience, very difficult to clearly observe and describe. For much that we tend to think of as memory is really imagination. "True memory" (Bergson) is not to be easily distinguished.[119] Thus my position is easily attacked. So, for different reasons is yours. For if the past is not given, is it merely inferred? If the knowledge is not immediate it is mediate, hence <u>in principle</u> fallible, even in God's case. Or is immediate knowledge not equivalent to knowledge by experience? And if past is never given could it be inferred?

You see perfect knowledge must have <u>some</u> sort of unity with its object. I should think a most peculiarly intimate and perfect unity. You appear to deny all unity whatever.[120] For after all I admit that the psychic whole is not in every sense one; in a real sense it is many. I only say that in some very exacting and perfect sense it is also one. Now if you deny this then I have not the slightest faint notion of what is meant by the perfection of God's knowledge, or even by his "knowledge," which seems to me in our experience always a unity of knowing and known,[121] except so far as there is precarious inference. Perhaps you really think God knows us purely by inference?

I think the debate about analogy is a misunderstanding between us. My point was an analogy between our minds and the divine. You don't avoid such an analogy. The very word "mind" means it. We are agreeing here I imagine. We both seek that in our experience to which certain features in God's experience can be thought analogous. For surely they are not identical with the features of our experience. In other words analogy means generalization here. You make God's knowing analogous to the knowing of past beliefs. Only I don't recognize your description of our knowing. <u>There</u> is the difference, not in employing or not employing analogical thought. The empirical fact you claim to be such is a fact of our experience, not of God's. What but analogy can bridge the gulf?

In your last letter you state clearly what you hold against me. You hold James and Fechner did not at all know the nature of mind, which might be true of course, but still means my position is not to be brushed aside. You assert the sheer unity of mind in a sense elaborately criticized by James and Fechner, if by no others.[122] "A mind is a unity of consciousness, and when it acts, the whole mind acts."[123] Yes, when <u>it</u> acts, it, the whole, acts, of course. But the parts,[124] what the parts do, must the whole mind do it? That doesn't follow from the other proposition, but is a quite independent one. "Every act in a mind is an act of that mind." Now you don't mean that every act known by a mind is an act of that mind, and perhaps you don't mean that every act known by a mind is an act of that mind, and perhaps you don't mean that every act <u>immediately</u> known by a mind is an act of that mind—or do you? This would imply that all knowledge of acts not one's own is inferential. And when you say that social interaction is not found within one mind you seem to be saying it is not known immediately. Or else that by immediate knowledge one does not mean any sort of unity of knower and known?

If a belief within a mind is not an act of that mind you cannot imagine what it is an act of. Of course, [it is] an act of some other mind within the first mind. This you hold to be impossible, but that is the question once more. You have only reasserted your position.[125] But you argue: if God contains my act as mine but not as his, then my act is not his in any personal sense, and "contain" is impersonal or abstract. This assumes there are but two possibilities: personally containing an act by enacting it, and impersonally containing it. Naturally this only gives a verbal shift to the same old question. I hold that there are two ways of personally containing: concretely as a person containing, a belief, or an act, by believing it; and by suffering it as enacted, believed by an included mind, included by virtue of the "suffering" relation, as one's own beliefs are included by an active relation. There is some activity in the suffering in a sense, for God's doing is necessary to our doing, but it is not sheer doing but is also a being done in and to.

But now do we experience any such things as the passivity referred to? I hold that we never stop experiencing it, and only so do we know we are not all that exists. If we only had our activity, relative to no other activity as we immediately have it, no inference to the acts of others would be suggested. This is a rather common doctrine (Dilthey, Peirce, etc.), which doesn't prove anything except that mere assertion is never going to go far on the other side. But there is a radical difference between us and God, as you probably agree, only you don't look for the difference in the same region. We are not able clearly to experience any mind other than our own so that it stands out individually and unmistakably as such. Hence your doctrine has plausibility. But then I can argue that were this not so we would be much nearer to the divine than we are. For ability to handle other minds on a high level as vivid elements in one's own mind means to be on a much higher level oneself. It is because God is so vastly above us that our activity, clear as you please as such, within him does not deprive him of his own integrity. In other words I can argue that, assuming my view, experience ought to suggest, superficially taken, the truth of your view. It follows that your view is not helped against mine by experience unless there is good reason to deny the "superficial." And so far, in many letters, I see little appeal to experience and much appeal to your beliefs and to words. You may feel that way about me, of course. But Fechner and James are in my boat not yours, and they surely were not wholly careless about the deliverances of experience.

Yes, the fading of one of my sensations is in a sense my fading, but not the same sense. For I may be more vivid as a whole than before. I was merely showing the danger of simply identifying properties of wholes and parts. "All psychic acts are done by the whole, and all properties are properties of the whole."[126] Clearly this needs qualification. All properties of parts imply correlative properties of their wholes. Thus an active part, a passive whole? I certainly agree that every property of the part makes a difference to the whole, and that suffering parts mean a suffering whole, though the proportion of the suffering to the rest of the experience will be different in the two cases. But I hold, as you know, that only passivity in the whole can be correlated with activity in the part.

Again, as to experience. How is either of us to prove that memory of the past is or is not experience of the past? That experience of a pain in the finger is or is not experience of feelings as both mine and something not mine. That the sense of activity is at the same time the sense of passivity to another activity, since otherwise it would be activity upon nothing, in a void, or that this is not what is x experienced.

Not only can I show that on my view we ought <u>not</u> to have clear experience of other high level minds, but that the low level minds being individually unimportant ought to appear, as they do, in confused masses, so that philosophers may reflect this confusion in their theories. Thus my view agrees with experience. So, you feel, does yours.

Where do we go from there? One thing you might do is to consider my questions about the immediacy or mediacy of knowledge, human and divine.

As to panentheism, it can be and has been rigorously proven that there are two senses in which God may be seen as the whole of things, senses as different as either is from the view that God is not the whole. He may be the whole as consisting simply of the parts it has, so that no part could be otherwise if God is to be God. This has all the bad consequences attributed to pantheism, consequences equally distasteful to both of us. But suppose God is the "flexible self-identity" of the whole (we agree, surely, that personal identity is "flexible," so here I am not contradicting experience), able to be himself whether the parts be this or be that. If the parts are this but not that, then God will be in one accidental state not another, but either state will be a state of Himself, and then there is no logical inconsistency in holding that God has freedom in relation to the parts and parts in relation to him, since the identity of the whole has not been said to consist in or depend upon the parts, or the parts upon the whole. "I could have done otherwise" would mean God could have taken on another state, but this may be passively settled on his part and actively (to some degree, that is) on mine. In the history of pantheism I doubt if you can find these simple distinctions anywhere clearly stated or adhered to. Certainly not in Spinoza, Hegel, Bradley, or what have you, or in the Stoics. And the distinctions follow from certain others that are even more easy to state with radical clarity. I submit it is not fair any longer to used the swear word pantheism for all views that make the world immanent to God. On panentheism, indeed, the world is immanent in one aspect of God and outside entirely another aspect of him, and in the latter aspect God is infinitely independent and wholly exclusive of every created thing, namely in his self identity.

We deserve some sort of medal for keeping this up. Philosophers are not long in patience with each other usually.

Sincerely,
Charles Hartshorne.

[Hartshorne continues under his signature.]

Note. Although my theory implies that you must be interpreting one aspect of experience superficially, this refers only to this one aspect. I recognize the care and depth of your thought about many matters, such as the necessity for limitation in God. It is always hazardous to explain why the other fellow thinks as he does, but it appears to me that your attitude toward the present problem has three reasons. One is the fact that the things I claim to be in experience and overlooked by you are subtle things, easily overlooked if one is prejudiced against seeing them, or even if one merely is not on the alert for them. Second is the tradition of personalism, with its trend toward an extreme monadism or pluralism. Third is the general tradition against pantheism.[127] This is the element I have least respect for. I cannot claim to know it has influenced you, but it seems extremely probable. I have two grounds for not thinking it a respectable basis for your opinion. One is that my view is not pantheistic, unless this term is used highly ambiguously, and in the sense in which it is pantheistic pantheism does not involve the horrible things it is in the other sense rightly accused of involving. The other ground is that the moment one admits limitation in God, one has given up the only theological barrier to panentheism. So long as God is held to be purely absolute, he cannot contain the relative as factors in himself. The absolute as such is exclusive not inclusive. Here Thomas was right and Bradley and Spinoza wrong. But if God[128] has a relative aspect there is no need to consider that to which it is relative as outside it. For a whole is relative to its parts, naturally. Consequently, to whatever extent your decision here is influenced by the anti-pantheistic tradition it is influenced in contradiction to your own best insight. Of course you won't believe this for a moment probably. But I seem to see it clearly enough, I must say.

You may say there is a religious as well as metaphysical or theological tradition against pantheism. But I am ready for that. When one suggests to an ordinary person that we are in God he probably does have some feeling of resistance. But this is explicable on my terms. We are not in God as something is in a box, or a brick in a brick pile, or an idea in a human mind. God is the most distinctive of all beings and relations to him are the most unique of relations. The "in" is of course a radically unique case of "in." It is easier and more comfortable to avoid trying to see this unique case by denying the "in" altogether. Then it is not directly necessary to think about it, since if we admit that God has supreme control and supreme knowledge and supreme love, in principle the "in" is fully covered without our having to see it as a single abstract aspect by itself. (That's why I say you and I are quarreling almost merely over a word or two.) Further, there is the traditional emphasis upon the world-maker idea, which suggests that God is outside the world as an artisan is outside his product. We do not try to conceive this maker relation directly and positively, realizing that we cannot do so. All that is achieved is the sense that God is responsible and in control, with some limitations or other. But we feel that "in" ought to be simpler to grasp than "made by," or is it merely that we are used to the latter and do not really examine it as a problem? Once we do it becomes clear that the artisan product relation is little used. God as mind is to the world not as the watch-maker but as the watch-maker's mind, and that mind acts immediately only on the watch-maker's body and only thus upon the watch. Since God as mind acts directly on all things it is the watch-maker's body that corresponds to the world and there will be no watch outside this body. Besides, the externality of product to artisan is essentially related to the fallibility and incompleteness of his knowledge of the product, which he may even have forgotten.

Every religious person knows we are within (not "beyond") "his love and care,"[129] and if this be said not to mean literally "in God" then it is a fair question what it does literally mean. Is the love outside God, or the objects of the love outside the love? Then the unity of love and its object is a third principle. That is why I say you do not really use the religious insight as decisive but subordinate it to sub-religious categories. I would suppose that the case of unity in multiplicity, a whole with real parts, is a supreme love-and-its-objects. You cannot draw a line around the lover (his actual state, not his mere self-identity) leaving the love, or around the love, leaving the objects, "outside." *Ipse dixit!*

Charles Hartshorne

Box 35, Newton Center 59
Massachusetts

July 12, 1943

Dear Hartshorne,

Your letter of June 5, coming in the midst of my accelerated program, has had to lie for a while on the table.

Our correspondence is both discouraging and encouraging. Discouraging, because we do not yet understand each other and have tended to take out our peeve by the use of epithets like "superficial" (which I thank you for partially retracting); and also discouraging because, where we do seem to understand, we disagree so sharply in principle. Nevertheless it is more encouraging than discouraging, because, as you point out, we keep at it. And I hope we'll continue to.

I. Comment on our agreements.

1. God knows (a) all things (b) perfectly, including all our acts. (a) Means (for me) all past, present, and fore-knowable future events, not future free acts.

(b) Means (for me) in the best possible way, fitted to the nature of the object. I.e., God's knowledge of another person is not knowledge by acquaintance, but knowledge by description. No mind can, in the very nature of knowledge, have acquaintance with anything but itself.

2. What we do, our acts, are done by us not by God. Here is an instance of (1 b). God obviously cannot know our doing as we know it, if this be true. What God does not do he cannot know himself as doing.

3. In so far as we are active, God is passive. Yes, I'd agree that he suffers what we do. He is also passive as regards the existence (validity) within him of eternal truths and the presence of eternal qualia (*vérités de fait*).

On 1, you bridle at the thought of knowledge by inference as being perfect. All merely abstract considerations of the nature of perfection seem to me metaphysically irrelevant. I define perfection as the best possible under the given conditions of being. If "inferential knowledge can be adequate only to abstract objects,"[130] then skepticism is the only inference I can draw. In fact, you seem to confine inference to analytic judgments. I see no possible way of knowing any concrete object (other than my present self) without inductive inference. There must be postulated trust of memory, of objective reference, and of some sort of rational order before any knowledge of any concrete object can be. It seems to me that this is the nature of knowledge—to refer, to describe, to understand, to infer—rather than to be. To tell the truth, I find it difficult to say (what I did say verbally) that there is knowledge by acquaintance. Acquaintance is pure immediacy of experience, pure being. But it is not understanding, relation, true comprehension. I think God's knowledge is perfect as knowledge,—that is as dualistic reference—not as being—that is, as monistic identity of idea and object.

Of course I'd not suppose that we know the past without inferring. The specious present—the datum self—contains a time-span of present, past, future, which, by acquaintance, gives us clues to pastness, otherness, and inferential reason. Knowledge (in memory or otherwise) is an elaboration of those clues. True memory is, of course, subtle and hard to disengage. But we trust it, not because of its memory-claim (which may be fallacious); but because of the fact that certain memory-claims enter into the structure of a rational whole, and thus render inference well-grounded (although never absolutely immediate!).

The unity of knowledge with its object is something that should not be arbitrarily presupposed, rather empirically investigated. I suppose my ultimate category of unity is based on a combination of telepathic communication between minds—rapport (*vide* J[ames] Ward)[131] and kinship in rational nature of minds. This principle, in a measure, applies to memory as well as to knowledge of other minds. At any rate, I'd say that so far as we know or can think in terms consistent with experience, God knows us purely by inductive inference.

Your appeal to the authority of James and Fechner could be answered by appeal to other conflicting authorities, if that were worth while. Leaving them aside, you ask, "What the parts do, must the whole mind do it?" Here is a very delicate problem. If you ask: Is everything in a mind the willed doing of that whole mind?—the answer is plainly negative. If you ask: Is every doing in a mind consistent with other doings?—the answer is again negative. But if you ask: Is every suffering or doing of a mind the experience of the whole mind, inseparable from it, present in the unity of its consciousness?—then I'd give an affirmative answer. I cannot find within my mind any direct or indirect evidence for other selves within my self, although I can find plenty of evidence that other selves, not within me, can affect me. In that sense, of course we experience passivity within us. But in thinking that the selves which produce that passivity must be within us in some sense, you seem to me to reject the category of interaction among selves, which (*pace* Leibniz) seems to me fundamental, <u>at least</u> (come back Leibniz) between God and other selves, anyway.

I can accept panentheism for the physical universe, which I do not regard panpsychically, but idealistically; for the personal universe, the social categories of interaction and communication are more enlightening than your analysis.

It seems to me that you are wrong in ascribing my analysis to personalistic tradition. I was not born a personalist, but came to it after hard struggles, having been first an absolutist and second a pragmatist. My antipantheism is due solely to the logical difficulties I found in absolutism, which even Miss Calkins[132] admitted to me were serious difficulties, although you do not view them as such.

Quantum Sufficit.

Cordially,
Edgar S. Brightman

[September 1, 1943][133]

Dear Brightman,

Thanks for answering my questions so carefully. Since you gave pretty much the answers I thought must be given I cannot be without some understanding of your position. On the other hand, there were one or two little surprises, not as to your interpretation of your own position but as to implied interpretations of mine. Probably in pointing out that, for you, perfect knowledge does not include knowledge of future free acts you did not wish to suggest we could disagree on that? Certainly we agree there. But when you say that I, unlike Miss Calkins and yourself, do not feel the difficulties of absolutism I must think that you are forgetting that I am not an absolutist and that I hold the absolutist position to be plainly <u>impossible</u>, since the wholly absolute being cannot include relative being. The absolutists were not and could not be panentheists. They did <u>not</u> believe the whole suffers rather than acts the activities of the parts, that it increases in value and is never the utmost possible in total value, that its self-identity is <u>independent</u> of particular parts, etc. The whole for me as for Fechner or Whitehead or Montague is absolutely inclusive of what actually exists, but not because it acts all activity. It acts-or-suffers all activity, but that means it (not in its mere identity) is <u>relative</u> to what the parts decide to do. Even Miss Calkins, if I remember rightly, did not have this idea. So your paragraph seems directly to confirm my notion that you are allowing your just repugnance to pantheism to carry over into your attitude toward panentheism. For me, God in his aspect as absolute (immutable and at an unsurpassable maximum of value) is <u>non</u>-inclusive of relative beings like ourselves. This aspect of God is <u>no more the "whole"</u> than your God is held to be, though it <u>is</u> a factor in us—unlike your God.

However, this issue just mentioned last is verbal, it seems. For by "part of a thing" in the widest sense I mean: "whatever <u>must</u> be described if the thing is to be fully described." To leave out the character of the part is to omit something (but not everything) of the character of the whole, and this I make a <u>definition</u> of part and whole. Now it seems pretty clear that you have a narrower (implicit) definition of whole and part. Or, do you hold that if A "interacts" with B, A <u>could</u> be fully described without fully describing B, and B without describing A? If you say the description of A must be included in the description of B, then by definition A is "part" of B in <u>my</u> sense. If you say that inclusion of the description is not necessary, then I think your concept of interaction can be shown meaningless or inconsistent.

However, the issue becomes more than verbal, as usually happens, owing to the effects of verbal associations. Thus your use of words leads you to hold that all knowledge of selves by other selves must be inductive. Now you mean by inductive what logicians do mean by it, I think. And at once several problems arise. (1) Is the idea of a "best possible mode of induction" any more meaningful than the idea of a greatest number? Perhaps the series of better and better inductive reasoners has no conceivable upper limit except in the form of something outside the series, namely super-inductive knowing, knowing by direct inspection? (2) Could inductive knowledge of my feelings be as good in all respects as <u>my</u> knowledge of them by inspection? I should think not, so that you ought to admit that there are ways in which we know ourselves better than God can know us. (1) and (2) are connected. Inductive knowledge is by <u>aspects,</u> and is abstract. (This did <u>not</u> mean that I thought it was "analytic.") An hypothesis is not as concrete as an actual situation. Of course you may believe in a special divine kind of verified-hypothesis that is wholly concrete, indeed you logically must hold this. But then that too is open, I seem to see, to very grave objection.

So the issue becomes more than verbal, though I think it is verbal misunderstandings that are partly responsible, and not merely the evidences of experience, for your taking the position you do.

As for the real issue, and the evidences of experience, by citing high authorities in psychological observation I sought only to show that your authority as an observer is insufficient for anyone except yourself, or one who inductively infers your depth as an observer. That is, you cannot say, "I have refuted panentheism," when all you have really done is to say that what its supporters (claim to) find in their experience you (claim to) find absent from your experience. That and not refutation is what you have, is it not?

Since my authorities are, as such go, good ones, the only reasonable conclusion is that experience is obscure upon the issue and that only the greatest caution and all-round survey can justify any decision. I am logically bound to think that either or both of us must have failed to achieve such thoroughness, or else that the issue is practically undecidable, since experience is utterly obscure on the matter. In the last case both of us may be equally superficial in daring to decide it! But if experience is not hopelessly obscure then one of us must be reading it superficially. Peeve hasn't much to do with the possibilities here. I only said that either my position is wrong or you are superficial on this issue. I cannot assume that my position is not wrong, or that you are superficial. I am, however, naturally on the alert for evidence that you are. I ought to be on the alert for evidence that I am!

There seems some verbal confusion about "interaction." You seem to say that interaction between selves mutually immanent to one another would not be interaction. True if you define interaction as wholly external action. I suspect such absolute "within" and "without." Where one self is active, [and] the other passive, the first acts on the second even though it is within it. Also, if we experience our own passivity we also experience that to which we are passive, the other-activity, for "passivity to" is nothing. In this connection, to be a panentheist about the physical world is to believe, by the definition of panentheism, that matter can be self-active, for a panentheistic whole has by its formula self-active parts. Now a non-psychic self-activity is one I, in your phrase, find nothing of in experience. So I must remain in doubt if you can really be even that much of a panentheist (officially, for implicitly I think everyone is a panentheist).

Please remember that the seeming absence of other selves within experience is what my theory implies would characterize human experience, since a self on that level could not conveniently manage other selves as clearly and distinctly manifest to it, but only selves on such a low level that only vague mass awareness of them would reach full consciousness, for individually taken they are too trivial to notice. (Only God notes everything consciously, however trivial).

You will note that my definition of whole and part—and query as to its applicability to interaction—is the chief point where I need light as to your position. For as to the problem of perfect induction of divine knowledge by indirection I almost think it certain nothing further can be said. It's my idea of a really ineffable mystery or paradox. But then, who can be <u>quite</u> certain in these things?

Sincerely,
Charles Hartshorne

September 5, 1943

Dear Hartshorne,

Yours of the 1st is the clearest statement of the thing we are puzzled about that one could well ask for, and I am answering it immediately. If I don't write now, when can I? The University opens on Tuesday, and my father-in-law has been lying at the point of death for a week.

The difficulty arises partly from the difference between pantheism and panentheism. I see no reason why, in some sense, panentheism is not correct (although the "en" needs most cautious definition—more cautious that I think yours is). I know, of course, that you are not an absolutist, yet I used the Calkins illustration as against the pantheism which I had understood you to avow. Knudson calls personalism panentheistic, and if you had stuck to that term we'd have understood each other better all along.[134]

But the real nub of the matter comes out in your definition of "part of a thing" in the widest sense as "whatever must be described if the thing is to be fully described." It seems to me that this definition is question-begging from the start, and implies (when taken concretely) that there is no real thing isolable from others in any important sense. In the widest sense, you have really stated (what I know you abhor) the Hegelian principle that "das Wahre ist das Ganze."[135] I do not see how we can avoid saying that nothing can be fully understood until it is understood in its relations to what it is not. Hence, a full description of anything also involves a full description of not-that-thing. Nothing can be fully understood apart from God. All that is true. Yet I have a very different definition of the part-whole relation in the empirical-personal sense. I define a person as whatever is now or has been present consciousness of a remembering and anticipating self capable of ideal values. "The whole" of a person would be the completed series of that consciousness—a situation never empirically attained (since I believe in immortality). "A part" of a person would be any consciousness less than "the whole." I adopt this definition on empirical grounds, and also because of my aversion to holding that everything is everything else. If the brain, or the neurons, or the air, or the sun, or my grand-parents are all "parts" of me, then everything is so mixed up with everything else that I see no place for individuality, freedom or privacy.

Your difficulty about induction is at least partly met by my theory of tele-pathic knowledge (which I share with your "authority" James Ward, for once).[136] However, even telepathic knowledge, I admit, could not be "as good as" my knowledge by self-inspection, in the sense that it could not be identical with it. In my sin God would not sin; in my ignorance, he would not be igno-rant. But God's knowledge would, in the rational sense, always be better than mine; he would grasp all the evidence as I could not; he would understand me as I could not. He would be excluded only from identity and sin. I think that exclusion is good for God and for me.

Did I send you my "Christian View of Nature"—a chapter in *Christian Bases of World Order*?[137]

Most cordially yours,
[Brightman]

January 13, 1944

Dear Brightman,
Re[garding] your Sept[ember] letter. I said long ago that we differ chiefly in language. This becomes clearer when you concede that the things I say are parts of God must be described to describe God. You don't say this in so many words but rather that nothing can be understood apart from God. But I take it you admit the converse, that God can't be fully understood apart from other things. So in my language this becomes: things are parts of God.

However, there are some differences, since I do not think that everything must be described to fully describe anything, and I doubt if you do. Must all the future be known to know the present? Is it any part of the description of Jane Austen that we like her? It certainly describes us to say this, but not Jane Austen. True, that she is capable of awakening love is part of her description, but this, so far as really descriptive of her, can be stated without mention of us as concrete individuals. The types of individuals that she can appeal to would suffice. Even more clearly perhaps is it untrue that to describe abstractions we must also describe all the concrete cases involving them. I think "whiteness," but what I mean by this term as a public concept is what it is whether I happen to think of it just now or not. I-thinking-whiteness describes me but not whiteness. That whiteness can be thought by certain types of beings belongs to it, but these types are themselves universals not requiring just this or that instance.

If Hegelianism means to deny this unidirectionality which internal relationship sometimes assumes, then it is the vicious organicism or block universe which most of us are done with. If it doesn't deny it, so much the better. But then, even in my language, I am no part of Jane Austen, though she is part of me. Also, we are parts of God as he is now but not as he once was or as he might have been now. We are contingent parts and only after a certain time.

Thus it is not true that all distinctions are lost if my terms are adopted. Further, a part is not its whole, so A related to not-A may be a whole related to its part. Also, there are effective or high grade ways of having parts as compared to low grade, ineffective ways. One may have a part in full consciousness or not in full consciousness, and this involves infinite gradations. Only God effectively or fully consciously involves all things. This means that if I were other than I am, God's consciousness would be other to the full extent of the otherness, while you would be other consciously only to a trivial extent in some cases as compared to the difference in me or in God. No doubt such a mode of differentiation is not crudely obvious and easy; possibly it is not legitimate. But no philosophy is easy and obviously true. The difficult points are shifted around from system to system. The question is, which system is freest from hopeless difficulties, real contradictions or lapses from experiential meaning, even subtle and difficult meaning. No one can judge this until he has tried <u>hard</u> to find meaning in all the systems. With this you probably agree.

Your whole and part of a person is only one sense in which person has parts, a sense recognized in my language of course. But then the only whole of personality that is <u>given</u> is really a part, the person up to now. But here I am somewhat puzzled by you. Taking present experience in its integrity, is past experience of the same person no part of this present experience? Then the whole of personality consists of segments each entirely outside the others? A quite usual view, but Hume's exploration of it—you know.[138] Then you fall back upon the doctrine that things imply other things, this impl[ies] being an ultimate, not further analyzable relation. Anyhow it is a relation, and I maintain that the unity of a relation must include both terms (or there are the terms and the relation to be related together, a real vicious regress), and I further maintain that some term must include the relation and hence include the terms. For relations cannot be themselves substances, and to say they fall between substances rather than in them is to forget that "between" is a relation. Something less abstract must have the relation in its being (how can it have it not in its being?)

I repeat my charge that your language was adopted largely to avoid a pantheism which I have shown is avoidable without your language, while at the same time my language enables one to analyze many other problems hard to handle in yours. That is, while the difference is verbal in good part, I think the advantage of your language is chiefly temporary (until the fear of pantheism has been exorcised by making panentheism generally understood). As to making the difference between the two carefully, I will boast: if any man ever made it nearly so carefully as I have done I really have missed his work. See November *Review of Religion,* "A Mathematical Analysis of Theism."[139] (By the way, an article on Schelling by Singer of some interest in that no.)[140] See also the Dictionary of Theology, articles on panentheism and pantheism (if and when it comes out).[141]

Pantheism makes the whole identical with the parts in relation in such fashion that if the parts were otherwise the whole would not be itself; whereas panentheism says that the self-identity of the whole-being (it isn't just the whole, but the being inclusive of the whole) is absolutely independent of what parts there may be (provided there are parts). Also (the same point from another angle) the parts are self-active even in relat[ion] to the whole-being, which is acted upon and not just acting. Also the parts are real substances and not just modes of the one substance; they are member substances. And so on. There is a precise logical pattern here, which no older pantheism ever had, and it is radically different from the pattern the latter did have when it was most exact.

Cordially,
Charles Hartshorne

[P.S.] Telepathy, if a fact, interpreted my way wouldn't help you, and interpreted your way would be only another case of what bothers me in you.

Box 35, Newton Center,
Mass.

May 19, 1944

Dear Hartshorne,
Dire physical necessity compels me to lag in our discussion, while agreeing that most of our differences are linguistic. But my physician has told me to call a halt on everything haltable and I must write very briefly.

I have read your article on the ontological argument with some care.[142] It shows your acute analysis at its best and makes many sound and brilliant observations. To me, however, the nub of the whole thing lies in your use of the word "coherent" and your interpretations which hinge on the meaning ascribed to that term. To be coherent is far more than to be formally consistent; it is to be systematic, both within itself and in its relations. Now, if this is what you mean, is your argument not much nearer to an Hegelian proof than to even a revised Anselmian?

Most cordially yours,
[Brightman]

[postcard]

May 25, 1944

Dear Brightman,

Many thanks. It's kind of you to write, under the circumstances. One hears so little from readers of articles. I give Hegel some credit (very likely too little) for appreciating the systematic nature of philosophy—and some discredit for the way he did it. I like Peirce's or Whitehead's or Fechner's ways better.

C. Hartshorne

[It seems likely that Brightman answered this postcard, perhaps with one of his own, but it has not been preserved.]

[postcard]

June 30, 1944

Dear Brightman,

Question one of degree perhaps? The more an argument is integrated into a system the stronger it can be. But I doubt if Anselm or Spinoza or Leibniz was wholly unaware of this. And I do feel there is considerable analogy between my argument and Anselm's. The incompatibility of "perfect" with "mere possibility" or "mere essence" is in both. And "coherent" need only mean neither inconsistent nor meaningless for [my] argument to hold.

Thanks for putting me in Russell vol.[143]

Thanks,
Hartshorne

[Brightman apparently did not answer this postcard, or if he did, it has not been preserved. Hartshorne wrote one letter dealing with a nonphilosophical matter on August 9, 1944. Thereafter it seems that Brightman must have written a more detailed criticism of Hartshorne's article on the ontological argument, but that letter has not been preserved. But Hartshorne did send the following postcard in response.]

[postcard]

March 15, 1945

Dear Brightman,

Harts-horne. (Horn of a deer). Thanks for your prompt response to the article. "Gulf" a metaphor for qualitative difference. To prehend a quality as datum is <u>not to have it as one's subjective form</u>. We have the being of God, but not as he has it, fully and adequately. It seems we can only tease each other on this.

C. H.

[Brightman scribbled some notes on this postcard that relate to Whitehead's books, but if he answered the card, it has not been preserved. This ends the substantive correspondence, although there are two more letters of recommendation written by Hartshorne for a student in 1945 that are preserved in the Brightman papers at the Mugar Library. In one of these (July 17, 1945), Hartshorne makes some remarks that indicate nicely how the correspondence had begun to subside: "I've had, like you, to cut down on philosophical correspondence. I see students of yours now and then. It is nice talking to them. Sometime we'll all be meeting again." However, this does not end the intellectual exchange between the two thinkers, as the appendices demonstrate.]

Brightman lecturing, circa 1945

*(From the Edgar S. Brightman Collection,
Department of Special Collections, Boston University)*

Hartshorne, 1937

*(Photograph courtesy of the Center
for Process Studies, Claremont, California)*

Hartshorne, circa 1928, when he was at the University of Chicago

(Photograph courtesy of the Center for Process Studies, Claremont, California)

Brightman, circa 1939

(From the Edgar S. Brightman Collection, Department of Special Collections, Boston University)

APPENDIX I

🎋

Brightman's Review of
The Divine Relativity

Hartshorne, Charles. The Divine Relativity; A Social Conception of God. *New Haven, Yale University Press. 164 pp. 21 cm. (Yale University. The Dwight Harrington Foundation Lectures, no. 24) $2.75. 48–7802.*

This expansion of lectures delivered at Yale University makes a searching criticism of traditional theistic absolutism. The idea of God as personal is retained and even enlarged, but the author, opposing tradition, holds the concrete and relative aspects of deity to be even higher in worth than the immutable and absolute aspects. His book, indeed, is an able attempt to defend divine relativity in somewhat technical detail. The perfect, for example, is defined as "the self-surpassing surpasser of all." To Dr. Hartshorne, God is a being in social relations such that all persons exist in him without losing their own identities. The absolute, he asserts, is "an abstract feature of the inclusive and supreme reality, which is precisely the personal God." The absolute, to him, therefore, is less real than the personal. The customary idea of God is criticized because the author believes it to involve absoluteness in a sense which precludes relationships. "How," he asks, "can we know God as causally related to the world, if he . . . has no relative being?" Nicolai Hartmann's atheism is similarly criticized as being relevant only to a non-relative God, a God who could not take into account human freedom.

Thomists will question the arguments advanced; non-Thomists may not agree that human beings can be included in God without contradiction. But all readers interested in theistic philosophy will find reason to respect the historical and critical powers of the author.[1]

৯

Brightman's Theory of the Given
and His Idea of God

Charles Hartshorne

Edgar Sheffield Brightman (1884–195[3]) was the principal founder of American Personalism. He was a forceful writer and teacher.

In his last book, *Person and Reality*,[1] published posthumously (1958), Brightman appears to agree with the following three propositions: Reality in general is the same as experience in general; momentary experiences are connected with others by one-way relationships of logical requirement, rather than by mere Humean constant conjunctions; temporal order is the basic order established by these relationships. Apparently, also he concedes something of the contention that the unity of the present self, which he calls the datum self, with its personal past, is akin in principle to that which connects my present with the past of other persons. But whereas for me this means that both the personal past and the past of others are actually given, this givenness being the same thing as causal conditioning, Brightman denies the givenness in both cases and seems (influenced by Hegel, I recall) to take causal conditioning (or the "rationality" of reality) as a primitive self-explanatory term. The present experiences only the present; however, it can "understand" itself only by accepting an order of causes and effects inconceivably more vast than its own internal content.

From some points of view the differences seem but verbal. For I actually *define* the given as the independent causes of experiences; Brightman apparently admits that experiences have independent causes but does not *call* them "data." What then does he call "data"? They are those I should term "*obvious* data," those whose givenness is easily accessible to conscious detection. Such are qualities of red, sour, painfulness, activities of perceiving and thinking, emotions of love, fear, rage, etc. Concerning these, he accepts Donald Williams's principle of the "innocence of the given." In themselves, it is held, they tell no tales about what is not given, that is, the absent portions of the world-system conditioning the experience. At the same time Brightman holds that the rational explanation of the given data drives us far beyond them, to their causes, near or remote. The doctrine I uphold is the innocence of the given is the same as the limitations of human consciousness as such, in the sense in which a baby is vastly less conscious than an adult, though what is given to the baby may be rather similar. Brightman brushes aside this distinctive ("Whiteheadian") meaning of "consciousness"; but then he should give us another term for the same very important distinction. The lower animals and infants have but little introspective power; they have data but can not judge that they have, at least not on a scale comparable to the judgments of human adults. Now either-or: Either the human adult possesses the possible maximum of this power, or not the maximum. If not the maximum, then there are data that even you and I cannot detect introspectively. How then does one prove that the causal conditions which Brightman says are not given are indeed simply not given, whether with or without possibility of conscious detection or noticing? I see no way in which he could prove this.

Early in the book, Brightman does offer an argument for his view, but as it stands, the argument is a simple formal fallacy. He protests that the absent factors (which I suggest mean those not obviously given) cannot be "identical with" "the shining present," the momentary experience or datum self. He appears then to infer, "not included in," from "not identical with." But, of course, identity is but a degenerate or improper case of inclusion. So this reiterated argument is, to be frank, absurd. Who wants to identify "the absent" with present experience as a whole? The given is, some of us hold, a constituent of experience; a constituent, however, need not be and normally is not identical with that of which it is constituent.

No doubt the formal fallacy referred to is not quite what Brightman had in mind. Perhaps he was thinking of this: Granted that the absent is constituent of experience, can we really admit that each experience is a whole of which all causal conditions are parts? Am I inclusive of the totality of my past selves, and your past selves, as well? My present self seems to lack any such superiority to all that conditions it. And even God as supreme cause would by this logic become a mere part of me, as I am now! This must be what Brightman had in mind. Does it establish his position? I believe it is the strongest argument available for that purpose. And the issue is subtle. Present experience cannot in an unqualified sense be a whole of which any causal condition you please of that whole is a mere constituent. By that principle a mouse which I influence must be more than I was when I influenced it, must be my superior, absolutely.

In reply, we must refer once more to the difference between conscious and unconscious possession of data. If I were absolutely conscious of all my data, then indeed I should be superior to all the causal conditions of my experience. But in truth my conscious experience includes no causal condition whatever without a more or less drastic loss of distinctness or adequacy. If all data are "innocent," it is because all nondivine experiences are but imperfectly conscious and it is for consciousness that the question of innocence arises. Mere feeling or sensory experience puts no general question like that which Williams and Brightman are answering. But, you may persist, if conscious experience does not embrace its causes, does not—on the Bergson-Whitehead-Hartshorne view we are discussing—unconscious experience embrace them, and are we not still faced with the paradox of an experience surpassing all that influences it? In a certain technical sense it does appear that the view assigns to an effect a total complexity greater than that of any of its causes. However, if value is finally measured by consciousness, then experience so far as merely unconscious is inferior to those of its causes which are conscious.

This defence may seem an evasion. But we can perhaps strengthen it somewhat by remarking that, so far as the human self-conscious individual is concerned, what he cannot bring into consciousness is not really "his" in the full sense, so that, granted that my experiences grasp God, for example, it does not follow that I consciously possess God as constituent of myself. On the other hand, God as the sole fully conscious being will without qualification contain every item of reality.

I am well aware of Brightman's reasons for rejecting this view of God (we once corresponded at length about it); but I see in these reasons only a partial neglect or denial of the passive-active structure of experience as such, or of the distinction between what Whitehead calls the subjective forms and the objective forms of feeling. In each case of feeling another's feeling, the first feeler feels the other's feeling in a different manner from the other and yet feels his very feeling. The doctrine of feeling is precisely the view that not only is this not contradictory, but that its denial is indeed contradictory. For, if we feel, what do we feel? Merely our own feeling itself? This is like a sign that means only itself. A basic epistemological issue is whether or not there is an essential subject-object structure running through immediate experience.

Brightman spoils his discussion of "epistemological monism" by taking it to mean the identity of subject and object. It may for some authors, but for others it means rather that the object, as nonidentical with the subject, is directly given to it and *thereby* made a constituent with the subject, of its total actuality. The subject includes the object, but for that very reason does not coincide with it. My (or your) feeling always embraces feeling which initially was not mine at all. This prior feeling does not thereby become my feeling of it, it becomes rather an objective affective part-content of my total affective state. I feel *how* the other felt, I do not feel as the other felt. I see no contradiction here. I may feel how some of my cells feel, for instance, their pain; but for them this feeling was existence itself, while for me it is but one item of feeling among many. So, if God feels our feeling of trust in a false hypothesis our feeling is on the far side of the duality, "feeling of feeling," not on the hither side. True, the first or divine feeling includes the second but surpasses it as the inclusive surpasses the included. God feels how we trust the hypothesis but does not trust it.

Peirce's definition of belief fits neatly here: Belief is willingness to act upon; God is not willing to act upon our belief, though feeling the full quality of our trust in it. God also feels many other things; and the total divine reaction to the world is negative with respect to the hypothesis. We do something like this in remembering vividly how we formerly felt trust in something that now we distrust. Ability to feel objectively and vividly the quality of the former trust does not at all mean that we now trust the object of the former trust. For we now have additional feelings *about* the former feeling, and its object or context, that we previously did not have. The whole question is whether a subject can become direct object to another subject. Some of us answer this by another question, how can a subject composed basically of feelings have an object otherwise than by a social structure of immediate feeling whereby the other subject is one's own directly enjoyed object?

There are many reasons why this social structure has been missed by most philosophers. It is the stone rejected of the builders, the almost secret bond of intuitive love that holds the universe together. I cannot imagine any other bond that can do this. "Intentionality" is a name for the problem, not a solution.

What does it mean to say, as Brightman does, that though the causes of the given are entirely hidden behind the given, yet their being is included in that of the given so far as we understand it? How does this differ from my contention that all causes of experience are data, though data in large part resistant to human introspection? The more conscious we are, the more we grasp experiences as effects of certain causes. At the ideal limit what could this mean if not that the causes, too, would be consciously accessible as data? How else could the supreme consciousness be aware of the causes of its experiences than by having them as fully inspectable data? Must infallible knowledge infer worldly causes by inspecting divine effects in themselves totally "innocent" of their causes?

Let us put the matter in terms of internal relationships. Does Brightman hold with the Humeans that all relations of immediate experience to past, future, or contemporary events are external? This is the clear implication of the "innocence of the given." But then what is the basis of trust in causality or in the inference to a larger world? Does Brightman hold that the relations of experience to previous events are constitutive or intrinsic? Then he is on my side. For the more conscious we become of what an experience is, the more its components, including relational components, will be not only data but consciously introspectable data. So I wonder if there is any real difference between us except that I take an unequivocal stand concerning internal relations. Of course, I equally posit external relations: for things experienced by a given subject are entirely independent of being experienced by it. Internality runs backward from subjects to objects, not forward from objects to subjects.

Some of my main objections to the *denial* of the thesis that causes are always given are as follows. First, it makes causality an entirely independent principle, an arbitrary conjunction that remains inaccessible to direct, and hence, I should think, indirect, awareness. Second, it makes love a derivative principle, whereas my most basic intuition about the meaning of life is that love or feeling-of-feeling is the primary principle, explanatory of everything, including givenness. Third, relations between events must be in some events, and thus be internal; but to say that relation to X is in Y, but X is not, is I hold meaningless or contradictory; moreover, if relations to causal conditions are in experiences (and where else?), then to the degree to which we can be directly aware of what an experience is we must be directly aware of its components, including intrinsic relations and their terms.

I should like to comment upon Brightman's notion of the datum self or shining present. I find this a somewhat ambiguous idea. In my view, the given self is not identical with the self to which it is given. The subject-object duality is never simply collapsed. If the shining present is the given self, then there is another self *for* which it is given. This I take to be the subsequent self. The datum self is then the immediately past self. It is a case of what Brightman calls "the absent"; but it is also present, not however, in the sense of being the present subject, rather in that of being the present object. Not only is it false that the past is never datum; it is also false that the present is ever presently a datum. The subject-object structure is basically the present-past structure. All direct awareness is "memory"; but memory has two forms, personal and impersonal. Take the first experience by an unborn infant; at first it can remember no predecessor of its own kind; it has no personal memory. Does this mean it is a mere present with no feeling whatever of past (or future)? I suggest that this is a monstrous assumption. More reasonable is the view that in the first experience in an individual's career the individual feels the immediately past state of its own organic components, cell or the like. Thus it has what we might call impersonal memory. Perception in its entirely may be viewed as simply the impersonal form of "memory" or direct sense of the past. This effects an enormous simplification of all our concepts of experience, a simplification whose grandeur suggests genius. And the source of the generalization was the genius of Whitehead, partly anticipated by that of Bergson and Peirce.

If memory is direct sense of the past, then the belief in the pure innocence of the given is mistaken. Note that memory itself is remembered. Immediate retrospection gives us ourselves as just having, in another act of memory, retrospected still earlier experience. So the datum is here past, and the datum is here also an act of experiencing whose own datum was still farther past, and so on indefinitely. Since perception is impersonal memory, and since the nonhuman feelings which are given are also experiences with data and causes, hence are themselves mnemonic in structure, all experience is in principle memory of memory of memory, and so on. That this does not appear in an obvious way to introspection (really retrospection) is the very thing that Whitehead sought to explain by his doctrine of "transmutation." The obviously given in sense perception is a universal, abstracted from the more concrete datum; consciousness is largely limited to the result of this abstraction, for reasons which psychology can, I think without great difficulty, explain. Thus is produced the illusion of the innocence of the given. To recognize it as an illusion is to be out of the solipsistic prison in which Brightman and so many others gladly put themselves, before proposing some ingenious device for sawing through the bars of the prison. There is no present self-contained event, given as such. Givenness is itself a causal and temporal arrow pointing backward and outward in space-time, or better, time-space. As Milič Čapek keeps telling us, time, or as Buddhists say, "dependent origination" is the key to the cosmic structure. Givenness is an actual grasp of actual past events whose being was independent of the present event.

I have been critical of Brightman's theory of experience. I wish now to express my admiration for him in another connection. I think Brightman's defence of what he called the "temporalistic" view of God was a valuable and well-reasoned contribution. Here he was one of the pioneers and a courageous and clear-headed one. I am indignant when he is referred to as a believer in a "finite God," even though he used this expression. He also said repeatedly that he believed in a finite-*infinite* God, and that is not only different, it is infinitely different, from believing in a finite God *tout court*. It should also be said that he believed, not in a temporal God but in an eternal-temporal God, and here, too, the difference is infinite. (It is, of course, the same difference.) Brightman's book *The Problem of God* is his most original one and his essay "The Temporalistic View of God" is one of the better essays in American philosophy.[2]

The finite aspect of God, about which Brightman speaks, not altogether clearly, as "The Given," is, I suggest, the same as the truth of certain things, but not all possible things, are *given* to God. All possible things are indeed given to God as possibilities, and the divine infinity is in this: Whatever possibility were to be actualized, it would be fully and consciously represented in the data of the divine experience, so that to say, such and such is possible, is to say, God could know it as actual. But God does know as actual only what is actual.

Brightman and I disagree as to how each actuality is represented in the divine experience. I say, by inclusion among its data, he says, by inclusion in the rational or causal implications of the data. I find this at best a distinction without a real difference. But the relation to finitude is essentially the same: To know that *this* world is actual and *that* is not is to fail to know what might otherwise have been known and is to be finite in a clear sense.

Brightman's view has the, to me, objectionable feature of making God not simply finite but fragmentary, a part of the total reality consisting of God and the created individuals. However, this is largely verbal, since every item in the totality has to be somehow represented in the divine knowledge. And in any case, the clear and the bold insistence that even divine experience or knowledge, will, or love must recognize a difference between worlds experienced, known, willed, or loved as actual, and those dealt with only as possibilities, so that even the divine reality must be finite in a definite sense, was a landmark in the history of religious thought. I suspect Brightman will be honored for this long after the details of his epistemology are largely forgotten. I certainly think he ought to be honored for it. I honor him also for refusing to accept dualistic theories of mind and mere matter, theories which the advance of science will, I am persuaded, cause to seem less and less attractive.

Brightman comes close to solving Plato's problem: What can "God is good" mean if "good" is defined as divinely commanded? A finite-infinite or temporal-eternal deity has volitions that are not eternal and hence (Aristotle, Peirce) are contingent. Our obedience to divine commands (if we know them) because they are divinely commanded is good somewhat as, in a well-governed state, it is good to be law-abiding. Traffic rules, for instance, are partly arbitrary (drive to the right—or to the left) but it is well that they be obeyed. However, the eternal principle of good is God's eternal essence and is in no sense arbitrary or contingent. It is what God could not choose not to will and what we can fail to approve only by failing to understand it or ourselves. It is the beauty of holiness, of incorruptible all-embracing love.

Brightman includes in what God eternally is and knows the principles of rationality (logic, mathematics) and calls it the Given. What this has to do with the given in the sense in which it occurs in perceptions of concrete actualities is inadequately clarified.

Like many another, Brightman seems to imply, without quite stating, a doctrine of dual transcendence. He allows the impression to haunt his discussion of the divine finitude and temporality that the traditional affirmation of the sheer, exclusive infinity or eternity of God was excessive praise, that God falls short of a too absolute ideal. He does not really mean this. But he gives his classical opponents a little too much assistance in believing what they are by habit desirous of believing. Berdyaev takes the right tack here: the sheer immobility of the medieval deity was a "deficiency," objectionable precisely as such. As Plato seems to have known, self-change is essential to soul on all levels, including the highest, that of the World Soul; and so is changeability by others, as is deducible from the truism of Aristotle, accepted by the scholastics in all applications except that to deity: to know something is to be influenced by it. On its own showing, medieval Aristotelianism, which broke with the master at this point without refuting his argument, was inconsistent in attributing omniscience to a wholly independent deity. Brightman was only returning to classical insights after a long detour.

ॐ

Interview with Hartshorne
December 1, 1993

Randall E. Auxier

Auxier: I have not run across anything that you have said about your notion of human beings being created in the image of God, and I was wondering what your position is on the imago-dei?

Hartshorne: Yes, that question I have thought about. I think what I would say is, in a very broad sense, everything is in the image of God, and it is only a relative difference between us and the other higher animals. For example, as I conceive God, God is the all-others surpassing, excellent being. God is; in the New Testament, the text is "God is love"—but God is *pure* love, is love for *all* the creatures not just for us. Now, we have a much more general love for the other creatures than the other animals do. The other animals specialize their interests in their own kind, and maybe the kind that they prey on or the kind that preys on them. But human beings can be interested in any animals that they know. . . . We are special thanks to our possession of speech, which is what distinguishes us; we're the speaking animals, and no other animals speak in the sense in which we do. . . . On the other hand human beings have a lot of defects, they can't possibly claim to love all the creatures (they don't even *know* all creatures). Think of all the other galaxies, the island universes in which there may be all sorts of inhabited planets that we know nothing about. God would be supposed to love all of them. One of my main points is that it is quite foolish to say that we differ from God because we are finite and God is infinite. For all we know, the whole of space (all the island universes and everything in astronomy)—most scientists don't want to think (and I refuse to think) that that is infinite, I think it is finite, but it's vast and you and I are just tiny fragments and all human beings are only a collection of such fragments. We are fragmentary, but so are all the other animals, but we're the fragmentary animal that can love. If we can get to know about them we can have some love for all the other animals, but we can't love them in the intimate direct way that God loves them all.

Auxier: So, in our capacity to generalize our interest and our love for other species, we are similar to God?

Hartshorne: Yes, and so therefore we can conceive God.

Auxier: Does God speak? You focused on the point about language.

Hartshorne: Well, God must be considered fully aware of our speech and what it means for us. I think God has to be considered as above language. The other animals are below language and I think God is above it. You can't put . . . all truth . . . into language. All language is more or less abstract. You say, "well, he's a person," but there are lots of persons—and just exactly what distinguishes this person from that person? Nobody knows. I can't tell you. Even an infinite number of statements about me, wouldn't be the whole me, because I'm more unitary than these statements, and they're only abstract. Nothing is fully concrete.

Auxier: This leads me to a question that has not been written on and which you have alluded to already: in your book *The Divine Relativity* you seem to come out rather in favor of the idea that God has a personality—this may be Edgar Sheffield Brightman's influence on you at that time in your life, perhaps. You talk about this less as your work goes on. I was wondering where you stand on the personality of God.

Hartshorne: I hold with Brunner . . . [that] God is more personal than we are. Yes, he surpasses us. He's the ideal of personality. He's the most excellent person. And I'm inclined to agree with that. On that point, I think he's right. God is the most excellent. God is in any possible situation incomparably more excellent than any other person. He is the ideal. When people talk about personal identity as though it were an absolute identity, as though an almost mindless fetus is the same as an adult person, they are talking nonsense in my opinion. The real mystery is not the abstract attributes of God which distinguish God from everything else. The real mystery is the concrete. There is no human person who fully knows that human person. Each moment of the day, I have maybe a dozen separate experiences. A dozen experiences per second—that runs into the hundreds of thousands per day. Now how many of those do I ever remember? What do I know about my own past experiences? Not a great deal at any moment. As I conceive God, they are all still present to God.

Auxier: Your philosophy of history seems to have a cosmic base. As time unfolds, everything is taken up and preserved in God. I was wondering about the relationship between human history and its seeming capacity to lose information—to forget slowly but surely. God doesn't forget. Humans beings do. I was wondering about the relationship between your cosmic philosophy of history in which everything is remembered in God and your account of human history.

Hartshorne: Yes. You see, it's awfully hard to conceive a mind that wouldn't forget anything. On the other hand, you [would] have the same problem even if you were an atheist. Then you have the question of truth. Isn't it true [for] the American Indians, who have been in the Americas for at least ten thousand years, maybe a good deal longer, [that] each one of those Indians must have had his or her own personal experiences? But what makes it true that they had these experiences? There's nothing you could find now in the universe that could tell you what they were. And how could there ever be anything that could tell you what they were? So the idea of truth gives you the same problem that the idea of God does, and that to me is one of the reasons why I believe in God. I don't see how without God there can be any truth. How can it be true that they [the American Indians] didn't have their own personal experiences? They were persons. But the whole question of what history is about comes in. Is history only about what there are present proofs of? Then it isn't about very much of what must have happened. That's one of my reasons for believing in God, the problem of God is the same as the problem of truth. How can there be truth about the past when there's nothing in the present world which seems to tell anything about them?

Auxier: One of your disagreements with John Dewey would have been over this point.

Hartshorne: Yes, I wrote to Dewey about this, but I couldn't make out what his answer was. Dewey very often was pretty clear and I very often agreed with Dewey; he said a lot of things that I think are quite right.

Auxier: So, you haven't given up on truth?

Hartshorne: No, I don't see how you could say, "well, it happened but now it isn't true that it happened." These things must have happened.

Auxier: That seems true. I wanted to ask you this because it raises yet another question which is written about a lot, but which I have never seen adequately treated. You demand on one hand, in theology, that it be a literal discipline, that the things we say about God must be literally true of God.

On the other hand, you do not hesitate in your work to use analogy in order to describe God—not negative analogy or some via negativa. You are quite clear about the capacity of an analogy to indicate something positive. But an analogy doesn't strike me as literal. And so I'm wondering about the place of analogy in theology.

Hartshorne: I think an analogy is literal, but it is very abstract. It's not concrete. God knows me as I am. But I don't know what that phrase, what "me as I am"—I have very scant knowledge of what that is. So—this is a very abstract thing—that God's [knowledge] is unlimited in the same way in which truth is unlimited. Everyone of us should know there is a lot of truth about him- or herself that he or she doesn't know. The very idea of truth as far as I can see must be more concrete than any of our knowledge can ever be. The mystery is the concrete. I don't know how I appear to God. I only know how I appear to myself, and my neighbors, and friends and enemies, but that's not the same as how I appear to God.

Auxier: You argue throughout your work that self-knowledge, human self-knowledge, is a matter of coming to know ourselves in a tiny part at least of the way that God already knows us.

Hartshorne: Yes.

Auxier: It's a curious view of self-knowledge, if there were no God there could be no self-knowledge—in your view.

Hartshorne: Well, I quote Whitehead on this. Whitehead says, "That truth itself, is only the way all things are all together in God as consequent upon the world." God is influenced by the world because God loves and cares for all the creatures. And that must mean that each of us makes a certain difference to God. We could never know exactly what that is, to know that would be for us ourselves to be God.

Auxier: You make the point about self-knowledge in this regard, but you don't make this point explicitly—anywhere that I've seen—about God's love: that in order to love ourselves, we have to love God, and learn to love the things that God loves. Is that an accurate representation of your view?

Hartshorne: Yes. My ethics is basically an ethics of *how* we should look at things. And I accept the New Testament thing—and you can find the equivalent in most religions—that we should love God. We should evaluate ourselves and other people by the same principles. If I didn't love personality in myself how could I love it in anybody else?

Auxier: So you disagree with Reinhold Niebuhr, who says that we have to hold ourselves to a higher standard than we hold others?

Hartshorne: Well, I am more responsible for myself. I have more control over myself than I have over any other. It's easier for me to know what kind of person I am than for any one else really. If I remember my history back to my childhood no one has that same set of memories. It's really memories which distinguish us. We have more responsibility for our own careers than for anybody else's. But we value our careers on the same principle that we value [those of] others. That's why when you say love others as you love yourself, that means that it's not only all right to love yourself, but you ought to love yourself. And Kant thought we have no duties to ourselves because automatically we care about ourselves, but he was mistaken there. Lots of people do things in the present moment which, if they were adequately concerned about their own futures, they wouldn't do. So they are paying disrespect to their own future selves. They immediately feel like doing something so they do it, regardless of what it will do to their own career[s] afterwards. We should love ourselves. If we don't how many others will?

Auxier: Does this translate into any kind of political philosophy? I realize that there has been a book written in the last couple years that you did not necessarily agree with, by Randall Morris.

Hartshorne: Well, Morris was partly right in the views he attributed to me, and he was partly just as wrong as he could be. But whenever philosophers fail to communicate it's always a question of who's most responsible. The paragraph that he based most of his book on—one paragraph written fifty years before he was writing, and it happened to be a pretty obscure paragraph even to me . . .

Auxier: And you wrote it.

Hartshorne: I thought it was far from the best paragraph I'd ever written. And it was way back in the past. At the time when he was writing the [issue] was Hitler and what we were to think about Hitler and whether the country should be isolationist or should go into a war against Hitler. That issue hadn't arisen when I wrote that paragraph. And he guessed what this obscure paragraph meant and he guessed wrong. But some of his points were valid enough.

Auxier: One thing that has been said about both you and Whitehead is that your political philosophies are difficult to discern on the basis of your cosmologies.

Hartshorne: Well, I maintain that political principles concern the human species of animal, which is a very contingent thing, and so it's very complex and subtle. Political questions, I think, are much harder than philosophical issues. And theology is more than just a definition of God. As far as it concerns human beings it's a question about some very empirical contingent things. There haven't always been human beings, and nobody can show how from the dinosaurs it was bound to be that there should someday be a human species. There's no way you can do that. Biology is one of the most unpredictive sciences. The best you can do is show how it was possible that we came to be. They can't possibly show that it was inevitable that we would come to be. We might not have for all we know.

Auxier: What might be next on the evolutionary horizon? I'm assuming that you don't take human beings to be in any sense necessarily the pinnacle of evolution. What might be next?

Hartshorne: The earth won't be here forever. In spite of science fiction, it's no light matter to be traveling light years. Suppose we got messages from another planet? They'd be years old when we got them. What would an answer mean? They would've changed. So I think we will never know more than a minute part of the truth about the cosmos.

Auxier: But our knowledge does grow?

Hartshorne: Yes. But there's also some regression. I think that in philosophy there is genuine progress. But every great philosopher has regressed in some way. I think the mature Plato had truths that in the whole Dark Ages and Middle Ages nobody had retained. We had to go back to them. The Reformation didn't help much. They substituted an infallible book, written by human beings or translated by human beings. I don't worship a book. God isn't a book. And God didn't write a book in any reasonably definite sense.

Auxier: But one thing that you do in your work is sort out the Hebrew theological ideas from the Greek theological ideas.

Hartshorne: You bet.

Auxier: For instance, on the question of eternity, you say that it is a Greek idea. The Hebrew equivalent, the closest equivalent they have, is the notion of everlasting. In many cases, you seem to favor the Hebrew ideas over the Greek ideas.

Hartshorne: Yes, but that's where there are two Platos. The Plato that most philosopher's think that they know, and then there's the Plato that they didn't know. Plato said, "In God there is being and becoming," so he did not disagree with the Jews about that. The fact that that is overlooked by so many Christians and Islamic people, seems to me to be a very important regression in the history of philosophy. Plato didn't say that God is unchanging. Not at all. He said that there is change in God. . . . Furthermore, Karl Barth who's considered one of the most conservative theologians in the twentieth century . . . I had twenty minutes to talk to him—his wife assigned him only twenty minutes. We had a great time. I began by saying that I think there's change in God. His face lighted up and he said that, "I say that too!" I looked it up in his great systematic work. Oh, yes; and not only that, he said that there is wholly change in God. He also says there is contingency in God. In other words, there are accidental things which God didn't eternally know would happen. He knows when or as they happen and afterwards. . . .

You mentioned Brightman a moment ago. Let's go back to him. Brightman did not say God is finite. That's often said about Brightman. Brightman said that God is finite *and* infinite or infinite *and* finite. God has an infinite aspect and finite aspect. He meant both terms. He meant the infinity just as much as the finitude and vice versa.

Auxier: You influenced one another? You modified his personalism and he modified your view?

Hartshorne: We argued. Brightman was a very serious man. He was not a witty man. He didn't make witty jokes the way some philosophers do. Bertrand Russell, for one. You could have a serious argument [with Brightman]. We really found out exactly where we agreed and where we didn't agree. I thought Brightman was exactly right. This is what I call dual transcendence. God is infinite in a sense in which nothing else is infinite and God is finite in a sense in which nothing else is finite. The finitude of God includes all the finitude there is. All the finite beauties in the world. The beauties in the world are all finite. Definiteness: This definite person, that definite person, this definite animal, this definite little cell, or this definite animal or molecule.

Auxier: You use the word transcendence, but you use it in a unique way.

Hartshorne: Dual transcendence.

Auxier: You do not use that word the way most philosophers use it.

Hartshorne: Most philosophers use the word transcendent as though it meant "beyond," or "out of," or something. That's a stupid spatio-temporal metaphor. It's a question of *excellence*, divine excellence. You're talking values when you talk about God. You're not talking about some strange place where God is, as though eternity were some place you might be in. If there was a special kind of place called eternity, what super container would contain this special place in the ordinary space/time?

Auxier: So when you say transcendent, what you mean is unsurpassable?

Hartshorne: All-surpassing. It's dangerous to put it in the negative. If you say "unsurpassable" then God can't even surpass himself. That means God is changeless. Change in us means change for the worse. And of course you wouldn't worship anything [changing] if it changed for the worse. That would make it too much like us. So God's change is never degeneration, or decay. But you have to be careful not to say that there's no suffering in God. Suffering is not a good thing. But there's a vicarious suffering in sympathizing with those who suffer. There is an old heresy, called the Heresy of Patri Passionism, that is, "the suffering of God." Now I believe—and Whitehead believed, and there have been others who believe—that God vicariously, through sympathy, suffers with the sufferers. Whitehead says God is the fellow-sufferer who understands. Now what makes us different from God is that we're the fellow-sufferers who *don't* understand. We can sympathize with other people; we can't fully understand them. God can. So there Whitehead said something that nobody had ever quite said. And he also came to this conclusion: that tragedy is not just the conflict of good with evil, it is the conflict of good with good—your good with my good.

There was a poet in California who fell in love with a married woman. What could be done about it? He couldn't see anything that could be done. He finally committed suicide. He wrote some exquisitely sad poems about it, then he gave up. He couldn't find the solution.

Auxier: Is that an acceptable solution?

Hartshorne: I don't think he had any great responsibilities that he gave up, so he may not have done much harm to anybody.

Auxier: So suicide is not inherently bad?

Hartshorne: Well, some people have even said it's the worst sin of all, and I think that's nonsense. Now for young people to do that, that's pretty dubious. Can you be sure that there's no way in which you can find a good role for yourself? How can you be sure of that, if you're young? But suppose you're old and have an incurable disease.

Auxier: Like your brother recently?

Hartshorne: Yes. He had done what he could do for the world. There was no chance that going through chemotherapy would enable him to do any more, so he said "No, I've done what I was to do."

Auxier: Did Socrates commit suicide?

Hartshorne: Socrates was better about death than Plato. Plato thought we would be reborn. Socrates reserved judgment. He wasn't sure about death. Maybe death is the final thing. And I admire Socrates there more than Plato. But in the Book of Job, there isn't a whisper about rebirth, or about heaven or hell. But most Christians couldn't pass an examination on the Book of Job. I bet they don't know that about Job. . . . That's why I admire the Book of Job. Not a whisper about heaven or hell, and yet it's all about God. Some people think that if you believe in God, then of course you believe in heaven, or maybe in hell. Nonsense. God is the immortal one; God is the one who can go on forever with new experiences. We are not just finite, we are little fragments in the finite. In all of cosmic history, my whole career is just a fragment.

Auxier: This reminds me of another very unusual doctrine of yours, and that is your view of human immortality.

Hartshorne: Here I'm very dependent on Whitehead. And yet, what he says is pretty obvious, and everybody who believed in God should have seen it all along. If you think of God as conscious, then you have to think of God as knowing the past. And then you have to decide whether God knows *all* the future. But if you say God knows all the future, you're swallowing up temporality into eternity—you are making everything eternal. If God knows future events, then the future events, for God, are not future. They are all equally present. And that really eternalizes everything, and then temporality is gone. . . . Karl Popper said that the whole of cosmic history wouldn't be very interesting to God if he knew all that would ever happen. And the Socinians, a little sect that was exterminated (except a branch of it survived in Transylvania) said God is not immutable, and does not know future events, because events that haven't happened—there *are* no such events. There are no "tomorrow's events." There is nothing fully concrete that will happen tomorrow; there are just various possibilities, things that may happen. And Charles Peirce was the first one to say that very clearly. The future is irreducibly a matter of the potential. What *may* happen is what defines tomorrow. Definite events are all past, and if that's not the way it is to God, then we're just wrong to see it that way [ourselves]. Then we should stop worrying about the future, because there isn't any future really, [as] distinguished from the past.

Auxier: It's just an abstraction?

Hartshorne: It's all utterly, hopelessly abstract. And we shouldn't be trying to decide what to do next. What would we be doing [in so deciding]? Living is deciding. And if we are alive, we're deciding; and if God is alive, God is deciding. We are all deciders. If God decides everything, then what is our deciding got to do with it?

Auxier: But we're immortal in the fact that God doesn't forget our lives, that we contribute to God's experience?

Hartshorne: For us the past is more or less real, but if there's a complete truth about the past, it can only be in God. And that's the objective immortality of the past. It doesn't swallow up the future, so there is a future even for God. That's true with the Greeks, and it's true with Plato in his maturity.

Auxier: That's not very consoling as a view of immortality.

Hartshorne: Well, but it means that if we have had a good life and helped others to have good lives, that goodness is still there—whereas it is lost otherwise.

Auxier: But if Hitler had an evil life, then the evil is still there in God's experience.

Hartshorne: God suffers that. Hitler was an actual person. He wasn't absolutely bad in every possible way. There was some goodness in him. Nobody lives for no good. Nobody lives who doesn't get what Whitehead called some satisfaction from living.

Auxier: Hitler loved his mother?

Hartshorne: Did he?

Auxier: And so that would be an example?

Hartshorne: Yeah, that would be an example. Certainly. No human being can ever become human without sympathizing some with other people.

Auxier: So there is no such thing as pure, unmitigated evil, at least evil that is real for humans.

Hartshorne: No, there isn't. Nobody lives very long without getting some satisfaction from life. It's complicated because each cell in his body has its own little will to live on my view, and on the view of many other people.

Auxier: This is what people call your "psychicalism."

Hartshorne: Yes. The Buddhists had this phrase: "Mind only." In two words, they state a very important philosophical position. And they meant it. All the other animals are involved. They all get their satisfactions. They refuse to say, as Immanuel Kant did, that since we are the only rational animal, we're the only one that has any intrinsic value. That's ridiculous. It assumes on the one hand that we are perfectly rational, which we certainly aren't, and [on the other hand] that the other animals are absolutely, in every possible sense, irrational. And neither of those makes very good sense. I think the Asians are right, that we are not absolutely different from the other animals; we are only relatively different.

Auxier: Your philosophy is more deeply influenced by Eastern philosophy than any American philosopher I can recall having read. And I wanted to ask you, it is common to Taoism that the existence of consciousness itself is an indication or a pointer to some fall from a more natural state, or from a more unified state. They are dualists, and they accept the idea that consciousness is something that is set up over against nature. You seem to reject that.

Hartshorne: Well, I follow Whitehead there. I haven't worked it out entirely for myself farther than Whitehead. Whitehead would say, you shouldn't say a baby is "conscious." The baby has feelings, and maybe little bits of thoughts. But the word "consciousness" he reserved for the capacity not only to think, but to think about thinking, and have judgments about thinking.

Auxier: What many people would call self-consciousness?

Hartshorne: Well, no, it's much more than that. A baby cannot talk. Buddha was said to have been born talking, but that's a miraculous thing. There's nothing else like it in history. It's really claiming a miracle, and there are lots of miracles in Buddhism. And one reason why I refuse to be a Christian by believing in miracles, is because then I have to decide what to do with all these other miracles. I don't know how to choose among miracles. How do you do that?

Auxier: Do you believe there are miracles?

Hartshorne: Well, I haven't said I could prove there aren't any. But I don't see how I could know that there were. I've certainly not seen any. And I've not seen any people that have seen any. There's a book talking about them. Well, how much does that prove to me? I don't know. That's just something too hard for me.

Auxier: Thank you for answering my questions.

Hartshorne: You are quite welcome.

༈

God, Process, and Persons—Charles Hartshorne and Personalism

Randall E. Auxier

It has been noted from time to time in the literature that Hartshorne's thought had a number of affinities with personalism, and this is a special case of the relationship between process and personalist thought. The latter is a tangled problem at best, but it is clear that among the important founders of the process perspective—specifically Peirce, Bergson, Whitehead, Dewey, and Hartshorne— it is Hartshorne's work which comes closest to being a kind of personalism.[1] Whitehead explicitly sets aside the personalist perspective in *Religion in the Making*, considering its claims beyond the possibility of being established.[2] On the other side, a number of personalists have been sympathetic to process thought, and Brightman is surely principal among them.[3] Here the focus will not be the investigation of whether personalism in general, or even the idealistic type, is reconcilable with process thought. It will be enough if something can be established about the first question, Hartshorne's "personalism."

The crux of this question will rest upon epistemological commitments that Hartshorne and Brightman slugged out in their correspondence. But before getting to that, one must first contextualize the correspondence by surveying the history of personalist influences on Hartshorne. After that some of Hartshorne's metaphysical commitments in relation to personalism will be examined, and then the differences between Hartshorne and Brightman regarding the nature and origin of knowledge. It will be necessary always to distinguish among three levels of discourse that are generally mixed together in the correspondence. These are metaphysical convictions, methodological commitments, and epistemological results. Obviously these are all related—method properly followed is how we *know* what there *is*, and what there *is* sets the boundaries upon what can be *known*, while method attempts to join these two for us. Hartshorne and Brightman agree to a great extent about what there is. They agree less about what can be known, and they have profound differences regarding how we know it. With respect to metaphysics, the effects of these differences upon the notion of "person" at three existential levels: the monadic, the datum self, and the divine will be estimated. The discussions of knowledge and method must be carried out within the context of this metaphysical agreement. This leads in the end to the more interesting question of what a personalist account of knowledge and method requires. From that standpoint an assessment of the extent to which it is accurate or fair to treat Hartshorne as a personalist is possible.

Personalist Influences and Statements of Hartshorne

Although Borden Parker Bowne was never an important influence in Hartshorne's thinking. The only reference to Bowne in any of Hartshorne's books appears in *Philosophers Speak of God,* and that occurs in an excerpt written by Brightman that is reprinted in the book. Further, Hartshorne identifies Brightman as "the principal founder of American personalism" in an article written in 1960, which suggests that he was practically oblivious to Bowne or to the other Boston personalists older than Brightman, such as Knudson and McConnell. G. H. Howison does occasionally appear in a reference, but Hartshorne never shows any awareness that Howison is considered a personalist. Nikolai Berdyaev was also an important influence upon Hartshorne, but Hartshorne does not associate Berdyaev's thought with personalism. This does not mean that it would be fruitless to investigate the contribution Berdyaev's personalism may have made to Hartshorne's, but it will not be undertaken here.

This narrows down the historical question of Hartshorne's personalism (or at least what Hartshorne *calls* personalism) to his debt to Brightman. This we will discuss. But it must also be added that a commitment to personalism is not dependent upon an historical connection to those who espoused it. There is also the matter of philosophical affinity with its viewpoint, which is far and away more important. Since Hartshorne's entire notion of what personalism is derives from what Brightman says about it, these two questions may be fairly treated together, but with the reservation that there may be more to Hartshorne's personalism than he himself recognized, since he chose to understand the perspective narrowly by identifying it almost exclusively with the views of Brightman.

Among the reasons that Hartshorne might be called a personalist, Sterling McMurrin has noted:

> Hartshorne claims for his dipolar (absolute and relative) metaphysics that it overcomes the traditional antinomies of unity and plurality, being and becoming, the infinite and the finite, eternity and time, necessity and freedom. His attempt to justify this immodest claim by logical analysis is impressive. I find it

rather surprising, however, considering his habit of frequently referring to the work of others, that in this and other connections he appears to make no references to the work of Borden Parker Bowne, whose personalistic world ground was intended to serve the same purpose—the resolution of the metaphysical antinomies. He refers on occasion to the work of Bowne's successor, Edgar S. Brightman, but usually in consideration of Brightman's somewhat unique finitistic theology. Of course, Hartshorne gives considerable attention to the concept of God as personal, and he might well be regarded as a personalist, though he doesn't fit the idealistic mode typical of American personalism. It would be interesting to have his comparative commentary on Bowne's personalistic idealism which, though in a manner different from the influence of James or Hartshorne, has had, through Brightman and Ralph Tyler Flewelling, a considerable impact on the philosophy of religion. I can see marked similarities as well as differences in comparing Hartshorne with Bowne.[4]

The marked similarities and differences are what are worth noting here. There is no point in pursuing this matter in relation to Bowne, however. Hartshorne's relationship to Bowne is a special case of the more complex relationship between the thought of Brightman and Bowne. I see few similarities between Bowne and Hartshorne that are not also similarities between Brightman and Hartshorne. However, Bowne and Hartshorne do share an interest in psychology that one does not discover in Brightman.

Unfortunately Hartshorne did not comment on McMurrin's question about personalism in the "Reply" to it that he wrote. But if there is a crucial similarity between Bowne and Hartshorne, it lies in their negative views on materialism. Hartshorne uses a refutation of materialism in his first book that Bowne himself could have written—except that if Bowne had written it, it would have been clearer.[5]

As McMurrin indicates, there is certainly *prima facie* reason to think of Hartshorne as a personalist. At the three metaphysical levels previously distinguished, the monadic, the datum self, and the divine, Hartshorne's panentheism commits him to the existence of increasing degrees of consciousness at each level. If, as Brightman holds, the phenomenon of consciousness is really the key to understanding "persons" and the presence of consciousness can be identified with the presence of personhood, then Hartshorne is certainly a personalist as far as this goes. Acknowledging in one's metaphysics that personality permeates the cosmos certainly seems an important step towards personalism.

A second important metaphysical commonality is that both Hartshorne and Brightman assert a certain passivity in God and in human selves.[6] Brightman refers to this as the Given, and Hartshorne is willing to accept the reality of the Given, although the two thinkers disagree about what it is and how it is known. As a metaphysical point, however, the Given exists for both. If the Given is an indispensable feature of consciousness and personality, as Brightman holds,[7] then it is significant to analyzing Hartshorne's "personalism" that he accepts this point.

On the negative side of their agreement, both Brightman and Hartshorne make a strong distinction between the personhood of God and the anthropomorphic conception of God, denying any mutual implication between the two.[8] The anthropomorphic conception of God is a phase in the development of human ideas about God, and an important one, but prereflective in character and not very helpful to modern humanity. Whatever it means to say that God is a person, it is clearly different from saying that the divine nature is adequately understood by simply generalizing upon human nature. If anything, human consciousness is understood by the two thinkers as a lesser, contingent—or even fragmentary—icon of divine consciousness.[9] Not much more can univocally be said about the divine/human relation. Analogically much can be said, but such assertion is always hypothetical for Brightman, while it is both abstract and literal for Hartshorne.[10] We strive for logically consistent analogies among the three levels of being, but not identities. Hartshorne and Brightman agree, then, that humans are not identical to God and that monads are not identical to God, which is to say that both reject pantheism.[11] Brightman and Hartshorne both accept the reality of the monad, although Hartshorne is much more willing to speak about the experiences had by subhuman entities than was Brightman.[12] This foreshadows their epistemological differences.

Another bit of *prima facie* evidence that might be considered in favor of Hartshorne's "personalism" is that in Virgilius Ferm's 1945 classic *Encyclopedia of Religion,* a work to which Brightman contributed forty articles[13] and in which Brightman had particular editorial input,[14] the article on "God, as personal" was written by none other than Charles Hartshorne.[15] This, along with Brightman's review of *The Divine Relativity* (cited below), suggests that Brightman himself considered Hartshorne a personalist. Brightman never said outright that this was his view of Hartshorne, but the indications are persuasive that he did think in this way. This, if true, is a nice complement to the fact that Hartshorne considers Brightman a process philosopher.

But to focus the issue a bit more, when asked about his commitment to the personhood of God in a 1993 interview (see Appendix 3), Hartshorne said: "God is more personal than we are. . . . He is the ideal of personality. He is the most excellent person."[16] This shows a basic continuity with Hartshorne's position as developed almost fifty years before in *The Divine Relativity,* which is the most personalistic book Hartshorne wrote. There, in a section entitled "Divine Personality," he says, "Maximizing relativity as well as absoluteness in God enables us to conceive him as a supreme person. . . . but it is the divine Person that contains the Absolute, not vice-versa."[17] In short, "personhood" provides the broadest possible conception of God, containing all God's relations, and even the part of God that is independent of all internal relations, God's absoluteness. Personhood is God's mode of existence, and since God's mode of existence, in Hartshorne's view, encompasses all possible and actual modes of existence,[18] one would think that this commitment fairly well establishes Hartshorne as a personalist, at least in his metaphysics. Certainly he never retracted this view or even expressed any doubts about it.

Yet, Hartshorne expressed privately in the correspondence his worry that personalism "is in danger of under (or under really) generalizing specifically human type of social relation" (letter of May 8, 1939). The question becomes, then, in what does the divine personhood consist, and how is it similar to and different from, on the one hand, the human datum self, and, on the other hand, the monad? What can be known of this and how? It is in the light of these three levels of "selfhood" that we must approach the letters exchanged by Hartshorne and Brightman.

The Correspondence

Our focus now shifts to questions of knowledge and method. When Hartshorne and Brightman began pointedly to argue about the nature of the self in the correspondence (July 19, 1935), the question was "how much and what is 'given' to the self?" Hartshorne refers Brightman to the following passage from *The Philosophy and Psychology of Sensation* in an effort to convince Brightman that there is *more* given to the self than just the "datum self," which Brightman refers to as the "datum-self" in the correspondence and as the "shining present" in his most mature work:

> He who thinks that the world, without any such unity of significance as constitutes an experience, would still have been or might be a real world, and who deduces this from the fact—which spiritualism accepts—that the world without a particular human personality, Mr. X, is perfectly possible, must also be one who thinks that if from "himself" those qualities which make him Mr. X were to be subtracted, nothing of the nature of mind would remain—in short, he is one who does not believe that other minds are members of himself. Such sheer privacy is the essence of what I call "materialism."[19]

Brightman's commitment to a particular interpretation of empirical method led him to resist this idea that more is given to the self than the datum self and that other selves can be known as "members of himself." If other selves cannot be known as being members of ourselves, then for Brightman there is no warrant for saying that they *are*. He insists that Hartshorne is using abstractions (e.g., "experiences" of which we are unconscious) to build his epistemological case.[20] One might, according to Brightman, infer or construct such "experiences," but only on the basis of what is truly given to the consciousness of the datum self, which is nothing more or less than the datum self. On this epistemological basis, Brightman opposes Hartshorne's claim that selves literally participate in one another's being. In Brightman's view, one may, by a rational process (e.g., analogy), come to the conclusion that selves literally participate in one another's being, as Hartshorne has done, but one cannot find conclusive evidence for it. This is Brightman's fallibilism, and it points to Hartshorne's overwillingness to have faith in the results of his deductions.

Here the monadic and divine levels become relevant. For Brightman the monad and God are constructed concepts, a rational extension of empirical method. For Hartshorne, monads and God are realities—which make it *possible* for human consciousness to emerge and construct more or less adequate ideas and accounts of them. Hartshorne does not seem to either appreciate or understand the force of Brightman's repeated point that monads, God, and other selves are not given in our conscious experience—which is why Brightman thinks their existence must be inferred or constructed. Brightman also holds that, even though what is given to God—and what God knows, which is everything that *can* be known—is vastly greater than what is given in our experience, a similar limitation applies to God. God must also make inferences and constructions in confronting the Given. God does not need a method as do we, but God must both remember the past and anticipate the future, which is to say that the past and future are not given to God in the same way as is the present. To deny this is to say that God is not temporal.[21] Hartshorne concurs on the point about temporality, but not on the claim that God must make inferences in order to know the past. This latter point will be addressed momentarily.

But for now the question is whether all of our present experience is also a part of God's present experience? Or must it be constructed and/or inferred by God? Does God need imagination and the capacity to reason in order to know us as we are? For Hartshorne the answer to this is a qualified no: "If God knows all the universe, then God-and-the-universe contains no more items than God (as omniscient). Omniscience means immediacy, indirect knowledge cannot, I should suppose, be perfect" (letter of January 22, 1942). God's present awareness is sufficiently complete to encompass all of our experience and the *way* in which we experience it, and although God does not believe our erroneous beliefs, God does "suffer" them and in that sense "contains" all of our experiences as we experience them. Still God does not have to infer or imagine us, for Hartshorne.[22]

But Brightman is less clear on this point. For him, our experience *as* we experience it is not given in God's conscious experience, it is known indirectly by God, albeit perfectly (since God's reasoning cannot fail), and God wants it that way: "When God intuits me, I am not a part of him, but he wills that I should be other than himself, yet known by him. May not his immanence be construed as reasonably in his purpose to maintain my otherness as in the theory that I am included within him?" (letter of December 10, 1934). Brightman thinks that to deny this, as Hartshorne does, forces one's epistemology towards pantheism, since it leaves no difference to us between God's experience of our experience and our experience of our experience.[23]

The point for the present is this: while Brightman aims to start with an empirical epistemology and to allow it to guide his conclusions about what is metaphysically real, Hartshorne starts with metaphysical convictions about ultimate reality and a transcendental epistemology to support that metaphysical account (with logical rigor trusted to support our reasonings about the conditions for the possibility of our knowing anything at all., i.e., that God first knows us). The relationship between Hartshorne's metaphysics and his epistemology is therefore the primary problem in Brightman's view at this early stage in Hartshorne's career. Hartshorne believes that his method is sufficiently empirical to support his claim to having an empirical epistemology, but he does not exclude transcendental argumentation from empirical method.

Brightman resists this approach in both the correspondence and in his published discussions of method,[24] but the question is whether Brightman (or personalism) can self-consistently maintain such a narrow version of empiricism. In any case, Brightman *attempted* to maintain this position to the very end.[25]

An example of this problem might be helpful. In a single paragraph of his important article "A Temporalist View of God," Brightman makes the following assertions: ". . . nothing real is timeless. . . . Eternity is a function of time . . . all things change except the logos of change. . . . God is not an abstraction, but a concrete, living reality." In the very next paragraph he says: "The only source of evidence for God is immediate experience, . . . what I have elsewhere called the 'datum self' . . . All of the reasons for belief in God are but interpretations, more or less trustworthy, of this datum."[26] How can empirical method and epistemology, narrowly defined, ever support such categorical claims? These claims circumscribe an epistemology but may not be knowable according to the very epistemology they circumscribe.

Brightman, already in his maturity during the years of the correspondence, has his view well worked out, and he endeavors to abide by the limitations this places upon him, even though he is willing to admit that a gray area exists between "what is given in experience" and "the *definition* of the Given." This is where Hartshorne could, and in some implicit ways *does,* drive a wedge in Brightman's view, because Brightman is willing as a point of method to collapse metaphysical questions into epistemological questions.[27] Hartshorne is not as willing, and he thinks personalism must employ both inductive and transcendental argumentation to support its own claims. This methodological point is the key to Hartshorne's criticism of Brightman, since it later issues in an extreme epistemological problem.

Brightman's unwillingness to acknowledge a kind of "literal participation" of selves in one another derives basically from his epistemological conviction that we *experience* the datum self as separate from other selves. From this he concludes that "monads have no windows through which existences or concrete realities may interact. Only purposes may interact."[28] Thus our interaction with one another and with God is not literal participation, but a commingling of purposes. The question Hartshorne continues to press is not whether we do or do not *experience* other selves as a part of us, but whether other selves must *be* a part of us in order for us to experience them at all. Brightman will not go beyond an interaction of purposes.

An interesting question, then, which does not come up in the correspondence—but which is crucial to the case—would be "what is the *being* of purposes for Brightman?" On the one side, if purposes are a part of what is given in experience and not merely a part of its definition, then would this not constitute a kind of literal participation, since "what is given" must certainly exist? In this case, even though purposes may be a part of what is given in experience, in order to be known they must still be inferred or constructed *post hoc*. Yet, how could we know whether they are *mere* constructions (abstractions) or truly reflect something given in experience? And the case is not even this simple, because on the other side Brightman sometimes speaks as though purposes are *not* given in experience. This is part of what he means by "the innocence of the given"—that what is given is neither theory-laden nor value-laden and it is not knowledge at all until it is reflected upon rightly, which is to say, until it has been analyzed according to the proper empirical method.[29] So if purposes are given, then there is literal participation (whether it can be adequately known or not), while if purposes are not given, then what are they? Mere chimeras? How are they known? Do they exist?

This makes Brightman's view of the given incoherent, in Hartshorne's view. Too great an attachment to the datum self as a methodological starting point commits one unwittingly to solipsism, he holds, since one could never achieve a sound epistemological basis for inferring the existence of anything beyond the datum self by this method.[30] Further, if it is true that human beings are social all the way down, resistance to a literal participation in the being of a person by others (including their literal purposes) is also a form of impersonalism, according to Hartshorne's analysis—a charge from which Brightman would have reeled, had he realized that this was Hartshorne's implication. The absence of literal participation would force one to assume that the human self is not essentially social but is rather essentially alone and capable of existing without other selves. Thus, if it is true that the social nature of the self is "basic," as Hartshorne believes and Brightman agrees,[31] then the denial of literal participation isolates what is most personal about persons, which then deprives them of their essentially personal, or social, character—i.e., no man is an island unto himself; to live alone is to be a beast or a God, etc. *Ergo,* it is impersonalism.[32]

Brightman seemed to realize that he was up against a genuine problem here and that it would be necessary to work out the ontological status of purposes. Otherwise his "privacy of method" might end in privacy of both knowledge and existence. He could not accept that result, and so he set out to provide an account of the status of purposes in his last work.[33] Had it not been for Hartshorne's repeated challenges regarding this in the correspondence, Brightman may never have addressed the problem in detail. To summarize perhaps without doing full justice to the subtlety of Brightman's view, his mature account states:

> Purposes are associated with efficient and final causes, and with substance:

> All cause is purposive. All substance is purposive. This does not mean that cause and purpose or substance and purpose are synonymous. What it means is that purpose is an essential and integral aspect of every efficient cause and of every substance—namely of every person. The fundamental empirical basis for such a telic metaphysics is, of course, to be found in the shining present. . . . Every moment of the present includes (along with much else) a striving, a conation, a choice, a preference, or a purpose in some stage of development.[34]

Not content to stop with saying that purposes are given in all conscious experience, Brightman then extends himself beyond this to that which makes conscious experience possible:

> It would seem strange indeed if all experience were purposive and truly real while the "illuminating absent" were devoid of purpose! Further, all that can rationally be said about that absent requires it to be viewed as interacting with human purpose, as itself conforming in all respects to the purpose of order and law, and also as exhibiting telic adaptations serving the ends of life and beauty and sublimity.[35]

From this one learns that purposes do indeed have being in Brightman's view and that they are given in experience—which seems at odds with value-free "innocence of the given"—and are a part of the absent as well. There are purposes that have being in spite of the fact that they are not given in experience—and since God has a datum self, or a shining present, as well as an illuminating absent (e.g., God's past), then one may assume that there are purposes that are not given to God—ours for example. It does not follow that there are free-floating purposes out there, but it does follow that there is no unity of purpose in the sense of a place and time where all purposes are fully related to one another. This would seem to point to a thoroughgoing pluralism in Brightman, but he admits no such view.

Instead Brightman goes still further in asserting that there is a total conformity of the nature of purposes beyond our experience to purposes given in our experience. But how can one know this on the basis of Brightman's method?[36]

One may rephrase this question as follows: How are purposes given? Insofar as this question is addressed by Brightman, it is with a distinction he makes in the concept of "the given." Brightman distinguishes between the Given (with an uppercase "G") and what is given in immediate experience (lowercase "g"). This distinction is not explicit in the correspondence, perhaps because Brightman had not recognized the necessity of making it until after Hartshorne had shown him the difficulty. Brightman says in his last work that "the 'shining present' as a whole is given as immediate experience, while the past, the future, and the absent are inferred, postulated or believed in. The Given, however, is discovered by analysis as an aspect or constituent of every given experience. The Given is never given by itself."[37] Thus, there is an identification of the shining present with the given (lowercase "g"), while The Given is the given plus all our hypotheses, analyses, inferences and abstractions tacked on, along with whatever else we are passive toward.

Clearly this has an effect upon the question of whether purposes are given; since purposes are an essential aspect of all causes and substances and since all causes and substances are persons, and at least one person is given in the shining present, then purposes are given.[38] But they are not recognized as a part of the Given without inference and construction. When given purposes come to be known, they are known only abstractly and indirectly, in spite of their immediacy in a given experience. Thus the purposes of others may be experienced as given, but only known as Given.

Those familiar with Hartshorne may immediately notice that Brightman's distinction between the given and the Given precisely parallels Hartshorne's distinction between relative and absolute—and the whole host of phenomena that may be distinguished as either externally or internally related to one another.[39] In Hartshorne's language, the Given is only externally related to the given, while the given is internally related the Given. It is likely that neither Brightman nor Hartshorne was aware of this parallel. But if this is an accurate accounting of Brightman's mature view of givenness, then he has added something significant to Hartshorne's view of this period, in that he has shown how not only God, but we, and whatever subhuman persons there are, have a dipolar nature analogous to God's. This provides an important point of contact between Brightman and Hartshorne and between personalism and process thought.

In any case, this distinction between the given and the Given is anticipated in the correspondence, as seen in Brightman's willingness to admit some degree of faintness in the given.[40] The real difference may lie in Brightman's methodological desire to have the self—and what is given to and as the self, the shining present—clearly defined, while Hartshorne insists that not only the self, but also the given "is more or less vague," and must be so. Brightman in turn is willing to allow distinctions of faintness and clarity in the given as experienced, but not in the definition of the Given or in the datum self. Consider the following passage from Brightman's letter of January 1, 1939:

My view must indeed take as a postulate that there is a faint givenness, so
faint that it is for the most part totally absent from the given—a given that is
not given. I see no contradiction in my postulate; yours seems to play on the
term given in such a way as to assert that the very faint is both given and not
given. I wish you would pull [my] criticism to pieces, for I am deeply interested in the problem and in your ideas.

Insisting upon clarity in the definition of the Given and the datum self is
not the same as insisting upon clarity in the given phenomena of experience,
and Brightman is again charging Hartshorne with mistaking abstractions (definitions) for concrete realities—of misplaced concreteness. In *Person and Reality,* Brightman takes up this problem of "the given that is not given" in
tremendous detail,[41] and it is quite likely that Hartshorne's criticisms provide
one of the primary motivations for this undertaking. Indeed Brightman might
never have distinguished between the illuminating absent and the shining present if not for Hartshorne's prodding.

Hartshorne answers Brightman's invitation to cut his criticism to pieces
both in the correspondence and in the 1960 essay on Brightman.[42] In the essay
Hartshorne attempts to show the incoherence of Brightman's final statement
of the nature of the self in *Person and Reality.* He never does address the difference between the Given and the given, however. Hartshorne's criticisms in the
correspondence and the review essay are quite technical and difficult to summarize. Perhaps the best way to present them is by looking at a test case—the
question of whether the past is or is not a part of the Given. As will be seen, this
has an effect upon the matter of the ontological status of purposes.

The Past as a Test Case

In further elucidating this view of the self, Hartshorne believes that Brightman
is cutting off the datum self, the shining present, from its own past. He points
out that Brightman logically must allow the past self to be given to the present
self immediately:

> . . . one's *past* self is not merely inferred but is given, *and . . . this givenness of
> past in present is an essential aspect of what is meant by the endurance of the
> "identical" self.* . . . The specious present includes all preceding presents of the
> self, but the succeeding only in the vague or outline form <u>constitutive</u> of futu-
> rity. (<u>This</u> vagueness is not merely in the givenness but in its object, though
> subjective and objective sides coincide only for God since <u>our</u> foresight is
> much less definite than the laws of nature, which themselves are, however, not
> absolutely definite.) Though past specious presents are still given they are nev-
> ertheless past, because they are the less definite parts of <u>the</u> present. Thus my

youthful aspirations and plans are less definite than my actual accomplishments since, even to absolute (divine) memory.[43]

Brightman responds, some eight years later (since this remains a point of contention between them throughout the correspondence):

> Of course I'd not suppose that we know the past without inferring. The specious present—the datum self—contains a time-span of present, past, future, which, by acquaintance, gives us clues to pastness, otherness, and inferential reason. Knowledge (in memory or otherwise) is an elaboration of those clues.[44]

Hence, for Hartshorne the past remains vague not only as given, but as Given (i.e., reflected upon, analyzed, and known to the extent humans are capable), whereas for Brightman the past may be vague as given, but not as Given. Not even our most heroic acts of analysis of the past can make it as definite as the present for either. Hartshorne is willing to concede that " The own-self is the only individual distinctly given. All our difference of opinion concerns vague givens."[45] The argument turns upon the status of what is not distinctly given to the datum self—in this case, the past, which both thinkers agree is not distinctly given.

But if Brightman admits some vagueness or faintness of either the past self or other selves, then he abandons the clean lines of his empirical methodology and begins ranging into its metaphysical presuppositions. The Given is no longer adequate to or exhaustive of the given, nor is the definition of the Given, or some parts of it, necessarily derived from the given. Hartshorne wants Brightman to recognize and admit that empirical methodology is always based upon metaphysical convictions and that we cannot evade talking about them, even though we must use abstractions to do so.

Thus, using the vagueness of the past self as a test case, we can also see that there is a difference of "distinctness" in the way the datum self is given as opposed to other selves.[46] Yet, literal participation of the one in the other is maintained, for Hartshorne, since the present self must at least literally participate in its own past self—otherwise, personal identity is problematic, and this threatens personalism with precisely the sort of solipsism that Hartshorne indicated from the beginning. For Hartshorne the self is continuous with its earlier states, but even the present self, although given, is still vague to some degree; for instance, the experiences of each of my cells is not *distinctly* given. The self is made more definite through inference and imagination, Hartshorne and Brightman agree, but the past self is constructed entirely out of the shining present for Brightman, while Hartshorne thinks that the only reason that any such construction is possible is due to the literal participation of the present self in its past states. For Hartshorne the difference between a self and its past (and other selves) is understood as a matter of degree and is known by *how much* inference and imagination is required in order to make the idea of that other self distinct.

For example, one is required to use much more inference and imagination in the case of the way that the self called "Plato" is given to one than the selves of one's current colleagues, while one must use more inference and imagination regarding one's colleagues than is needed in order to infer and construct one's own past self. Nevertheless what inference and imagination accomplish for Hartshorne is identical with the object to be known, insofar as it accurately represents what is truly given, albeit vaguely. Under the best epistemological circumstances, i.e., God's, there is an identity of knowledge and givenness when knowledge is truly knowledge, for Hartshorne; on this point he departs from Brightman, who maintains a firm distinction between knowledge of the given and the given—this is a part of the general thesis about the "innocence of the given." For Brightman even God confronts this difference. Hartshorne is quite willing to accept the distinction, but he does not see in it the same limitations as Brightman, especially regarding God. It is *our* limitation, as Hartshorne says:

> . . . the <u>seeming</u> absence of other selves within experience is <u>what my theory implies would characterize human experience</u>, since a self on that level could not conveniently manage other selves as clearly and distinctly manifest to it, but only selves on such a low level that only vague mass awareness of them would reach full consciousness, for individually taken they are too trivial to notice. (Only God notes everything consciously, however trivial).[47]

But Brightman holds firm to his empirical method when faced with such assertions: knowledge must be knowledge *of* something; otherwise it is not knowledge at all. For Brightman that is always knowledge *of* the given; for Hartshorne only God can know the given with complete clarity, and the rest of us cannot be certain—because of the vagueness of the given to *our* consciousness—of *what* we know when we reflect upon, imagine, and infer things from the given. Inference and imagination can go astray, but the laws of nature and logic are reliable enough, in Hartshorne's view, to guide us in making inferences and imagining "the other" as it really is; otherwise the knowledge of nature, God, and the self could not increase through history, as Hartshorne is convinced it does. Hartshorne concludes then that "all selves are identical as well as different, and thus the cosmic identity of God (and of being) is accounted for. All real questions, as Peirce said, are questions of degree, on this view."[48] This may seem paradoxical unless one realizes that for Hartshorne the question of truth (and true knowledge) and the question of the existence of God are the same question. In an interview in 1993 (see Appendix 3) Hartshorne gave the following analysis:

Isn't it true [for] the American Indians, who have been in the Americas for at least ten thousand years, maybe a good deal longer, [that] each one of those Indians must have had his or her own personal experiences? But what makes it true that they had these experiences? There's nothing you could find now in the universe that could tell you what they were. And how could there ever be anything that could tell you what they were? So the idea of truth gives you the same problem that the idea of God does, and that to me is one of the reasons why I believe in God. I don't see how without God there can be any truth. How can it be true that they [the American Indians] didn't have their own personal experiences? They were persons. But the whole question of what history is about comes in. Is history only about what there are present proofs of? Then it isn't about very much of what must have happened. That's one of my reasons for believing in God, the problem of God is the same as the problem of truth. How can there be truth about the past when there's nothing in the present world which seems to tell anything about them?[49]

Aside from being an excellent example of Hartshorne's commitment to transcendental argumentation, this shows the relationship between the question of the self and the nature of God for Hartshorne, and how the question of the past ties them together. Coming to an adequate view of God is a condition for properly understanding the human self and also the monad, for whatever the truth of the lesser beings may be, it is a vague and specialized case of what the supreme being knows. This is a peculiar epistemological stance, but Hartshorne insists that it is empirical; it is merely abstract, which is not the same thing as a priori.

The tie with the past is seen in the related issue of literal participation in the being of the creator by the creatures—which is the only way Hartshorne can make sense of the idea of creation.[50] Yet, Hartshorne is at pains to distinguish his sense of "participation" from Plato's *methexis*. Hartshorne later says that real creativity "is not content with actualizing 'images' which are antecedently, or eternally, in being, but rather produces 'new images,' sheer additions to the 'forms of definiteness.'"[51] Both the question of creativity and of truth are modes of God's givenness to human experience, and it is through the problem of relating to our past selves, the past selves of others, and the past of the universe that this question becomes focused.

Hartshorne insists to Brightman that

. . . unless God is given I do not see how he could be inferred, for the foundation of inference beyond immediacy seems to me necessarily the reality of God as the ground of world order. If God were not given could he be constructed? Is the idea of God the expression of what is directly apprehended, though vaguely, or is it a pure hypothesis to explain data in an experience which has no immanent transcendence, which experiences only its experience?[52]

Hartshorne thinks that this difference on the nature of the self and the nature of God is a mostly verbal dispute and that he and Brightman do indeed share the same view.

Brightman is less sure, and it is now *his* turn to charge Hartshorne with inviting solipsism:

> "The given" surely does not mean <u>my</u> given, does it? If so, it sounds solip-sistic, in spite of mutual immanence; it would have to be at least "our given." Yet the belief that any aspect of my given is also ours would be an additional postulate, akin to the postulate that what is totally absent from consciousness is really faintly given. If I were to grant that all principles of explanation are ca-pable of illustration in someone's given sometime, and were allowed to locate the principle of interaction in the given of God, I could follow this principle. Otherwise, not. It seems to me that my postulates are less arbitrary than the ungiven given, my absolute less absolute than yours![53]

But for Hartshorne this amounts to saying that, so far as we can know, there is no God and there are no other selves, and thus Brightman is really the solipsist—for our experience cannot just spontaneously occur; it is made possi-ble by what is not our present selves (and this includes our past selves), whether all that is distinctly given or not. Brightman is saying, in effect, that the experi-ence of the datum self is (or can be) knowledge, but only *of* what is given to the datum self. For Hartshorne this would imply knowledge *of* something that can, and perhaps even must, exist independently, *without* us and without our knowledge *of* the things upon which its existence depends. Hence Hartshorne is claiming that Brightman's account presupposes knowledge—of independent, ungiven existences, e.g., the past—of a sort his method cannot provide, and therefore it requires us to know what we cannot know. That is the contradic-tion Hartshorne sees in Brightman's view.

Where Metaphysics and Epistemology Touch

The key may lie in understanding Brightman's statement that "My heart is dual-istic, yours monistic. For me, I am directly aware only of my own experience."[54] Hartshorne is willing to begin with the metaphysical reality of God and other selves, not just as a postulate, but as concrete existences, and then to use infer-ence and imagination to provide an account of their nature and relations—an ac-count that *can be* more or less adequate to its object, given the limitations of our form of consciousness. Brightman insists that we must start with our own human experience and infer the metaphysical reality only of what reasonably follows from that experience and that the contents of these inferences will never be more than hypothetical—and it is difficult to be certain how adequate they are to the phenomena, since those phenomena are not given as they are in themselves.

Hartshorne's reasoning is from the "outside in," or transcendental—metaphysical reality makes certain experiences possible—regarding metaphysics and from the "inside out," or empirical in epistemology—that metaphysical reality is inferred and imagined upon the basis of what is experienced, abstractly but literally. Brightman's reasoning is from the "inside out," or empirical, in both cases; in this regard he calls himself an "empiricist of consciousness,"[55] and it also explains his willingness, evidently motivated by a fondness for his method, to collapse epistemological and metaphysical questions. Brightman is more Humean, then, while Hartshorne is more Kantian, methodologically speaking. Both are fallibilists, but by all rights Brightman should be more of a skeptic and naturalist than Hartshorne. Interestingly Brightman is the one professing idealism, and Hartshorne naturalism.

In a very real sense Brightman's metaphysics has been reduced to his epistemology[56] that he then, ignoring Hume's skeptical warnings, tries to extend out into the metaphysical world—building a bridge over the river of doubt with an abutment on only one side. This is why Brightman is a "dualist at heart"; he recognizes the difficulty, nay, the near impossibility of safely gaining the other side, while being convinced, for no clear reason, that there *is* another side; he is in consequence a thoroughgoing fallibilist and, given his method, should perhaps even be a skeptic. In Humean fashion Brightman does not expect to complete this bridge, given the tools he has to build it, but what was skepticism in Hume becomes fallibilism in Brightman, and in direct proportion to their willingness to trust philosophic method—a matter regarding which Hume had a more thorough suspicion. Hume would perhaps say that the other bank is more a useful habit of our thinking than a real bank while Brightman is not so diffident.

Meanwhile Hartshorne's has *two* starting places: he is building a bridge over the river of doubt in his epistemology, while digging a tunnel under it from the other side with his metaphysics. This is why Brightman calls Hartshorne a monist and an absolutist—Hartshorne is adequately convinced of the unity of reality as to think that such a dual strategy operates upon the same unified reality; in short he expects to finish both the bridge and tunnel and to be able to have conquered the river of doubt in the human way—it remains a river, but one that can be negotiated without getting overly wet. We might suppose that James and Dewey are willing to try their luck at wading across the thing, while Peirce is busily building a ferry out of the somewhat flimsy materials of language. The classical pragmatists have a closer relation to doubt than do the personalists and more speculative process thinkers such as Whitehead, Bergson, and Hartshorne.

But Hartshorne uses his tunnel to gain an abutment on both sides of the river for his bridge and uses his bridge to do the needed surveying for his tunnel. His conviction that this can be accomplished rests upon his faith in God on the one side and in logical rigor on the other—his belief that his tools are indeed adequate (for humans to have the kind of knowledge humans *can* have); that our knowledge of God, although partial, is really knowledge of God as God is. Hartshorne affirms neither a narrow empiricism nor wholly unempirical a priorism; yet, neither can he abide a narrow rationalism or absolutism. He says, "if there is no a priori metaphysical knowledge, then I think agnosticism is the right conclusion,"[57] and of course he rejects agnosticism. Yet, he also makes it abundantly clear that all a priori knowledge must be based on some kind of empirical experience.[58]

Brightman has serious reservations about Hartshorne's tunnel, and the tools he is using to dig it: transcendental arguments as applied to given experience about what *must be* in order for us to be what we are. And he is also dubious regarding the bridge, although he sanctions the tools—reason, inference and imagination—in a more limited way. Hartshorne acknowledges that his tools are not perfect,[59] but he is unconvinced that the fact that "probability" enters into all deduction means that we should seriously doubt the conclusions of those deductions—any more than we should doubt the conclusions of deductive mathematics. Here it is clear that Hartshorne is working with a Peircean idea of "genuine doubt," while Brightman is taking seriously the broader hyperbolic doubt of the Cartesian tradition. In this regard Hartshorne is probably more truly an empiricist than is Brightman, and Brightman's professed epistemological dualism was bound to expose its Cartesian heritage at some point. This is that point.

There is some measure of resolution of this issue in that the two thinkers can agree upon the fact of mutual immanence among selves, among monads, and of God in relation to both. However, what they mean by this at first appears quite different. For Hartshorne this "mutual immanence" is literal participation in one another's being. For Brightman it is *only* mutual immanence of purpose.[60] This brings us back to the all important question of the status of purpose for Brightman, for it is here that Brightman is willing to acknowledge some real interaction among the three metaphysical levels of personhood. Brightman perhaps concedes Hartshorne's point in the following:

> Starting with my actual experience, which is the datum self, I am led to distinguish between those hypothetical entities which were once or which may become my actual experience (and which as a whole history are my total self) and those other hypothetical entities which constitute the environing universe, interacting with me yet never a part of me. Among such entities I should count my body, my subconscious, society, the natural order, and God. My fundamental category is not "in-ness" but rather purpose. I can understand my universe only in terms of the purpose that there shall be otherness, which at the same time is a purposively cooperating otherness. Hence I deny windows through which parts of anything else can come in or go out, but not windows through which purposes may interact.[61]

Hence, monads, other selves, and God all have windows—there is a positive relation between purposes on the one side and selves on the other.

What then *are* "purposes"? We are back to the question of whether they are given to the datum self. We have seen that Brightman answers this question in the affirmative. Clearly the datum self's own purposes are given to it, but this cannot contain the "otherness" of which Brightman spoke, nor can it exhaust the positive relationship between God's purposes and the datum self.

In order to understand the simultaneous givenness *and* otherness of purpose, one may have two options: first, sometimes one's own purposes conflict and one is at odds with oneself, and sometimes this conflict cannot be resolved except by giving up one purpose or the other. Is this how one learns about otherness of purpose? That seems untrue to experience, and likely Brightman would have to reject it. Rather, and this is the second option, one learns about otherness of purpose by the brute resistance of the other to *one's own* purposes. Whether this is a child who has been told "no" or a plant that is thwarted by a pair of pruning shears in its effort to grow toward the light, otherness of purpose is, at its ground, *metaphysically* other at the outset, and epistemologically other only emergently. We reflect upon what thwarts our purposes only *because* we have in fact been thwarted in what is given—and this is how we come to the abstract idea of the Given. But if we are concretely impeded by something in what is immediately given, the otherness of purpose, then is this otherness the purpose *of* some being beyond what is immediately given? Or is it simply free-floating otherness of purpose?

We have already rejected the idea that we ourselves are the source of the given and of otherness of purpose. What further alternatives have we besides saying either that the otherness of purpose we experience has its source in the purposes of another being or that purposes other than our own are somehow just loose in the universe? Brightman acknowledges that at least some of the other purposes we experience are God's. But in this case God must be more than inferred or constructed—God is given in the otherness of purposes, and our awareness of the discrepancies between divine purposes and our own; common terms for this are sin, fallenness, guilt, conscience, and the moral sense. This requires that there be a moral God as a transcendental condition of our experience, and Brightman's method cannot give warrant to such a claim.

Thus, by construing otherness of purpose as basic to his philosophy, Brightman is digging a metaphysical tunnel of his own under the river of doubt; but he digs only at night, while wearing a blindfold, and does not remember doing so in the light of day. This boils down to saying that Brightman has a metaphysical theory of providence or purpose that is not grounded in his experiential method, except *post hoc,* abstractly. He is caught in a vicious epistemological circle, not unlike the Cartesian circle. Furthermore, for him God has the *same* epistemological problem as we do. God knows us only by inference and construction and knows our purposes only as

an otherness of purpose in what is given to God—in their disvalue, their fallenness. Hartshorne says as much of Brightman in discussing him in *Man's Vision of God:*

> [Brightman's] notion of the Given as an intrinsic limitation of God's
> power, a passive element in his activity, analogous to sensation and emotion in
> us, can be defined and defended only in the context of an adequate analysis of
> what is or can be meant by "passivity," "sensation," etc.; and the exploration
> of such concepts taken in their most fundamental or general senses, as they
> here must be, can only amount to a metaphysical system whose defense is not
> merely empirical, since the very meaning of "experience," "facts," etc., will
> have to be grounded in this system.[62]

Regarding God's part in this, Hartshorne says: "I hold that the experience
of God as the principle of interaction is useless as explanation unless we can
reach God on the basis of what we experience, and on this basis must rest also
the knowledge of interaction between us and God which enables us to conceive Him."[63] This is why Anselm's version of the ontological *proof* for the existence of God is so vital to Hartshorne's thought, while Brightman never
placed much stock in it—but perhaps should have. Brightman basically concurs with the point about God's importance, but he objects to the necessitari-
an phrasing and adds:

> . . . any God must confront a given. However, the nature of such a given must
> always be deduced from experience. In general, any God (as creative will) must
> confront within the total unity of his consciousness a twofold Given, consist-
> ing of Form (logic, mathematics, Platonic ideas) and Matter (brute fact con-
> tent, a "receptacle"). What amazes me about the traditional view of God is
> that it admits the eternal nature of form, but will not admit this as a given.[64]

Hartshorne agrees:

> Your notion of the "given" to God seems close to what I think of as the
> dependence of God upon the past as the sum of acts of more or less free be-
> ings, to whose activity God is passive, since otherwise it would not be real ac-
> tivity. Since the past never began, as I take it, God never at any moment, or in
> any act, for all his acts were at a moment, had a clean slate to just make a world
> out of the realm of logical possibilities, but always had to make the best of a
> world that could have been better.[65]

What is apparent here, as has already been noted, is that the two thinkers have
emerged on the far side of their epistemological differences here and are finding agreement on metaphysical issues.

Hartshorne's Personalism?

The question this leaves is whether this epistemological dispute places Hartshorne outside of personalism in any important way. In Hartshorne's own view it does, but I think that conclusion rests upon Hartshorne's willingness to treat Brightman's version of personalism as being the only real or important version of that philosophy. On the contrary, however, ought we not ask ourselves whether Brightman's commitment to a narrow version of empirical method, his subsequent willingness to collapse metaphysical and epistemological issues, and his account of the datum self are crucial parts of personalist philosophy? These are the ideas to which Hartshorne objected. Not only are these not important elements of a personalist philosophy, they are in fact Brightman's greatest weaknesses. They expose him to the charges of solipsism that Hartshorne mentions in the correspondence, and even impersonalism, which is implied but not mentioned. Hartshorne's charges are not proven, but he has a case. Brightman was intellectually honest, and the following expression of his uncertainty seems to suggest that he knows Hartshorne has raised issues his philosophy cannot handle:

> Your worry about my philosophy is the idea that other selves are merely inferred but never given, you say. It is also my worry, a worry such as one experiences when one has a debt far larger than one can possibly pay. I'd like to be able to make sense out of the idea of a literal participation in other selves. But I have not yet been able to do so. Whenever I try, I find myself landed in contradiction, in epistemological chaos, and in unfaithfulness to experience— all of which is hopelessly unenlightening, I know.[66]

The demand, then, that Hartshorne must meet is to give an account of literal participation that avoids contradiction, epistemological chaos, and unfaithfulness to experience. The fact that Brightman could not accomplish this, although he did not give up the effort, does not mean it cannot be done. It is interesting, to note, however, that Hartshorne has sought throughout his work to avoid precisely these pitfalls while maintaining a doctrine of literal participation. His success in this endeavor has been enormous if not complete. In many ways this argument with Brightman can be seen as a formative moment in Hartshorne's thinking that taught him as much about what he could not allow into his thought as about what he could.

One cannot settle the question here beyond all dispute, but one view of the matter is that Hartshorne's approach is actually an enlargement and corrective that personalism needed[67]—that it saves personalism from tendencies that would lead it toward the reification of personality at one extreme and a sort of solipsism that implies impersonalism at the other. In short, then, Hartshorne is a more thoroughgoing personalist than Brightman, and any version of personalism that does not treat Hartshorne's thought as personalistic is missing out on the most important corrective to and updating of personalist metaphysics and epistemology in the second half of the twentieth century.

There is neither space nor time here to delve deeply into the particulars of *how* Hartshorne has corrected and expanded personalism, but one final passage from the correspondence suggests much about his expansion of personalism. The question of the literal participation of selves in one another's being finally worked its way beyond the question of purposes and into the question of whether one mind can "contain" another mind. Hartshorne insists that it can—because mind is dipolar. God can contain all our beliefs, including our erroneous beliefs, without believing them. Rather, God suffers our errors passively. Brightman thinks that any doctrine of that sort is pantheistic and that no mind contains other minds, because a mind is a unitary mode of being for Brightman. Any act of mind is an act of the entire mind. In this context Hartshorne writes:

> If a belief within a mind is not an act of that mind you cannot imagine what it is an act of. Of course, [it is] an act of some other mind within the first mind. This you hold to be impossible . . . but you argue: if any God contains my act as mine but not as his, then my act is not his in any personal sense, and "contain" is impersonal or abstract. This assumes there are but two possibilities: personally containing an act by enacting it, and impersonally containing it. Naturally this only gives a verbal shift to the same old question. I hold that there are two ways of personally containing, concretely as a person containing, a belief, or an act, by believing it, and by suffering it as enacted, believed by an included mind, included by virtue of the "suffering" relation, as one's own beliefs are included by an active relation. There is some activity in the suffering in a sense, for God's doing is necessary to our doing, but it is not sheer doing but is also a being done in and to.[68]

Here we begin to get an indication of the nature of Hartshorne's expansion of personalism. Where Brightman had remained ensnared in a Kantian view of mental activity—and it would be hard to miss that his difficulty with the given and the Given parallels Kant's difficulties with appearances and things in themselves relative to the production of knowledge, and the phenomenal and noumenal with respect to valuation—Hartshorne has broken through. The self and God is dipolar, and to be a person is to be both relative and absolute, to act in suffering the acts of another, and to be receptive, in the sense of organic sympathy, in acting. To be a person is to be social all the way down, which means to have one's being literally participate in the being of others. *This* is the advance that Hartshorne's dipolar theory offers to personalism. There may also be an important advance that Brightman's theory of the given and the Given can offer to process epistemology, but that question would have to be taken up in a further study.[69]

APPENDIX 5

꒳

The Pacifism Debate in
the Correspondence

Mark Y. A. Davies

Introduction

The most substantive portion of the Brightman-Hartshorne correspondence took place from November 1933 through the summer of 1944. Three major events in Europe and Asia during this time are well known: the rise of Nazi Germany, the expansion of the Japanese Empire, and the culmination of these in World War II. Considering that Hartshorne and Brightman intentionally relate their philosophies to the concrete issues of our human existence in the world, it is not surprising that at some point in their correspondence they would discuss some of the issues of the war and the United States' involvement in it. The bulk of their discussion concerning the war centers around the issue of pacifism, with Brightman defending the pacifist position against Hartshorne, who sees doctrinaire pacifism as an irresponsible approach, especially given the aggressive actions of Germany and Japan in the 1930s and early 1940s.

The Disagreement in the Correspondence

The pacifism debate in the correspondence was triggered by a short remark by Brightman in a critical review he wrote on Hartshorne's 1941 book, *Man's Vision of God*. In the review Brightman criticizes Hartshorne's stance against pacifism.[1] Hartshorne's antipacifism argument as it is found in *Man's Vision of God*[2] criticizes doctrinaire pacifism for its lack of social awareness. Hartshorne writes, "there is evidence enough that dogmatic pacifism is often the expression of a preference for a certain enjoyable sentiment as against facing the tragedy of existence, which even God does not escape, and which we all must share together."[3] Hartshorne stresses that love is not to be equated with sentimental humanism,[4] rather it is an effort to act on an adequate awareness of others, and this awareness may lead one to use force in order to coerce those who are oppressing others.[5] Hartshorne understands love to be "social realism" that recognizes the necessity at times of using "coercion to prevent the use of coercion to destroy freedom."[6] To stress this point against the pacifist approach, Hartshorne writes, "Freedom must not be free to destroy freedom. The logic of love is not the logic of pacifism or of the unheroic life."[7]

Hartshorne is convinced that although war is an evil, it is not an evil to be avoided at all costs. With Germany and Hitler in mind, he writes that "it is better that many should die prematurely than that nearly all men should live in a permanent state of hostility or slavery."[8] Adequate social awareness, which in Hartshorne's view is the primary factor in love, will not allow those who are unsocial to gain a monopoly on the use of coercion, and therefore it is appropriate at times to go to war in an attempt to avoid such a monopoly and its tragic effects on humankind. That love must sometimes choose the use of violent force is, according to Hartshorne, an unavoidable part of the tragic aspects of our existence in a world where human sin is a stark reality. He maintains that "to decide to shorten a man's life (we all die) is not *ipso facto* to lack sympathy with his life as it really is, that is, to lack love for him. It may be to love not him less but someone else more. . . ."[9] Thus, for Hartshorne, killing other persons may at times be the lesser of two or more evils.

The basis of Hartshorne's case against pacifism is that the consequences of absolute pacifism are often worse than the consequences of forceful intervention—based on adequate social awareness—which includes awareness of human sin and the precarious balance of power in world relations. Given this emphasis on consequences in his discussion of pacifism, Hartshorne may have been surprised by the remark in Brightman's review, which criticizes Hartshorne's rejection of the pacifist approach. In the review Brightman writes, "Perhaps the worst effect of a priori thinking in the book is the rejection of pacifism on grounds derived from the abstract nature of social awareness (pp. 166–68), without concrete consideration of actual long-run consequences."[10] The words to emphasize in Brightman's remark are "long-run consequences." Although short-term consequences may favor the use of violence or war, Brightman does not believe that Hartshorne has taken into consideration adequately the long-term consequences of a consistently pacifist approach. Hartshorne begs to differ, and the debate on pacifism in the correspondence begins.

Hartshorne responds to Brightman's review in a letter written on January 22, 1942, less than two months after the United States' official entry into World War II. In specific response to Brightman's remark about pacifism, Hartshorne writes the following:

> As to pacifism, I thought I pointed to the concrete consequences of pacifism. Do we differ there as to the conclusion? If so, in the Conference on Science, Religion, and Philosophy you will find my empirical discussion. I was primarily trying to combat the a priori argument *for* pacifism, in the book. I never yet met

a pacifist with much interest, as distinct from profession of interest, in the consequences, short or long, of his doctrine. I mean this and I know of no exception. I
am plenty interested in the empirical aspects of this issue I assure you.[11]

Brightman responds as follows:

> If all you were trying to do in the book was to combat the *a priori* argu-
> ment for pacifism, I am with you. The only valid argument is, I think, empirical.
> But when you write the following sentence, I am astounded: "I never yet met a
> pacifist with much interest, as distinct from profession of interest, in the conse-
> quences, short or long, of his doctrine. I mean this and I know of no excep-
> tion." It happened that your statement came to me about the same time as the
> copy of *Fellowship* with Nels Ferré's article in it, pleading for pacifism precisely
> on the basis of consequences. All the Quakers I know base their action and their
> faith largely on the successful consequences of peaceful behavior. Although not
> an absolutist, I call myself a pacifist, and argue solely from concern about conse-
> quences. The failure of the last war, the terrible revenge that the defeated coun-
> try has taken, has seemed to me good evidence of the failure of victory in war to
> secure desired consequences. At present there is less hope for victory and less
> desire for decent consequences than in the other war. If you are going to say
> that any pacifist who professes interest in the consequences of the method of
> love has profession but not interest, I do not see what you are basing that on. I
> know dozens of pacifists who are far more concerned about the consequences of
> their views and of this war than are most supporters of the war. As for your state-
> ment, I deny the allegation and defy the allegator in so far as it is proper for a
> pacifist to assume such attitudes.[12]

Brightman's remarks sparked a lengthy reply from Hartshorne in his next letter, written only five days later, on September 23, 1942. In response to Brightman's
astonishment at Hartshorne's claim that he never met a pacifist who had much
interest in consequences, Hartshorne makes the following clarification:

> Of course my sentence about pacifists not being much interested in conse-
> quences is at best elliptical. All of us have a tendency to make facts and real prob-
> abilities fit our views (or get out of our sight) rather than to make the views
> adjust to the facts and the knowable probabilities. Now my impression has de-
> cidedly been that pacifists do this even worse and much worse than other peo-
> ple, especially other people who are articulate and educated.[13]

Hartshorne picks up on Brightman's comment on Ferré's "Christianity and
Compromise" and illustrates how even Ferré tends to overlook the consequences
of the pacifist approach and, as a result, fails to make his argument on an empirical basis. Hartshorne writes:

I have read Ferré's article, also a long letter on the subject, and also talked with him. Interest in concrete knowable realities seems to me in the background even with him. He says, for example that the only way for Europe to get along is to have the German people united and strong. Yet every known fact about Europe and the Prussian tradition and many other aspects of the matter, including the elementary geographical facts, imply that such an arrangement would mean that only by a lucky miracle could the other peoples in Europe get their minimal rights, unless the other peoples had first been made strong in independence of German influence. Germans have every military advantage, and this one-sidedness is the great problem, made much worse by many facts about Europe's traditions and structure.[14]

After criticizing Ferré, Hartshorne turns to a criticism of Brightman's remarks about the consequences of the present war and the results of World War I:

To call the last war a failure has to mean, for your argument, that a German victory might have been as well or better, unless you think we might somehow have gambled for a draw. . . . Now I see no good reason to think that a victorious Germany would have done less harm than a defeated one has done. On the contrary. We might now have not even a choice but to give in to the Germans. But further. The results of the last war were not fatalistically determined by the war itself, or there is no freedom. Winning gives an opportunity, but opportunities are not guarantees. Now why was the opportunity not better used (it was not wholly wasted, in my view, far from it)? Well are pacifists honestly surveying the mass of evidence for the conclusion that, as one of the best German students of the problem, a very religious man, has said, the greatest help of all to Hitler in his catastrophic career was given by "international pacifism." (E. Heiman[n].) This seems to me a plain fact. Hitler need not have been successful in his villainous plans, had enough people believed in the wisdom of stopping him by force. Surely the failure to stop him had something to do with the widely diffused notion that fighting never accomplishes anything. Thus this very belief that fighting is useless is one of the chief reasons why the fighting of the last war was not more useful. A wise discriminating use of force is one thing, a panicky resort to force at the last gasp, followed again by a wave of vague pacifism, is another. I shall fight this vicious cycle all my life.[15]

Hartshorne goes on in the letter to argue that pacificism actually makes war worse when it comes because it weakens the wrong side, allowing those less hesitant about using force to get the upper hand.

In response to Brightman's criticism of Hartshorne's rejection of pacifism as an example of *a priori* thinking that fails to consider the long-range consequences of pacifism, Hartshorne counters with the following:

Is the argument *a priori*? Absolute pacifism must be *a priori*, like all absolutes. Relative pacifism can appeal to contingent facts. However, in evaluating a principle of action rather than a description of facts there is in a sense necessarily an *a priori* element. That is, one must ask what the principle implies, should it be adopted, and this adoption is largely a possibility not a fact. In short, ideal experiment comes in to show what *would* happen. Still, that is not *a priori* in the strict sense. My argument was, that if all good men adopt the principle, or all wise men, that they will never use force then force will be left as the monopoly of any men not good enough or wise enough to abstain from it. That there will be such seems sure enough on an empirical basis, and it follows almost *a priori* from the notion that there is at least some plausible case for fighting, and this again follows pretty certainly from the fact that most *good and wise men* believe there is.[16]

Hartshorne goes on later in the letter to focus on Brightman's remarks about the unlikelihood of desired consequences coming from the fighting or even from the winning of World War II. Hartshorne points out the differences between the consequences coming from victory or defeat, and he stresses the desirability of an Allied victory. He writes:

In any case, the primary consequences to be considered are those likely to follow from an Axis victory compared to those likely to follow from an Axis defeat. . . . You say there is even less chance of a good outcome if we win than last time. I see many facts on the other side, but anyway that's not the question, which is, is not the danger from defeat much greater than the danger from victory? This is not purely a question of your values or mine, there is a democratic principle involved. The United Nations are certainly much closer to being representative of mankind than the Axis, by any standard almost you choose, including the numerical.[17]

Hartshorne concludes that pacifists are representing the interests of a minority in the world if they argue that the consequences of an Axis victory would not be worse than those of an Axis defeat.

In a handwritten addition at the end of the letter, Hartshorne points to what he sees as one of the most devastating effects of the pacifists' lack of social awareness and disregard for consequences. He writes in closing:

I add one thing out of unpleasant sense of duty, perhaps perverted. The more you argue that there is nothing to fight for now and little hope of victory the more you in effect fight on Hitler's side. He'd pay you to do it, and wisely.
Sorry we have to argue this awful business.[18]

The debate on pacifism ends in Brightman's next letter to Hartshorne, dated September 25, 1942, only two days after Hartshorne's letter. Either there is an error regarding the date, or the United States' postal service was much faster than it is today. At any rate, at the end of the letter, Brightman gives what proves to be the last word on pacifism in the correspondence. He writes:

I believe that Russia was right in calling on the League of Nations to keep the pledge of Versailles for a general disarmament. If England, France, Germany (Weimar), and America had kept the treaty, this war would have been averted. Nations pledged themselves to a pacifist policy and broke the pledge. The number of sincere and intelligent individual pacifists is very small. I believe that it is their important function to work now and in the peace for a reconciliation of humanity, to which they can make a unique contribution. This is not the whole story, but it is part of it.[19]

Philosophical Bases for Hartshorne's and Brightman's Positions on Pacifism

Hartshorne's and Brightman's positions on pacifism are related to their general philosophical outlooks. Their positions hinge mainly on their understanding of value and their views concerning human nature. For Hartshorne, as for Alfred North Whitehead, value is connected to the complexity and enjoyment of experience, to the achievement of the satisfaction of an occasion of experience. That which adds to the complexity and enjoyment of experience adds to the value of the world and God, who is fully present in the world. That which inhibits complexity and enjoyment of experience subtracts from the value of the universe. Given Hartshorne's understanding of relations in which occasions of experience, and societies of occasions of experience, including humans, literally participate in one another's being, it is not surprising to see Hartshorne's emphasis on social awareness as the key to his rejection of doctrinaire pacifism. When certain human beings or groups of human beings subtract from the complexity and enjoyment of experience through various forms of oppression, aggression, or extermination, as in the case of Hitler's Germany, the most responsible and loving thing to do, in Hartshorne's opinion, is to use force in order that the oppressors, aggressors, and exterminators will be brought under control so that the value of human experience might again be increased. Hartshorne maintains that war "is better than to have a good part of mankind given over to slavery."[20] He believes that democratic nations have a particular responsibility to defend themselves and other nations in order to prevent injustices brought on by political tyranny.[21]

Hartshorne is apt to use organic metaphors to describe our relations with one another, and this carries over into his discussion concerning the use of force and warfare. At one point he even makes an analogy between war and amputation.[22] There are times when a certain part of the body so threatens the rest of the body that the tragic choice must be made to eliminate it. It should be noted, with a sense of caution, that such organic analogies have been used by such figures as Hitler himself. He attempted to justify the purification of the Aryan race through the eradication of "undesirable elements" from the national body. However, the difference between Hitler and Hartshorne is that Hartshorne advocates the use of force only to deter others who are not respecting the freedom of other persons, whereas Hitler used force in order to bring about the dominance of one group over others, without any respect for the value of their experience.

In regard to the conception of human nature, Hartshorne seems to be squarely within the "political realism" tradition that focuses on the prevalence of sin in human nature and on the necessary use of power and coercion in group relations. In criticism of Brightman's approach to world peace, Hartshorne remarks that in Brightman's thought there is perhaps an "insufficient stress upon the ever-present tragedy of sin, which no plans for peace can hope to banish."[23] Much like Reinhold Niebuhr, who is often described as a "Christian Realist" because of his "realistic" views about human nature and power relations, Hartshorne believes that various forms of coercion are necessary to maintain the balance of power among groups, and in certain circumstances this includes the necessity of going to war—World War II being but one example. Hartshorne hopes that a peaceful world full of friendly cooperation might one day be possible. He says that he can hope for this "because it is God's world; but on the other hand, we are human beings and not God, and so we remember our weaknesses."[24] In such an imperfect world, Hartshorne maintains that although persuasion is a preferable means of influencing others, love must be open to the possibility of using force so that those who are unloving may be coerced into a moderation of their aggressive tendencies. For Hartshorne, absolute pacifism fails to be aware of this "realistic" appraisal of human existence, and this he refers to as the pacifist delusion.[25]

In contrast to Hartshorne, Brightman has a much more narrow understanding of the locus of value. For Brightman personality is the seat of all value.[26] In agreement with T. H. Green, Brightman holds that all value is "for, of, or in a person."[27] He concludes that it is only in persons that peace can exist.[28] Consequently there can be no real peace without "respect for personality."[29] Brightman maintains that personality is free, that it is social, and that it grows through a process of dialectical tensions.[30] Because personality is free "an enduring peace must rest on plans for effective freedom in the whole world."[31] Because personality is social, a permanent peace is possible only when there is reconciliation among peoples, and Brightman notes that reconciliation is difficult to bring about through the means of warfare. Because personality is growth through dialectical tensions, "peace is tension raised to a constructive, creative, cooperative level . . . ; [whereas] war is destructive tension."[32]

The philosophical principles undergirding Brightman's pacifism are expressed in his formulations of the moral laws, which he describes as universal principles to which the will ought to conform its choices.[33] These laws are not to be confused with prescriptions for action in specific circumstances, rather they act in a regulatory way as principles according to which one should choose if one is to be moral. All of Brightman's eleven formulations of the moral laws undergird the vision that fuels his commitment to pacifism, but at least four of them warrant special attention.

First, in Brightman's formulation of what he calls the "Axiological Law," he maintains that "*all persons ought to choose values which are self-consistent, harmonious, and coherent, not values which are contradictory or incoherent with one another.*"[34] Given Brightman's understanding of personality as the seat of all value, it is difficult for him to reconcile the killing of other persons with a respect for their personality. If the end or value that is desired is respect for personality, then it would be more consistent if the means to reach that desired end also reflect this value.

Second, in Brightman's formulation of the "Law of Consequences," he writes, "*All persons ought to consider and, on the whole, approve the foreseeable consequences of each of their choices. Stated otherwise: Choose with a view to the long run, not merely to the present act.*"[35] Clearly Brightman believes that the consistent use of peaceful means will have more desirable consequences in the long run in respect to the value of personality than does war. His experience of the post–World War I years provided him with an example of how difficult true reconciliation is after such widespread hostility among nations, and he feared that the long-run consequences of World War II might not be much better. This fear led him to write the following in 1933: "[T]he probability that peace will involve greater evils than war is, under modern conditions, almost infinitesimal."[36]

Third, in Brightman's formulation of the "Law of the Best Possible," he states, "*All persons ought to will the best possible values in every situation: hence, if possible, to improve every situation.*"[37] Writing in the middle of World War II, Brightman maintained that "the War is man's revolt against the best. . . . War threatens the very existence of values at any level both by destroying persons in whom alone the good can be realized and by menacing the ordered society and the institutions which support and cultivate values."[38] In Brightman's view the cause of war can be traced to two sources: the failure of love and failure of reason. According to Brightman, "Co-operative, whole-hearted, universal love is the prime condition of the realization of the best possible world,"[39] and this is a love that constantly contributes to the true welfare of all concerned, regardless of response.

Finally, in Brightman's formulation of the "Law of Altruism," he writes: "*Each person ought to respect all other persons as ends in themselves, and, as far as possible, to co-operate with others in the production and enjoyment of shared values.*"[40] Here we see again a formulation of the principle of "respect for personality" that is so central to Brightman's position. The conditions of war make it extremely difficult to respect the enemy as ends in themselves; so much the case that Brightman feared that soldiers returning might need to undergo reeducation and moral rehabilitation after the war in order to recultivate a rational love that is grounded in respect for personality.[41]

In looking at Brightman's moral laws and his position on pacifism, it becomes obvious that he had a more melioristic understanding of human nature than Hartshorne. Brightman is aware of the foes of love and reason in the world:

e.g., persons' inhumanity to one another, racial hatred, economic exploitations, and wars.[42] Perhaps it is this awareness that keeps him from describing himself as an absolute pacifist. But his focus is on the ability of persons to realize the best that is within them and on the power of love to bring about reconciliation. If this type of unrelenting love were practiced in the years following World War I, perhaps the conditions that led to World War II would not have been created. We will never know since the Treaty of Versailles and other post–World War I actions were not based on the rational love that Brightman was advocating.

Strengths and Weaknesses of Hartshorne's and Brightman's Views

Hartshorne's recognition of the prevalence of human sin and the necessity of the use of coercive force in group relations is both the strength and the weakness of his position. It is a strength because, even in a world community, human sin would still be present and coercive force would still be necessary, if only in the form of international policing. Hartshorne's position seems to ring true in light of the tragedy of human existence in the world.

Hartshorne's stress on sin and the necessity of coercive power becomes a weakness, however, because it tends to keep him from developing constructive programs for a peaceful world community. It is true that human beings have been sinful, are sinful, and always will be sinful, but this can sometimes be overused as an excuse to avoid trying less coercive methods in societal and world relations. If we rely too heavily on forceful intervention to solve problems in world relations, we run the risk of simply continuing the cycle of violence by using violence as a solution to our problems, thereby making true reconciliation and mutual goodwill even more difficult to come by. Perhaps Hartshorne's emphasis on the reality of sin and the need to check it by coercion made him unable to see the pacifists' concern for long-term consequences and the need to have a persistent minority calling the rest of us toward a more peaceful world community. Pacifists and nonpacifists often share a desire for the same ends, but they disagree on the best means for attaining their ends. Hartshorne's failure to recognize the pacifists' deep concern for consequences is perhaps the greatest weakness of his position,[43] especially when he goes to the extent of blaming pacifism for contributing to the success of Hitler. A Hitler might not have been possible had more pacifist policies guided the leaders in the period directly following World War I.

The primary strength of Brightman's position is his emphasis on reconciliation and on long term consequences. I think he sees correctly that reconciliation is the principle upon which a lasting peace must rest. Otherwise the cycle of violence and war will continue. At the end of a time of open hostility the hatred does not disappear, and it often lies in wait for an opportunity to manifest itself anew in oftentimes more violent forms than in the past conflicts. Reconciliation is the only way to break this cycle.

In light of the modern situation and our possession of weapons of mass destruction, it is more pressing today than ever before to focus on a peaceful reconciliation of our differences. If wars continue to escalate and the wrong weapons get into the wrong hands, we may not have any long-term consequences to worry about. Brightman is right to see that the best possible long-term future belongs to a less violent world.

Hartshorne may be correct in surmising that one of the weaknesses in Brightman's position is a tendency to underestimate the power of sin in the world and the need for the use of coercive force at times.[44] Brightman does seem to be dreaming of a fantasy "world community" at times, but it is not a dream divorced from an awareness of the challenges and difficulties of the pacifist approach. Brightman is aware that peace based on respect for personality is often more difficult than war, but he believes strongly that the consequences of peace are more favorable than those of war.[45] One must still ask, however, "Is Brightman's position tenable in the face of Hitler's Germany?" Does there not come a time when the evil is so great that war is the lesser of the evils?

Conclusion: The Synthesis of Martin Luther King, Jr.

Reading through the disagreement in the correspondence as well as seeing Hartshorne's and Brightman's positions clarified in some of their other writings, one can come to the conclusion that their "realistic" and "melioristic" positions should be mutually corrective to one another. At least in the expression of their positions concerning pacifism, Brightman could be more cognizant of the role of sin and power in group relations, and Hartshorne fails to be more aware that the best long-term consequences will come about through more peaceful and persuasive rather than coercive measures, with reconciliation being the guiding ideal for our actions.

The thought of Martin Luther King, Jr., can be a viewed as a synthesis of the strengths of these two positions, while for the most part leaving the weaknesses behind. King's experience as a member of an oppressed minority in a violent and racist society, coupled with the intellectual influence of Reinhold Niebuhr's "Christian Realism," led King to be painfully aware of the role of power and coercion in group relations and of the complexities of social and economic structures. King admits that Niebuhr helped him recognize "the complexity of man's social involvement and the glaring reality of collective evil."[46] But King did not despair of the possibilities for social improvement. The influence of personalism on his thought during his studies at Boston University gave King a greater appreciation for the dignity of personality and a view that a personal God is working in the world so that this dignity might be enhanced. King was influenced by the moral laws with their stress on the respect for personality.[47] He became convinced that the only possibility for improvement for black people in American society was through the reconciliation of both white and black people based on justice and equality, the very ideals expressed in our Constitution, yet so inadequately expressed in our social structures.

King knew that injustices in society were not going to disappear magically, and he did not have a conception of God's somehow miraculously curing the ills of racism, classism, and economic exploitation. He rejected the extremes of passive nonresistance on the one hand and violent resistance on the other. Passive nonresistance did not meet the demands of the moral obligation to resist collective evil, and violence was an expression of despair that dimmed the hope for true reconciliation.[48] King chose the path of "nonviolent resistance," which can be seen as a form of what Brightman calls rational love. Its goal is not the annihilation of one's enemies, but rather their transformation and the transformation of unjust social structures so that injustice might increasingly be overcome within society.

As a strategy for justice for black Americans, King's nonviolent approach can be seen to be more fruitful than both passive nonresistance and violent resistance. Hartshorne could not accuse King of not being concerned with the consequences of his nonviolent actions. It was precisely King's desire for a certain set of consequences that drove him in his nonviolent struggle for justice. In the case of King and his nonviolent movement, we are dealing with a minority group within a country that has practiced slavery both officially and unofficially. The majority people had already shown a willingness to commit violence against black Americans. From a strategic point of view, a violent revolution was not and still is not a fruitful option. Force could not have achieved the desired consequences.

But is not the situation of World War II different? In this case a minority of the people in the world, the Axis Powers, tried to force its will on the majority of the world, exterminating millions of people in the process. The majority of the world had the power to resist, and Hartshorne argues that violent resistance achieved better consequences than the nonviolent options. There are extreme cases when killing someone for the sake of the lives of others might be the most loving and fitting action, as with the German theologian Dietrich Bonhoeffer's agonizing choice to participate in an assassination attempt on Hitler. But these cases are more rare than most people would concede. We must continually ask ourselves if forceful intervention is really contributing to a context for greater respect of personality, or are the issues of self interest and other ulterior motives clouding our judgment? We must ask ourselves if we are hindering the chances for reconciliation and a lasting peace by too often and too hastily speaking in the language of war. One hopes that by wrestling with the issues that Hartshorne and Brightman were struggling with over a half century ago, we will be able to derive some lessons for the construction of a more peaceful world, where the language of war will be heard no more, or at least less often than is presently the case.

☙

Immediacy and Purpose in Brightman's Philosophy

Randall E. Auxier

"Selves, subpersonal, personal and cosmic, are no part of each other, and yet their interaction and their inner experience as purposive unities constitute the structure of the universe."

E. S. Brightman, *Person and Reality: An Introduction to Metaphysics,* p. 279.

Introduction

In the previous essay on Hartshorne's personalism, the issue emerged regarding the role of purpose in Brightman's philosophy, since he allows that it is the only "window" in the monad he called the "datum self." Brightman allowed that purposes interact and are in some way immediate, and this was how he evaded the charge of solipsism. It is clear from Brightman's development after the correspondence had ceased that not only did Brightman continue to think and worry about this criticism, in many ways its solution became the motive force of his last works. Thus it is worth our effort in assessing the correspondence, its importance and meaning, to take a look at how it affected Brightman's thought.

An extended quotation from Brightman's relatively early work *A Philosophy of Ideals* states a basic point of orientation regarding this issue from which Brightman never departed:

> One of the chief differences between mind and physical object . . . is its immediacy. When we speak of the immediacy of mind, we mean the fact that it is actually present. We do not have to guess or hope or infer that we are conscious, or that *experience exists.* Consciousness is given as an unescapable fact. But the objects of physics and chemistry do not appear to be immediate or given in the same sense as mind is immediate and given. Certain perceptions occur in my mind; I interpret them and infer the existence of molecules and electrons. . . .

We may go even further and say that not only is mind immediate, but also nothing but mind is immediate. All that ever can be immediately present is mind. Science and philosophy seek to discover the cause or stimulus or interpretation of what is present in the mind. But all of thought and life is only an elaboration or explanation of what is at some time given as present experience. . . .

There has been a great deal of discussion in recent philosophy centering about the problem "What is the datum?" The word datum means "what is given." . . . The view which I have just presented is obviously the same as saying that the mind (or the self) is the datum. . . . Loewenberg . . . distinguishes between "pre-analytical" and "post-analytical" data. Applying his distinction to our problems, it is evident that the notion of mind as datum means experience as we live it and find it before the work of analysis; while abstractions like "sense-datum," "essence," or "biological situation" are arrived at after analysis, and so are post-analytical. . . . The most certain fact, and the only absolutely certain empirical fact, then, is my own self-experience. To say that the mind is datum emphasizes at least four aspects of experience: (1) that we find relatively confused and "raw" sensations in experience prior to their elaboration by scientific thought; (2) that we possess an unanalyzed consciousness prior to the work of analysis and the reference of thought to objects *and causes;* (3) that our present conscious experience is the ultimate basis of all our knowledge of and belief in whatever is not now present conscious experience, or in other words, present self is the sole basis of confidence in absent objects; and (4) self-experience is a name for a trait of all consciousness and is to be distinguished from reflective self-consciousness, a relatively infrequent process in which we think about ourselves. . . .This self-experience is an indivisible whole, yet ever-changing; private, yet in communication with other selves; present, yet remembering a past and anticipating a future. . . .Every answer of science or religion, poetry or philosophy, must be tested by its relevance and adequacy to the datum-mind. What do I mean by my sensations, my moral nature, my aspirations, my pleasures -by my whole life?[1]

From this it is evident that "immediacy" is a key term in Brightman's philosophy. The provenance of his idea of immediacy would require time to trace, and that is beyond the scope of the present essay, but there is *prima facie* reason to suppose that he takes his use of the term primarily from Hermann Lotze—perhaps as influenced by Borden Parker Bowne. There is no question that his propensity for taking seriously the idea of immediacy originates with Hegel, but Brightman's use of the term is less grandiosely metaphysical than Hegel's " *Un-mittelbarkeit.*"[2] Although Brightman was very impressed both with Hegel's method and the results of it, he regarded Hegel as "unempirical" about key methodological points, and this is for Brightman a serious flaw. Lotze's method and results are less flashy, but more sober and plausible, and Brightman (the quintessence of philosophical sobriety, which may in part account for the fact he is so little read these days) emulates Lotze's language. For example, a section of Lotze's *Logic* entitled "Determination of Individual Facts" reads:

> We cannot be certain about matters of fact unless we have ourselves per-
> ceived it, and even then only on the supposition that our interpretation of the
> sensible impression, which is all that is originally given, is correct. . . . There is
> uncertainty in all such inferences. . . . It follows that wherever anything is out-
> side the range of immediate perception, we are in our judgments of reality limit-
> ed to probabilities.[3]

Aside from the obvious similarity about everything beyond our immediate perception being inferred—Lotze's expressed view here—note particularly that his
quite un-Hegelian and even pro-Humean use of the word "fact" (*Sache*) both
here and elsewhere[4] is the same as Brightman's use of the word.[5] Lotze is a dialectical empiricist, and his methodological starting place (the datum self) is
Brightman's. Consequently they also think of immediacy in similar terms.

Wherever Brightman may have picked up his use of the term "immediate," it is not the original source of the philosophical problem. In the West the
problem really begins with Plato's notion of "participation" (μέθεξις). This is
a much debated topic, and it is worth pointing out that a distinction in this
discussion of immediacy has its roots in the "participation" debate. Plato allowed that there is one sort of participation between particulars and forms and
another sort of participation between and among the forms themselves.[6]
However we might argue about this, it underlies the problem Brightman is
confronting. But Brightman's version of this problem is distinctly modern,
which is to say post-Cartesian in form, taking for granted a version of
mind/body dualism that Plato would find peculiarly narrow. Brightman is trying to overcome a problem that Plato never really had. The main difference
between Brightman and Descartes is in the clear distinction the former takes
from Loewenberg, who is giving a Hegelian account, between the pre- and
postanalytical senses of the "*je pense*" in "*je pense, donc je suis.*" Descartes is not
ignorant of this problem either, having responded to an objection that in spite
of the "therefore" ("donc," or "ergo") his formula is not an argument, but a
self-evident utterance.[7] Whatever the case may be for Descartes, Brightman
was impressed by the idea that "immediacy" is most definitely *not* the product
of reflection. This sets him outside the Aristotelian tradition of treating thinking about thought as the ground of immediacy.

It is useful to distinguish among three senses of the word "immediate" and
to apply this distinction to Brightman to see if it sheds any light on the issue at
hand:

> (a) metaphysical immediacy: the being of two things is unmediated (i.e., there is
>   no third thing in virtue of which the being of x and y is related);

(b) epistemological immediacy: the knowing of two things is unmediated (i.e., there is no third thing we must know regarding x that makes it possible for us to know y);

(c) existential/experiential immediacy: the existence of a thing and the experience of it are identical (i.e., there is no gap between the givenness to experience of x and the existence of x).

It should be clear that while the sort of immediacy one finds in (a) does not depend on any act of reflection, it is unknowable except by means of reflection and not fully determinable by means of reflection, since reflection upon the metaphysical immediacy of x and y is not identical with the metaphysical immediacy of x and y. The moment of impact when one gets hit by a Mack truck going sixty miles per hour might be supposed by some to qualify as an "experience" of (a), where the victim is x and the truck is y, but metaphysical immediacy, as meant here, is more like the relationship between the Form of the Good and, say, Truth Itself, or Beauty Itself, etc. The Mack truck encounter as described belongs under (c), as the terms are used here.[8] Metaphysical immediacy in the sense[9] of (a) is certainly relevant to Brightman's view, as will be shown later, but while this *may* be the sense of "immediacy" that is first in the order or *being*, it is definitely not methodologically primary for Brightman. Whether this difference between what comes first methodologically and what comes first metaphysically causes Brightman problems is a matter that can wait. His tendency to collapse epistemological and metaphysical issues has been noted in my earlier essay.

It should also be clear that (b) takes for granted the accomplishment of certain cognitive operations. It is "post-analytical," to use Loewenberg's term (which Brightman continued to use for the rest of his career). There is indeed a sort of immediacy that accompanies *modus ponens*, but that sort of immediacy is the place where thought stops, not where it starts. Epistemological immediacy interests Brightman, but it is not the sort of immediacy he aims at in his metaphysics. Both (a) and (b) employ the term "immediate" in a way Brightman regards as misleading because they confuse genuine immediacy as found in what he calls "first person experience" with that which is either beyond the pale of experience altogether, (a), or the outcome of reflection upon experience, (b). It should also be noted that (a) and (b) endeavor to bring together two terms (*x* and *y*) that are initially considered different (hence the different variables) and then the immediacy of their relation is asserted. This raises issues about their identity that do not emerge when immediacy is approached like it is in (c).

The most fundamental sense of the term "immediate," as Brightman uses it, must be grasped under the general heading of the existential/experiential, or (c). According to (c) there is a moment in which there is no difference between the existence of *x* and the experience of *x*. Only later is it possible to divide *x*'s *existence* from the *experience* of it (by reflection) and pose questions about which

determines which. One should therefore reserve the term "being" for the postanalytical *existential* status of what is (or as Brightman puts it "analyzed *immediacy*,"
or *Sein*,[10] and the term "knowledge" for the postanalytical *experiential* status of
anything that is. The issue of immediacy as considered here initially concerns only
the preanalytic status of the "shining present," the "datum self," "self-experience," or the "whole self" (terms that are all interchangeable for Brightman),
which he calls "the level of unanalyzed synoptic immediacy."[11] But it is crucial to
note that there *is* a type of immediacy which is postanalytical, and it looks more
like (a) than (c) in our choices above. Brightman tries to build a bridge to make it
possible to say some things about this metaphysical type of immediacy that may
surprise some. But one must proceed from (c) to (a) because, as Brightman puts
it, "the 'arrow of intelligibility' has no one bull's eye; it must fly from the pre-ana-
lytic whole to its parts and then back to the whole, now reillumined with knowledge of the parts. It can never stop, because the whole is dynamic."[12]

Existential-Experiential Immediacy

The third conception of immediacy, then, is the one best investigated initially.
This sort of "immediacy" is not a type of relation for Brightman, but the absence
of a relation. Although it is not a privation, it is generally expressed in privative
language. Consider this for a moment. There is irony in it. As Hegel noted long
ago, the capacity to speak of something is already evidence of an unbridgeable
gap between the word and the object. This gap is the privation that makes *non*-
privative language possible.[13] Where there is no gap, only privative language
(such as the word "immediate") is appropriate. The irony is that *non*privative
language is evidence of a gap that has to be crossed, while privative language is
evidence of unity. Whenever there is *no* relation *to speak of,* one finds *immediacy*.
This is hard to grasp. But it is likely that this is what Brightman means by saying
that we have here a "problem" in *A Philosophy of Ideals.*[14]

   Some clarification on this point can be found in thinking of the following
analogy Brightman provides:

> . . . personal selves are not windowless monads but *interact* with other persons and
> the surrounding environment. Indeed the interdependence of immediate experi-
> ence and its environment is fundamental to the very quality of its existence. "As a
> drop of blood exposed to the air clots and dries and ceases to be blood, so any mo-
> ment of experience dries up into a dead abstraction when taken alone. But if the
> blood be left in the body, it circulates and plays its part in the life of the whole or-
> ganism. So alone can experience live; not by separating itself from past and future
> and environment, but by functioning in the movement from present to future,
> from here to there, establishing connections with the whole flow of time and the
> complex environment. The truly spiritual life is not a withdrawal into immediacy,
> but the construction of linkages between immediacy and what lies beyond it."[15]

Note that "the environment" determines the *quality* of the *existence* of immediate experience, but not the existence itself. The reason is that the existence of immediacy *is* the experience of it, and its fundamental, albeit mediated relation to the environment determines its quality only, not the brute fact of immediacy itself.[16]

It is now possible to say something about why Brightman's account of immediacy is important in twentieth-century philosophy. Brightman's experiential-existential account of immediacy brings together two other sets of important philosophers, *viz.*, the existentialists such as Heidegger and Sartre and the experientialists such as Whitehead and Dewey. The existentialists are better at providing accounts of the stubbornness of the immediate, e.g., Heidegger's existential structures of Dasein or Sartre's "facticity", while the experientialists are better at discussing its cooperative role in creating experiences, e.g., Whitehead's "subjective immediacy" or Dewey's "postulate of immediate empiricism". Many interpreters have noticed that there are significant points of contact between those one may call "experientialists" and those one may call "existentialists," but it is likely that no one before Brightman ever employed "immediacy" as a strategy for translating the insights of each into terms compatible with the other, and for constructive, as opposed to merely interpretive, ends. It is not that Brightman succeeded in preserving all that is best in each approach or that he succeeded in creating an adequate language to bring the two sorts of philosophy together in a lasting way. He sacrifices too much of the existentialists' insight and clearly favors the experientialists; perhaps his American roots are showing. But Brightman offers a path of interpretation well worth following, and perhaps also a promising path of metaphysical construction.

What, then, is "immediacy" for Brightman? Recalling the earlier point about privative language, it is easier to say a bit more about what it is *not* before saying what it is. As previously mentioned, immediacy is not a relation, it is the absence of relation. There is a sense in which immediacy for Brightman is "identity," but "identity" along with change, time, actuality, and potentiality are classified by Brightman as "categories of all possible realms of being" and a category is a tool of analysis. In other words, one may discover something about postanalytical immediacy as it refers to "being" by looking at Brightman's categories, but one learns nothing about experiential-existential, or "unanalyzed synoptic," immediacy by invoking these categories. Indeed, making this error confuses the issue beyond all help, so one must resist the urge to bring up the traditional philosophical problems in the traditional language in this context. The fact that experiential-existential immediacy is "no relation" does not mean it is an identity, nor is it an actuality or a potentiality. These ways of *being* are all inferences arrived at through a rational process, reflective concepts, and so are precisely *not* immediate in the primordial sense of the term.

Immediacy is the place where the experience of *x is* its existence, and the existence of *x is* the experience of it. It does involve what Brightman calls a "complex unity of consciousness" because immediacy is a feature of the shining present, the datum self, but complex unity is not what makes immediacy immediate. To say that the shining present is the complex unity of consciousness involves both mediation *and* immediacy. There are many forms of mediation in the shining present, but Brightman asserts that the most universal form of mediation is time. Space is not a universal form of mediation in the sense that one could do away with the spatiality of some experiences and the experience would still exist, but the same is not true of its temporality, which is indispensable to all experiences.[17] But temporality, that which brings the inferred past and the anticipated future into concrete relation with the shining present, is a kind of mediation in the shining present. It is not immediacy.

So what is the immediacy of the shining present? For Brightman immediacy is one of the "levels" of unity in the shining present. As we have mentioned, the unity of the shining present is "complex" rather than simple. This sort of unity is "organic" in Whitehead's sense of the term.[18] And indeed Brightman is willing to a great extent to analogize his concept of the shining present with Whitehead's "actual occasion,"[19] embracing Whitehead's idea of feeling but without his "highly specialized definition" of consciousness as the feeling of feeling[20] and with a mitigated account of its atomicity:

> As A. N. Whitehead declares, the actual occasions (which are shining presents of a peculiarly Whiteheadian type) are "incurably atomic." But thought also requires that they be incurably interactive (communicating, or prehensive in Whitehead's language). Without the rational postulate of interaction, all talk about knowledge of the outer world . . . would be groundless.[21]

The shining present, like Whitehead's actual occasion, "is always a whole, a gestalt of gestalten,"[22] which has parts, a definite duration, and a structure. Not all of the shining present is immediate, but rather, immediacy is a feature of the shining present—just as for Whitehead subjective immediacy is a feature of actual occasions. As Brightman says, "all that Whitehead means by feeling, prehensions, presentational immediacy, causal efficacy and consciousness is included in the shining present."[23] Each shining present is a unity, but its unity is also complex, like the unity of an organism. The unity of the shining present is derived from several "levels," and first among these is the level of unanalyzed immediacy:

> The level of unanalyzed immediacy is the ordinary shining present as it occurs without special effort or plan. It is, to be sure, highly complex and always contains more than sensory experience. It is a unity in at least three respects. Viewed as present, it is a whole of the complex of experience felt in a single time-span. Viewed as containing memories of the past, it is (more or less vaguely) recognition and acknowledgment of what I believe to have been my former experiences. Viewed as desiring or purposing, it is conation or driving for

something that is not yet present. . . . Strictly speaking, then, the exclusion of effort from the definition of this level is unempirical. There is always some effort at all stages. At the minimum level, the effort (or "subjective aim") may not be directed by free conscious choice toward a selected goal; in every instance, however, there is an urge of some sort toward the future.[24]

So the unity of existential/experiential immediacy has three "respects," corresponding to the three aspects of temporality: memory/past, feeling/present, and purpose/future. For those familiar with Whitehead, what follows is not unlike a personalistic version of the phases of concrescence of an actual entity.

Memory

Memory is the aspect of existential/experiential immediacy that orients it toward a past that is beyond it. The shining present cannot be what it is without presence of the unanalyzed immediacy of the past because this is the source of the self-identity of any particular shining present, making it just the shining present it is and not some other.

> Inherent in the complex unity of consciousness and in the experience of memory is the fact that memory always is an experience of self-identity. . . . Regardless of whether I have chosen my experiences or not; regardless of whether I brought them into being by my will or they were forced on me by known or unknown causes, they are my present self, a complex yet actually indivisible whole of experience. My self-identity at all times, then, is the experience of a unity in plurality. . . .[25]

So memory as the respect of existential/experiential immediacy that makes self-identity possible is therefore the ground of the atomicity of a particular shining present, and this is how Brightman uses the term "memory." How are we to understand this "self-identity" as a respect of its unanalyzed immediacy? To answer this question we have to know what self-identity contributes to the shining present. Brightman says that:

> . . . the minimum possible self is an experience of real duration (*durée réelle*). There is no simple indivisible instant of self-experience. Every self endures in time; in its lowest terms every self is at once a unitary experience and a succession of experiences. In one conscious grasp, many details are comprehended as the unitary structure of one self. The minimal unity of a self accordingly is the unity of self-identification, that is, the fact that all experiences of a self belong to that self and to no other. But such a unity is barren. . . . To bare experience a kind of unity is given, but a growing unity of quality is an ideal to be achieved, a task to be performed.[26]

This respect of memory, the ground of self-identity, brings home the existential side of the existential/experiential character of our unanalyzed immediacy. It is Brightman's way of saying with Ortega that "man, on a word has no nature, what he has is . . . history,"[27] and then he adds to this insight that whatever self-identity our history may produce in our present, it is barren of meaning without what Heidegger and Sartre call our "projects." Otherwise put, the peculiar history of any given shining present is what individuates it, factically. Thus this memory does not provide whatever moral value there may be in our unanalyzed experience of immediacy. But, leaving the existential side for a moment to invoke the experiential side, this memorial respect of our unanalyzed immediacy is *also* what makes any particular shining present "incurably atomic," in Whitehead's sense. Recalling that Brightman says the shining present is also "incurably interactive," one recognizes that memory as the ground of self-identity is only one respect of the unanalyzed immediacy of the shining present. There are two other respects, namely, feeling and purpose.

Feeling

Feeling is the respect of unanalyzed immediacy that orients it on the present, while purpose is the respect of present immediacy that orients it on the future. One may be initially tempted to say that feeling must therefore be mediating between past and future and is thus the only truly *immediate* immediacy in the unanalyzed immediacy of the shining present. But to assert this brings back in the temporality of the shining present, which is its most basic and universal form of mediation. The fact that each respect of the unanalyzed immediacy of the shining present corresponds to an aspect of temporality should not lead one into this mistaken interpretation. When the *analyzed* immediacy of the shining present is addressed later, this will be an issue, but for now it is not relevant to the unanalyzed immediacy of the shining present that it is necessary to use the *words* "past," "present" and "future" to describe the various respects of what is in its actuality indivisible. The consideration here is not the temporality of the shining present, but only its felt real duration, which is a far more focused issue,[28] and obviously in "analyzing" the "unanalyzed immediacy" of something, there is going to be at least a verbal violation of the integrity of the immediate.

The immediate presence of the present in the shining present is "feeling" or "affectation." It is the ground of the "duration" of the unanalyzed immediacy of shining present—a term Brightman takes from Bergson. As Brightman says, "One of the most important traits of the shining present is its duration. No experience occurs in a single indivisible instant. It would then have no structure, no process, no memory, no purpose. It would vanish as soon as it appeared. Every actual present is a present-past-future."[29] What follows from this quote is that the *presence* of the present unanalyzed immediacy supplies duration to the unity of the shining present in the way that memory supplies self-identity to the unity of the shining present. The shining present both *is something* in particular, that is, its history and *is here,* that is, its felt present. Even the other unfeeling respects in which the unanalyzed immediacy is immediate—memory and purpose—depend upon the presence of the present, innocent though it is, to provide duration. The "innocence of the given" emerged as an important issue in Appendix 4, above, and as a problem for Brightman. Observe how he handled that difficult problem in his development after the correspondence. The order in which Brightman lists the respects of the unanalyzed immediacy of the shining present as "present-past-future," he says, "is significant" since "nothing can be in my past that was not first in my present; and I can face no future if I have no present."[30] The importance of duration in Brightman's account, therefore, can hardly be doubted.

One may well be curious about the duration of the innocent, unanalyzed immediate presence of the present and ask "how long is it?" In order to answer the question one has to subject what is unanalyzed and indivisible to analysis and division, but Brightman is, perhaps surprisingly, willing to do that and offer a figure, once he has made it clear that he is not speaking of the notion of "present" that comes from analysis:

> . . . there is a complex experience of time which is a real duration composed of many pasts-presents-futures. "Present" then has a double meaning. It may mean the . . . imaginary instant which divides what precedes it from what follows it. Or it may mean an actual shining present, which normally endures several seconds, and yet . . . is never empirically discontinuous with previous shining presents. "There are no leaps" in the shining present. . . . When one grasps a time-span in a shining present, the situation is one of pure immanence.[31]

This final remark is a way of putting the point about the innocence of the given in other language. Reading further, it becomes clear that the unanalyzed immediacy of the present not only supplies the shining present with its unity by way of duration, but also by way of grounding the needed continuity of the entire shining present with the illuminating absent. A discontinuous unity would be like a square circle, and so the unity of the shining present has to derive its character of continuity with the illuminating absent from somewhere. It is evident that for Brightman this comes from the felt immediacy of the present that, taken alone, is purely immanent, but taken in relation to the entire complex unity of the shining present grounds a transcendence. How? One would assume that this has something to do with memory and purpose, although no mechanics could be described, since the felt present of unanalyzed immediacy needs no relation to memory and purpose—they are, after all, respects of the same immediacy.

Brightman uses the term "feeling" in much the way Whitehead uses it, but his more common term for this respect of the unanalyzed immediacy of the shining present is "the given." Its character—aside from its duration and continuity—

considered in its sheerest immediacy is its "innocence." That is, recalling the earlier essay, "from the mere presence of the shining present, nothing can be inferred about the rest of the universe. . . . As experience, the present is innocent, not only of good and evil, but also of cause and effect. . . . The innocence of the present, then, is its mere presence, from which nothing can be deduced."[32] Certainly the felt presence of the present is the heart of unanalyzed immediate experience, the place where the experience of x is most properly the same as its existence, and the existence of x is the experience.

> The present as given is innocent. Every present can be viewed in its innocence, but the point of view of innocence is important chiefly because it acknowledges the fact of immediate experience. It is not the whole truth about any experience except the [very] first, and perhaps even the first was too complex to be entirely innocent. For most minds, innocence is an affectation.[33]

What is this sort of "feeling" or "affectation"? Brightman says that "every self experiences feeling, that is, liking or disliking, approval or disapproval, satisfaction or dissatisfaction. All feeling is present experience . . ." and such feeling is "always immediate, present, and subjective in its being."[34]

There is a great deal more to be said about feeling, the given and its "innocence," and since the earlier appendix treats this issue in some detail, rather than following out what can be said of it here, it is worth noting that Brightman's efforts to accommodate Hartshorne's criticisms do not succeed. It is not clear that Brightman can ultimately maintain both the innocence of the given *and* his preferred epistemology, as noted before. Nor is he perfectly self-consistent in what he says about the given, but that issue lies beyond the present scope. Here it will be enough to note that the presence of the present in the unanalyzed immediate is feeling and that it does not point beyond itself for Brightman. Rather, the other two respects of the unanalyzed immediate do the pointing. Particular worth emphasizing is Brightman's view that feeling *as such* is free of good and evil and even of the category of causation.

By taking memory and feeling together, it has been possible to determine thus far that the unanalyzed immediacy of the shining present can *exist*, i.e., possess a self-identity in virtue of its past, and can *experience*, i.e., feel what it feels, endure, without having any apparent immediate connection to value and perhaps not even to causality. Whatever processes brought a particular shining present to its current self-identity, these are not a determinative part of that self-identity *qua* present immediacy. Rather, the self-identity is a respect in which the shining present is immediate and from which it may infer its past by means of reason, will, desire, or any number of other modes of transcendence by which a "whole self" becomes a "complete self." Also since nothing follows of good or evil, or even causality, from the immediate presence of the present, it is value neutral considered alone. Analogously, as far as feeling is concerned, the shining present has the level of unity it takes from felt unanalyzed immediacy from the latter's character of duration and continuity but nothing that implies value or cause emerges from this.

The importance of this finding is that insofar as value, perhaps even cause, has a grounding in the unanalyzed immediacy of the shining present—and one would hope that valuation is grounded in the unanalyzed immediacy of the shining present and not merely in reflection or developed emotion—it must come from the respect of the unanalyzed immediate that orients it upon the future: what Brightman calls "purpose."

Purpose

In the same way that memory is the ground of self-identity and feeling is the ground of duration and continuity, purpose is the ground of the *interactivity* of experiential/existential immediacy of the shining present. This is difficult to understand. What is "interactivity" as related to the unanalyzed immediacy of the shining present? Enough may be understood for the moment if one grasps that the term "purpose" applies to the unanalyzed immediacy of the shining present and brings "interactivity" to this immediacy. This is the only respect of the unanalyzed immediacy that points beyond the immediacy in such a way as to suggest value or perhaps even cause and effect. Purpose orients what is immediate in our shining present toward the meaning and value of what is not immediate. It is the futurity of our immediacy. Phenomenologists are wont to call it intentionality. And, yes, when we look at purpose as a part of our immediacy, it is also our essential incompleteness, which means it is fair to say with Sartre that it is the nothingness in our being. It is ineradicable from the notion of purpose that something that *is not* is immediate within that which most truly *is*. The purposiveness of purpose is a lack that finite selves can never fill, and our privative language here points up an absence of a relation grounded in an ontological absence. Heidegger's "nihilation of the nothing" comes to mind as a suitable phrase to capture the notion.[35] But what is interesting in Brightman's view is that this does *not* cut us off from others, depriving us of all realistic hope that authentic being-with-others, or with nature, or with God, or locking us into a mode of existing peculiar to *Dasein*. Rather, Brightman says it is the ground of interactivity as such. If this is true, then what Brightman is claiming is that what seems to be a hole in our being is actually the window through which others, God, nature, and even self-knowledge enter. And God has the same problem we have, by the way. We are monads with one window—the interaction of purposes as mediated by the universal category of time. To give a further promissory note, what Brightman likely means is that because there is a future that always already exists in our immediate experience—this is the eternal as a function of the temporal—we might always yet be redeemed. That is, Brightman, not unlike Marcel, is looking for an experiential grounding for existential hope. But we will not be able to assess his success in this endeavor until we have backed away from the unanalyzed immediacy of the shining present and discussed the analyzed immediacy of the shining present and what it contributes to the unity of the shining present.

Metaphysical Immediacy

With regard to the unity of the shining present, there are six levels at which it is unified for Brightman. The most basic level is unanalyzed immediacy. The second most basic level is that of analyzed immediacy, or what Brightman calls "*Sein*." After *Sein* comes "Causal Uniformity," or "*Wesen*," followed by "Normative Control," or "*Begriff*." With these levels of unity, Brightman gives his version of the progression of Hegelian consciousness with an important difference. Instead of immediacy being seen as abstract and the realized *Begriff* as concrete, Brightman sees immediacy as the source of concrete unity in the shining present while the *Begriff* is abstract. He is not so much rejecting Hegel as trying to avoid absolutism. It is true in Brightman's metaphysics that the Absolute is presupposed in every experience, but this is something the finite self must infer, not something about which it can be certain from what is given. If one starts with the finite self and tries to find God, nature, and others, one must begin with what is unanalyzed and immediate in one's first-person experience and work outward from there. If one proceeds in sound fashion, one can reach Hegel's conclusions, but the conclusions are what is abstract, not the experience with which one began. Thus is Hegel's dialectic subordinated to Cartesian method.

The shining present evinces two other levels of unity: functional unity, which temporalizes the shining present in relation to the illuminating absent—Brightman admits this level is not known by strictly empirical means—and the level of "whole experience," which is the place where the shining present actually confronts the absence of the illuminating absent as the source of new experiences. Putting aside the complete view of the six levels for the moment, if one can get from the first level to the second, from the unanalyzed immediate to the analyzed immediate, from the experiential/existential to the metaphysical, with one's philosophy still coherent, one can then take up the other levels.

Earlier Brightman was quoted as saying that "the truly spiritual life is not a withdrawal into immediacy, but the construction of linkages between immediacy and what lies beyond it."[36] But how do we get beyond immediacy? There are a number of ways, such as reason, desire, valuing, etc., but they all are mediated in the same two ways, and perhaps a third: time, purpose, and perhaps causation. These present different problems. In order to understand the problems, one must understand something more about how Brightman's metaphysics operates.

First of all, metaphysics is an activity mediated by reason. It arrives at conclusions that are only probable, but it proceeds from that which is certain—the immediacy of the shining present. This is Cartesian method modified by pragmatic fallibilism. When one tries to extend our experience of the shining present, in its immediacy, to knowledge of the illuminating absent, one is required to "infer" things. This recalls (b), epistemological immediacy, above. One strives to be as certain as possible about both the inferences that one makes from the shining present to the illuminating absent and the account that one gives of the shining present. Here Brightman fudges. Unlike Descartes, he recognizes that there is no methodological guarantee our inferences regarding the illuminating absent will be made properly and that there is no guarantee that an adequate account of the shining present can be given.[37] He does the best he can, but his metaphysics, like Dewey's, Whitehead's, and Hartshorne's, is descriptive at bottom.

The "best he can" involves distinguishing the shining present as immediate experience from the metaphysical theory of these things, as mediated by the mind's rational processes. In particular he favors, like Whitehead, the idea of identifying "categories" that apply to "realms of being." The shining present and illuminating absent as such are not "realms of being," but, rather, any account of the realms of being and categories that govern them presupposes the structure of the shining present and its continuity with the illuminating absent. Thus one has the functional equivalent of Heidegger's analysis of *Dasein,* but without the restriction that *Dasein's* form of being is peculiar to it. The three terms Brightman uses to bridge the gap between "the shining present/illuminating absent as experienced" and "the metaphysical account of what is" are time, purpose, and cause. That means that getting from where Brightman starts philosophizing—with his own immediate experience—to a metaphysics *depends* upon what he says about time, purpose, and cause.

Is Brightman counting on there being *more* than a weak, that is, merely probable, inference between what really *is* and what we experience? Brightman wants more, and it is most evident in *Nature and Values*[38] and in *Person and Reality,* but it may not be obvious that what depends on this is the status of Brightman's moral philosophy. There is no question that Brightman thinks his moral philosophy is grounded in his personalist metaphysics and epistemology, and the moral philosophy can have no more warrant than this grounding provides it. If the metaphysics is the product of a rational process and the rational process is a set of inferences from the shining present, then one wants as much coherence as possible between the shining present and one's metaphysical account of reality. The standard options for Cartesians—and make no mistake, this is Cartesian metaphysics—for solving this problem are well known: (1) Descartes's method of analysis, deducing the relation of mind and body by means of proofs about God's existence and benevolent character; (2) Locke's theory of ideas; (3) Spinoza's geometric pantheism; (4) Leibniz's algorithmic preestablished harmony; (5) Malebranche's benevolent occasionalism; (6) Berkeley's "seeing all things in God"; (7) Hume's skeptical naturalism. All these views find voice in Brightman, but post-Kantian philosophy approaches these "solutions" in a different way. Brightman's Kantian, or critical, orientation is expressed at the level of method and in the recognition that certainty with regard to metaphysical questions is not to be expected, except on the basis of certain rational postulates that, if made, enable us to bring the moral order into line with other ideas of reason. Brightman's post-Hegelian influences lead him to temporalism also. But much temporalism, and especially pragmatism, rejects the Cartesian method that Brightman embraces, and so Dewey, Peirce, and James do not try to solve the set of problems that Brightman faces, since they regard his methodological starting place as a mistake. Other temporalists, such as Husserl, Heidegger, and Sartre *do* embrace to a great degree Brightman's starting point of the Cartesian cogito and develop versions of a new method, the phenomenological method, to handle the very problems Brightman faces: how to get from immediate experience to what *is*. To some extent Brightman is definitely using phenomenology in his account of the shining present in relation to the illuminating absent. But he is not a sophisticated phenomenologist, and it is clear that his loyalties do not run along those lines. He shares their starting place and their conviction that philosophy, thought, or poetry provides a way out of this little patch of immediacy. And Brightman accepts the existentialists' conviction about the stubbornness and tragic character of the given. He recognizes that at bottom existing is a problem, even for God.

But Brightman does not follow the existentialists much further. Instead he goes with process philosophy. Only Kant and Hegel are cited more often in *Person and Reality* than is Whitehead, and they are not ahead by much. Whitehead's influence on Brightman is more prevalent than that of Plato, Aristotle, Lotze, and Bowne in this work. There is little doubt that when Brightman faced the full extent of his philosophical problem—how to get the shining present together with what *is*—he found the resources of process philosophy more appealing than any other approach. This is also not surprising given his correspondence with Hartshorne prior to writing *Person and Reality*.

Process philosophers, mainly Bergson, Whitehead, and Hartshorne, are not as far removed from Cartesian metaphysics as pragmatists are, but they are not as wedded to it as existentialists and phenomenologists are. And Brightman falls into this category of process philosophers. When it comes to solving the old mind-body problem, process philosophers are for the most part occasionalists, but unlike Malebranche they are temporal occasionalists. Like Malebranche process philosophers do not favor discussion of causation as if it were the very heart of metaphysics. Brightman never seems to have gotten clear about this issue. Process thinkers tend to think of cause as one *kind* of relation, and a derivative kind at that, the identification of which requires a process of abstraction. And although causation is a very important kind of relation, one deserving of categorical status according to most, it is not the only or even the main thing that one needs to grasp in order to solve the problem of the relation between what is immediately experienced and all of what exists. Brightman uses the notion of category in the way Whitehead does, and he recognizes it is a mediator, the outcome of reflection.

He argues that there are two categories that apply to all possible realms of being: time and cause. However, he is not consistent on the matter of cause. He exempted feeling—the immediate presence of the present in the shining pres-ent—from causation, along with exempting it from good and evil, when he dis-cussed its "innocence." If feeling is exempt from the category of causation, then it is clear that there is a mode of being exempt from causation, and Brightman should not have claimed that causation was a category that applies to all possible realms of being. Had he followed Whitehead more closely, he could have saved himself from this inconsistency.

But Brightman, like Whitehead, encounters a similar issue in the case of time. The problem is that there is no "time" in the unanalyzed immediacy of the shining present, in spite of the fact that its three respects, memory, feeling, and purpose, are described in temporal terms. Memory, feeling, and purpose consid-ered in their *immediacy* are not aspects of temporality, but rather *refer* to aspects of temporality. When considered *apart* from this reference, as one must do in order to understand their immediacy, one recognizes that they are one and the same immediacy. Their unity comes from "a power beyond them," according to Brightman, while their immediacy is the place where there is no difference be-tween the experience of them and the existence of them. They contribute that unity (at one level) to the shining present. The three aspects were earlier ana-lyzed, and that introduces mediation. But the complex, six-fold unity of the im-mediacy of the shining present comes whole, notwithstanding the constraints language places upon us to distinguish that which is "actually indivisible," to use Brightman's phrase.

Purpose and time are the keys to bringing together the unanalyzed immedi-ate with the analyzed immediate. So given that time is supposed to be a universal category and the mediator of all, how can the unanalyzed immediacy of the shin-ing present be timeless, when considered alone? And given that purpose is a part of immediacy, the ground of interactivity, and one's purposes are supposed to in-teract with the purposes of God, nature, and others in the illuminating absent, one wonders about their status, as noted in the earlier essay. To the degree one's purposes are immediate, they also seem atemporal, or pretemporal, but to the degree they point beyond themselves to something else, they do so by means of time. So what is time on Brightman's account, and how does it relate to this issue?

A full account of time in Brightman's view would require more space than available here, but Brightman summarizes the issue as follows:

> There is no simple indivisible instant of self-experience. Every self endures in time; in its lowest terms every self is at once unitary experience and a succes-sion of experiences. In one conscious grasp, many details are comprehended as the unitary structure of one self.
>
> The minimal unity of a self accordingly is the unity of self-identification, that is, the fact that all experiences of a self belong to that self and no other. But such a unity is barren. A self is significant in proportion as it achieves meaningful

unity through rich systems of moral activity or aesthetic appreciation within the limits of self-identity. To bare experience a kind of unity is given, but a growing unity of quality is an ideal to be achieved, a task to be performed. Following Brentano's classification, we may say that higher unities of representation, of judgment, and of love always lie ahead. But these unities find their realization in and derive their actual unity from the fact that they are the experience of one monad. . . . This interrelation between unity and variety and among different forms of unity further illustrates the organic nature of the finite self.

A different perspective on this complex, minimal, organic unity of experience, here called the shining present, brings into relief another phase of the same unity. Indeed, the first and most basic characteristic of the self is its temporality indissolubly connected with time-transcendence. In order to grasp any sentence or any sensory whole or any series of events, the mind must be aware, in one actual present, both of parts and of whole. It must grasp the temporal succession of the parts and their total meaning in one act of gestalt-experience. Thus every time-span is also time-transcendence. Likewise every present experience transcends present time by an explicit or implicit reference to past time of future time. Memory, on the one hand, and anticipation and purpose, on the other, are always present in consciousness and always are temporal experiences with transtemporal reference. Even experience of the so-called timeless illustrates this same principle.[39]

It appears that the issue of the relation between the unanalyzed immediacy of the shining present and its analyzed immediacy rests on the sense in which every time-span is a time-transcendence and how this enables purposes and memories to refer beyond themselves without giving up their immediacy. Brightman emphasizes the pervasiveness of the temporality of the self, saying that "temporal experience is necessary to the *existence* of a self under any conceivable condition. If time were abolished, nothing that could be called a self would remain. Further, *every* aspect of a self's *experience* is temporal."[40] Given the strength of his language here—regarding the very existence of the self, and what pervades every part of its experience—it would be difficult to limit his claim here to the analyzed immediacy of the shining present. It is clear that Brightman is vacillating between saying that the unanalyzed immediacy of the shining present is temporal and saying that it is not temporal. Whitehead faces the same difficulty. One should note this ambiguity at the very bottom of Brightman's metaphysics and move on to the issue of purpose. Brightman equivocates on the issue of time, and this enables him to equivocate on the issue of purpose and the issue of memory. Memory was treated extensively earlier, so the treatment of purpose is all that needs to be treated here.[41] Purpose is particularly relevant here, however, because, as mentioned earlier, unlike memory, purpose grounds our moral selves.

Brightman says the following regarding time and purpose:

> The experience of time is intimately related to, and involved in, the experience of purpose. Purpose is close to the very essence of selfhood—as James and Royce, and Hegel before them, taught. It is there to some degree in every moment of the shining present. To experience is, of course, to be aware of much that the self does not voluntarily produce or approve, but no experience is entirely devoid of purposive conation or striving.[42]

This begins to point us in the direction of why the issue of purpose in the unanalyzed immediacy of our experience matters to Brightman. We can *do* nothing about the past—its quality or meaning, and the presence of the present is innocent, that is, value neutral. What is before us simply is what it is as given, and we cannot will it away, reason it away, imagine it away, or desire it away. Taken together then, the presence of the present and the presence of the past can have no moral quality precisely because there is nothing *voluntary* about them. In order for an experience to have moral value, there must be some measure of freedom in it, and freedom is a feature only of our purposes. The only aspect of time in which freedom is operative is the future, and the only way in which we can appropriate the future so as to give our present experience moral value is by way of our purposes. Brightman continues: "It has already appeared that time is a pervasive category. Purpose seems to be equally pervasive, although the extent of its application to the illuminating absent is not now under discussion. What, then, are the relations of time to purpose?"[43]

This is an important statement because it makes clear that this discussion is aimed at relating the unanalyzed immediacy of the shining present to its analyzed immediacy and that the metaphysical immediacy of the interaction of purposes in the illuminating absent is a problem that eventually will need to be confronted. Whatever is to be said about time and purpose, then, has to do with how they pervade one another and somehow enable us to transcend our little patch of analyzed immediacy. Brightman then says:

> Ordinarily the word "end" refers to a process both telic and temporal and thus is used synonymously with purpose. It is the stopping place or conclusion of a process which aimed at this end from the start. End is *finis*, final cause. Yet to purpose is far more than to aim at a stopping place. All stations are on an unending road. The "end" (destruction) of the world is not the goal of all process. The richer meaning of purpose now becomes evident in two ways. On the one hand, the "end" is present (at least tentatively) in idea throughout the process and governs every stage of it—the artist's conception of the finished painting, the scientist's ideal of experimental method, the plan of achieving peaceful understanding among nations. Wherever the end drops from view, the process tends to develop confusion, and the end is destroyed. On the other hand, the highest ends are not stopping places at all; they are but moments in the inexhaustible hours of purpose. If love is a moral end, there is no time to

cease loving. Kant's argument for immortality, defective as it may be, rests on the truth of the endlessness of moral obligation.[44]

This passage makes it clear that the finite and the infinite meet in the relation between time and purpose. Everything that has a self—which is to say all persons—has the character of being both finite and infinite. The issue is whether this drives a wedge in the self or person that can never be removed. It is easy to say that the self or person is finite in some respects and infinite in others, but when the question is asked "is the self therefore two?" Brightman wants to say "no, it is a unity." The question that follows is "how are its finite aspects united with its infinite aspects?" The answer has to be something like "there is a mediation whereby what is finite becomes infinite, and what is infinite becomes finite." One really needs, therefore, two accounts: one that begins with what is finite and shows how it becomes infinite; and another that begins with what is infinite and shows how it becomes finite. Brightman, however, adopted a method that only allows one of these—the one that begins with the finite and tries to show how it becomes infinite.

However, it needs to be pointed out here that other process philosophers, such as Whitehead and Hartshorne, have no qualms about giving both sorts of accounts; some of the details regarding Hartshorne's willingness are in the earlier essay above. They recognize that their speculative account, the one that begins with the infinite and traces it into finitude, will be insufficient alone and be to some degree unempirical. They do what they can to counterbalance this weakness by providing an empirical account as well and by remaining fallibilistic about metaphysics. In *Person and Reality,* Brightman adopts this same stance in an explicit way for the first time. His theory of categories, as well as two of the six levels of unity in the shining present, he recognizes as being "unempirical" to some extent, but he tolerates this. This is a methodological departure for Brightman from his previous stance and from Bowne's method also.[45] Whether this counts as growth or a mistake for Brightman is an interesting issue. It can certainly be counted as growth and attributed to Hartshorne's and Whitehead's influence on Brightman. But it happened too late in his thinking for him to adjust his entire philosophy to its implications. Had he lived longer, it is likely that the adjustment was within Brightman's intellectual powers. The fact that he had so boldly launched into the unempirical and employed the results pervasively in the work that he had done on *Person and Reality* indicates that Brightman still had the intellectual courage to make the change.

Returning to the issue of the interaction of purposes in the illuminating absent, one can now see why the unempirical character of what here has been called "metaphysical immediacy" might not bother Brightman as much in his last years as it would have in his earlier years, as is quite evident in the correspondence. There Brightman was left with a choice between saying that purposes interact in the illuminating absent and that an account of this must be included in his philosophy or saying that this was simply beyond our understanding and that we really might be locked into our little patch of immediacy, with philosophy having no power to get us out of it. Brightman eventually opted for the former in *Person and Reality*, in spite of its methodological dangers.

The account of the interaction of purposes in the illuminating absent will be taken up shortly, but first it is needed to finish the account of how time and purpose make the finite infinite in making unanalyzed immediacy into analyzed immediacy. Brightman asks: "If purpose, then, does not have exclusive reference to finite stretches of time having literal 'ends,' does this mean that purpose is independent of time and essentially timeless?"[46] Recalling that the problem with memory and feeling in the unanalyzed immediacy of the shining present was that they were immune, apparently, to the mediation of time, the only way that this unanalyzed immediacy can be temporal is by way of the relation between time and purpose. Brightman poses this question here. If unanalyzed immediacy is to be related to time, it must be in virtue of purpose. Brightman had argued before that there is no such thing as the "timeless"[47] and then accordingly answers his own question:

> . . . purpose may be considered in relation to time in three senses. (1) Purposes may all be achieved in finite stretches of time; if a tree or a human body has a purpose, that purpose has an "end" when the organism dies.

Note that this is metaphysical immediacy: since bodies, etc., are inferred, not given, it must be the case that whatever purposes they possess as such is beyond what is in our shining present, and if there is interaction between their purposes and their ends so considered, this interaction has to occur in the illuminating absent.

> Such purposes are exhausted in time.

These are finite purposes whose immediacy resides in the fact that they may be achieved and pass into memory, and this would seem to apply both to purposes in the unanalyzed immediacy of the shining present, and the metaphysical immediacy of the illuminating absent—an analogy that one must not overlook, since finite purposes have the same character whether they are found in what is given or what is not.

> But it is possible that (2) purposes may be inexhaustible in any time.

Obviously these are infinite purposes, perhaps the same as what Royce means by "lost causes" in *The Philosophy of Loyalty* in urging us never to dedicate ourselves in any final sense to a purpose that can be achieved, for to do so is to aim too low on a moral scale; Niebuhr says the same sort of thing in pointing out the "value of impossible ideals" in *Moral Man and Immoral Society,* so Brightman may be referring to something of this sort, and this points up the importance of the interaction of infinite purposes in the illuminating absent.

> And (3) purposes may be wholly timeless, without reference, or relevance, to time experience. The third abstract possibility has no philosophical importance. By definition it can have no basis in, or meaning for, "the shining present." It is literally meaningless.

This implies much for Brightman: the reason he believes he can speak intelligibly, if not empirically, about the immediate interactivity of infinite purposes in the illuminating absent is that they have something fundamental in common with the interactivity of finite purposes in the shining present. That "something" is their temporality. He acknowledges that he cannot rule out the possibility that there is more to purpose in the illuminating absent than temporality, but he also knows that whatever that may be it can have no relevance to the way purposes are communicated to, and present in, beings who are finite and necessarily temporal. The interactivity of finite temporal beings with infinity is conditioned not by what can be known about the character of infinite things, but by how that interaction is conditioned by the forms of finitude with which it will be required to interact in order to interact at all. To put it in earthier language: If God wants to speak to or interact with finite beings, God will have to speak a human language or take on finite form. We do not know *why* we are finite, we only know *that* we are, and we hope with every fiber of our being that it is not some sort of cosmic joke that we are enabled to know that we will come to an end. What, after all, do one's infinite purposes, the ones that one *knows* cannot be realized, amount to if they have no immediate relations to something morally valuable in the illuminating absent? And if there is no such relation regarding these infinite purposes, in what way do finite purposes—the ones that can be achieved—have any meaning beyond transient immediate experience? If one's finite purposes are not held in some sort of positive moral relation to some greater, temporally inexhaustible, purposes, then one's life is meaningless—one may get retail meaning, but at the cost of wholesale nothingness.

This is simply not acceptable to Brightman. He thinks philosophy is capable of assuaging this fear. In many ways Bowne is more accepting of this possibility, and he always invokes "faith" when confronting this possibility in any of its many guises. But Brightman puts greater reliance on the power of reason, imagination, desire, and will to set our minds at ease regarding our existential malaise. One of the main ways in which he accomplishes this is by providing an account of the nature of God in which God suffers from the same problem that we have—even God has a shining present and an illuminating absent, and, as Brightman made clear in the correspondence, God cannot know our purposes (they are not given to God) and therefore cannot know whether his own purposes interact with ours in a morally productive way in the illuminating absent. This is the "problem of God," and faith for Brightman has to do with the way finite/infinite creatures have faith in the power and goodness of their finite/infinite creator to bring about moral progress in the unfolding of the universe.

But more needs to be said about this second way in which time and purpose are related. Brightman says:

> The second possibility remains. As has been shown, this possibility is involved with the very nature of valid scientific and moral ideals. Oddly, some who deny it with reference to moral ideals are most eager to affirm it with reference to scientific ideals like the experimental method.[48] Does the inexhaustibility of some purposes in any finite time render purpose independent of time? Far from it! . . . such ideals owe their force and meaning to their applicability at all times.

In short, even though the *immediate interaction* of God's purposes, and the purposes of others, is beyond what finite understanding can grasp, that interaction is *relevant* to anything and everything that finite understanding *can* grasp. Recalling that the *continuity* of the unanalyzed immediacy of the shining present is given innocently in the presence of the present, the brutest moment of existence/experience, we can be as certain as is possible regarding anything of the relevance of infinite purposes to finite ones. If infinite purposes in the illuminating absent were wholly irrelevant, contrary or contradictory to finite purposes in the shining present, our unanalyzed immediacy would be unintelligible to us. Or so Brightman believes. That is why philosophical, scientific, and moral thinking is not a waste of time. No, we cannot rule out the possibility that the universe is ultimately meaningless or that even God is defeated in the end. What we can say is that this cannot possibly matter to anything we can understand. Brightman concludes:

> The sum of this argument is that all purposes are temporal—applying either to finite stretches of time, like an architect's blueprint for a house,

This illustrates the temporal relation between unanalyzed and analyzed immediacy in the shining present.

> or else to all times, like the ideal of rationality.

Recall that earlier on one saw that metaphysical immediacy was more like the relation between the Form of the Good and Beauty Itself, than like the Mack truck experience. Brightman simply temporalizes the participation of forms in one another's being, while simultaneously accounting for how the forms can participate in the being of particulars in virtue of their shared temporality and the principle of continuity.

In every shining present, a purposive or telic process, a Whiteheadian "subjective aim," can be detected, either transient or permanent. Purpose and time
seem inextricably involved in each other. Certainly: no time, no purpose. Quite
possibly (although this remains to be seen): no purpose, no time.[49]

The second question, regarding how God's purposes are the ground of
time, Brightman provides later in the book, although it is unfinished. Needless to
say, the argument is empirical only to the extent that it rests on the account of
immediacy herein examined. However, it must be noted that a genuine break-
through or development in Brightman's philosophy is evident here. Before this
last work, Brightman was not dealing with the full extent of the problems created
by his method. He was overly rigid about his starting point. He maintained his
starting point in this last work, but finally became emboldened, largely because
of the influence of Whitehead and Hartshorne, to launch into new areas of
thinking—ones fraught with danger for a devoted empiricist. At stake was
Brightman's moral philosophy itself, as well as his formal epistemology.

Did Brightman succeed? He never got some of the most important basic
ideas, such as cause, worked out, and he never developed an adequate philosophy
of culture, or language, to make what he was doing clear. Hartshorne's philosophy is clearly superior in this respect. But it must be recalled that Hartshorne
stood on Brightman's shoulders regarding the way finite and infinite are related
to each other both in individual persons and in God's experience. Hartshorne always credits Brightman for this insight, and it is a feature of Hartshorne's philosophy that is worked out far more than one finds in Whitehead. In other words,
Brightman's influence on Hartshorne led to an important advance in process
philosophy, and it could lead to still more, since Brightman's notion of the person is far more developed than Hartshorne's, and his moral philosophy far excels
either Whitehead's or Hartshorne's. Neither of them can claim to have framed a
moral philosophy that grounded the civil rights movement in America.
Brightman, through the brilliant agency of his student King, could make that
claim. Perhaps it is worth retrieving and developing Brightman's metaphysics of
purpose for the sole reason of finding a metaphysical ground for his ethical philosophy.

Also Brightman's account of immediacy brings together its experiential and
existential character in a far more worked out fashion than the pragmatists have
so far managed. To the experientialists, then, Brightman contributes an important link to existence. He contributes also to existentialists: his account of immediacy offers a basis for an account of authentic being-with—God, nature, and
other persons—and that is no small contribution.

Notes

The Correspondence

1. At this time Brightman was beginning work on his book *Religious Values* (New York: Abingdon, 1925), and he very likely sent Hartshorne the bibliography he had compiled for it (interspersed in the footnotes).

2. Brightman published both of these books in 1925: *An Introduction to Philosophy* (New York: Henry Holt) and *Religious Values* (cited above).

3. Evidently Brightman suffered an injury or an illness during this time. He did not experience a death in the family, and his surviving family recalls nothing specific about this time.

4. Hartshorne, review of Martin Heidegger, *Sein und Zeit,* and of Oskar Becker, *Mathematische Existenz,* from *Jahrbuch für Philosophie und phänomenologische Forschung,* vol. 8 (Halle: Max Niemeyer, 1927), in *Philosophical Review,* 38 (May 1929): 284–293.

5. Durant Drake (1878–1933), professor of philosophy at Vassar College and author of numerous books including *Problems of Conduct* (New York: Houghton Mifflin, 1914); *Mind and Its Place in Nature* (New York: Macmillan, 1925), and *The New Morality* (New York: Macmillan, 1928).

6. Brightman refers to the American Philosophical Association, which was in those days still quite small.

7. Ernest Ward Burch (1875–1933), who also took his Ph.D. at Boston University (1913), was professor of New Testament interpretation from circa 1918 to 1933 at Garrett Biblical Institute (later Garrett Theological Seminary), affiliated with the Methodist Episcopal Church, North, and associated with Northwestern University in Evanston, Illinois. Among other things, Burch wrote *The Ethical Teaching of the Gospel* (New York: Abingdon, 1925).

8. Hartshorne, "Ethics and the Assumption of Purely Private Pleasures," *International Journal of Ethics,* 40 (July 1930): 496–515.

9. Hartshorne, "Redefining God," *New Humanist,* 7 (July–August 1934): 8–15.

10. Brightman, *Personality and Religion* (New York: Abingdon, 1934).

11. Hartshorne, *The Philosophy and Psychology of Sensation* (Chicago: University of Chicago Press, 1934).

12. *Idealismus* was a journal that Brightman helped to launch by contributing a long and significant article, "Immediacy?," to the initial issue. *Idealismus,* 1, no. 1 (1934): 87–101.

13. Brightman's concept of "the Given" is a complex and important idea that will be the topic of considerable discussion in this correspondence. One cannot do justice to it in a note, but, briefly, it is the idea that, insofar as conscious beings must be conscious *of* something (which is other than their consciousness itself), that other constitutes both a condition of and an enduring problem *for* consciousness. This is true even when consciousness is thinking about itself, for in so doing it makes itself into an object for consciousness, which is then

different from consciousness itself. One finds this notion in Hegel's account of the *Fürsich-sein* of the *An sich,* from which Brightman evidently develops it. See Hegel, *Phenomenology of Spirit,* trans. A. V. Miller (Oxford: Oxford University Press, 1977), 73–85. Cf. Donald Phillip Verene's *Hegel's Recollection: A Study of Images in the Phenomenology of Spirit* (Albany: State University of New York Press, 1985), 14–26.

See the interpretive essay in Appendix 4 of this volume for an analysis of the differences between Hartshorne and Brightman on the question of the Given.

14. See G. W. Leibniz, "The Principles of Philosophy, or the Monadology," in *Philosophical Essays,* ed. R. Ariew and D. Garber (Indianapolis: Hackett, 1989), 214 (sect. 7).

15. See Leibniz, "The Principles of Philosophy, or the Monadology," 220 (sect. 57).

16. Hartshorne refers to Brightman's "Personalism and Economic Security," in *American Scholar,* 2 (May 1933): 215–223.

17. Hartshorne's article was "The New Metaphysics and Current Problems, I," in *New Frontier,* 1 (September 1934): 24–31. This was followed by part 2 in the November–December issue, 8–14.

18. The title of Brightman's article is "A Temporalist View of God," in *Journal of Religion,* 12 (October 1932): 545–555.

19. William Pepperell Montague (1873–1953), *Belief Unbound* (New Haven: Yale University Press, 1930).

20. This is essentially the same criticism of behaviorism that Hartshorne advances in his book of the same year, *The Philosophy and Psychology of Sensation* (Chicago: University of Chicago Press, 1934), 154ff. What is more interesting in this letter is that Hartshorne is speaking here, apparently, as an apologist for synechism, or Peirce's version of the principle of continuity (as actual and more than just possible). Later in his thinking, not only would Hartshorne reject synechism, but he also identifies it as one of Peirce's greatest errors. Cf. Hartshorne, *Creativity in American Philosophy* (New York: Paragon House, 1984), esp. 82, 84–85.

21. See Bernard Bosanquet (1848–1923), *The Value and Destiny of the Individual* (London: Macmillan, 1913), 136. Brightman discusses this in *The Problem of God* (New York: Abingdon, 1930), 169–171, among other places.

22. Montague, *Belief Unbound,* 83

23. The American Philosophical Association's annual Eastern Division meeting, held at New York University in December 1934.

24. Henry C. Simons (1899–1946), *A Positive Program for Laissez Faire: Some Proposals for a Liberal Economic Policy,* Public Policy Pamphlet No. 15, ed. Harry D. Gideonse (Chicago: University of Chicago Press, 1934). Hartshorne reviewed this pamphlet in *Christian Century,* 52 (June 5, 1935): 761–762.

25. Hartshorne went back and wrote this paragraph in between the lines of the typed paragraph that begins, "Your letter. . . ."

26. This is an early statement of the doctrine that Hartshorne works out in detail in *The Divine Relativity* (New Haven: Yale University Press, 1948), esp. 60ff. The next paragraph contains an early version of his view of the sociality of God, which constitutes the first chapter of the same work. Cf. "Redefining God," cited above.

27. The paragraph Hartshorne refers to from his *Philosophy and Psychology of Sensation* runs as follows:

> An objection to the doctrine of mind as a congeries of simples is that it destroys the meaning of the idea of individuality. Simples have nothing to prevent their repetition in various contexts, hence they are universals. Complexes, externally derived from these universals, are only complex universals, and it is rather too

much to ask us to believe that this is all there is to the age-old problem of the *principium individuationis.* The fact is that individuality is only identifiable by direct grasp of a thing as a "this," that is to say through its relations to the experiential context. The individual and real is what acts upon and is acted upon by us. The relative or approximate independence of the real object from ourselves as subject is the protean and social character of the latter, its lack of absolute severance from other actual and possible selves. There is for idealism, or at least for spiritualism, no self except that which is a member of all other selves and of which they are members. He who thinks that the world, without any such unity of significance as constitutes an experience, would still have been or might be a real world, and who deduces this from the fact—which spiritualism accepts—that the world without a particular human personality, Mr. X, is perfectly possible, must also be one who thinks that if from "himself" those qualities which make him Mr. X were to be subtracted, nothing of the nature of mind would remain—in short, he is one who does not believe that other minds are members of himself. Such sheer privacy is the essence of what I call "materialism." For the contrary spiritualistic doctrine, Mr. X is a social organism seen in a unique perspective in one of its members. Imagine the suppression of that member and you do not imagine the complete destruction of the organism but only its more or less slight or profound alteration, according to the importance of the member in question. The self imagining itself to vanish, in another sense imagines itself to remain, namely, in the sense in which it already identifies itself with other selves, actual and possible, human and non-human, the sense in which it overlaps and is one with them. (100–101)

28. See Donald C. Williams (1899–1983), "The Innocence of the Given," in the *Journal of Philosophy,* 30, no. 28 (1933): 617–628. Brightman comments on this article in *Journal of Philosophy* 31 (May 10, 1934): 263–268, and Williams's reply is on 268–269. Brightman and Williams, in spite of many profound differences, agreed eventually upon this doctrine of the "innocence of the Given," and it plays a crucial role in defining the concept of the "shining present," which is central to Brightman's last work, *Person and Reality,* ed. Peter Bertocci, J. E. Newhall, and Robert S. Brightman (New York: Ronald, 1958), esp. 47–48. Hartshorne appears to endorse the "innocence of the given" in this letter, but a close reading shows that he is accepting only a modified version of it. He later identifies this concept as Brightman's chief epistemological error, which locked him in a "solipsistic prison." See "Brightman's Theory of the Given and His Idea of God," reprinted in this volume. It is also worth noting that in his final work Brightman may be read as having moved in the direction of Hartshorne's position on this issue and away from his statement of it here. See the interpretive essays by Auxier in this volume for fuller details.

29. Leibniz discusses this idea in many ways throughout his career, but, for an early example, see "Meditations on Knowledge, Truth and Ideas" (1684), in *Philosophical Essays,* 27.

30. Alfred North Whitehead, *Adventures of Ideas* (New York: Macmillan, 1933), 201–208.

31. No person by the name of Vincent Evaud was awarded a Ph.D. by the University of Chicago, or any other U.S. university, between 1934 and 1955.

32. Hartshorne refers to a list published by *Christian Century* of the American Library Association's of the forty most important books, for library purposes, of 1934. The list includes Brightman's *Personality and Religion.* See *Christian Century,* 52 (July 10, 1935): 924.

33. Brightman's "bezw." is the abbreviation for the German word *beziehungsweise,* meaning "relative to."

Brightman is mixing allusions here to both Whitehead and to Ralph Barton Perry (1876–1957). Perry was well known for describing the "error of exclusive particularity," defined as "definition by initial predication . . . ," which "consists in regarding some early, familiar, or otherwise accidental characterization of a thing as definitive." Ralph Barton Perry, *Present Philosophical Tendencies* (New York: Longman's, Green, 1912), 128. On the other hand, Whitehead's criticism of "simple location" and its relation to the fallacy of misplaced concreteness is in *Science and the Modern World* (New York: Macmillan, 1925), esp. 58. Brightman's statement is consonant with Whitehead's suggestion that this is the special vice of Enlightenment-style philosophies, whether monistic or, like Brightman's, dualistic.

34. Ralph Barton Perry, *Present Philosophical Tendencies,* 104.

35. Mahanambrata Brahmachari (1906–1999) became a significant religious leader of the Vaishnavite school in India. He went on to publish a good deal of work, most of it in Bengali; see esp. the journal *Indian Philosophy and Culture* in the late 1950s and throughout the 1960s for articles in English and the portion of his dissertation that was published in the United States, *The Philosophy of Śrī Jīva Goswāmi* (Chicago: Institute of Oriental Students for the Study of Human Relations, 1937).

36. Reuben Eugene Gilmore (b. 1903); B.A. Oklahoma City University, 1924; M.A. University of Oklahoma, 1925; S.T.B. Boston University, 1936; A.B.D. in philosophy, University of Chicago; Th.D. Boston University (1947). Gilmore was president of Northwest Nazarene College in Nampa, Idaho, from 1932 to 1935. Hartshorne likely refers to a visit Gilmore paid to Chicago, since Gilmore was no longer a student at the University of Chicago in 1937.

37. Hartshorne refers here to James Ward (1843–1925), the English philosopher and psychologist who authored among other things *Naturalism and Agnosticism* (New York: Macmillan, 1899), written in 1896–1898; *The Realm of Ends or Pluralism and Theism* (Cambridge: Cambridge University Press, 1911), his Gifford lectures, 1907–1910; and *Essays in Philosophy* (Cambridge: Cambridge University Press, 1927).

38. The theory of "*rapport*" was actually Hermann Lotze's (1817–1881) and was much discussed in the philosophical and psychological literature, both in America and Europe, throughout the late nineteenth and early twentieth centuries. Cf. Ward's *The Realm of Ends,* 215–219, 254–259, 513.

39. Written on the letter at this point in Brightman's hand is the word "purpose," no doubt hearkening back to his remarks in the letter of July 25, 1935, and earlier when this question had arisen.

40. For the annual Eastern Division meeting of the American Philosophical Association.

41. It is odd that Hartshorne says he is answering a letter of three years ago, since he and Brightman had exchanged letters in the early part of the previous year, but it is also possible that Hartshorne is looking with interest at Brightman's letter of May 30, 1935. The content makes this conclusion seem likely. It is also possible that he is answering Brightman's letter of July 25, 1935, which in the letter of July 31, 1937 he mentions he had never answered.

42. Brightman has underlined "mutual immanence" and written "rapport" in the margin, following the theory of James Ward, presumably, or perhaps Lotze.

43. Brightman wrote "as a postulate" in the margin at this point.

44. Brightman refers to the 1938 meeting of the American Philosophical Association in Middletown, Connecticut.

45. Brightman refers to the dissertation of Marion B. Stokes, entitled "Clarity, Vagueness and Knowledge," which was accepted by the faculty of Boston University in 1940.

46. The date at the top of this letter is typed as 1938, but (as is common immediately after a new year) Hartshorne was still in the habit of writing "1938," even toward the end of January in 1939. The internal evidence for dating this letter 1939 is overwhelming, making it

fit in both content and sequence with the on-going discussion. Otherwise this letter comes out of the sheer blue. Brightman's February 18 answer, which directly quotes this letter, is dated 1939. One of the letters must be dated wrong, and typing "1938" in early 1939 is much more probable than typing "1939" in early 1938.

47. Brightman wrote "God only knows!" in the margin at this point.

48. The previous passage, beginning with the words "If the items are," was a written insertion by Hartshorne after he had taken the letter out of the typewriter. After the insertion is concluded on the back of page 1 of the letter with the line "But that proves nothing," Hartshorne adds, "See last quarter of page 2." He is referring to page 2 of the same letter, to the paragraph beginning "Regarding clearness, there seem to be. . . ."

49. At this point Brightman wrote "logical and ontological" in the margin.

50. Albert George Wiederhold, M.A. in philosophy (1936) and S.T.B. (1937) Boston University; Ph.D. Stanford (1940), taught at Lakeworth Community College in Lakeworth, Florida.

51. Peter A. Bertocci (1910–1989), *The Empirical Argument for God in Late British Thought* (Cambridge, Mass.: Harvard University Press, 1938). Bertocci was Brightman's student, and he assumed Brightman's chair as Borden Parker Bowne Professor of Philosophy at Boston University when Brightman died (1953) and held it until his own death.

52. Hartshorne, "The Compound Individual," in *Philosophical Essays for Alfred North Whitehead,* ed. Otis H. Lee (London: Longman's, Green, 1936), 193–220.

53. This becomes the key distinction to the argument of *The Divine Relativity*. It is anticipated by a discussion of internal relations at the beginning of *The Philosophy and Psychology of Sensation* (21ff.).

54. See Leibniz, "The Principles of Philosophy, or the Monadology," 220 (sec. 56).

55. Ibid., 213–214 (sec. 7).

56. The term *prehend* is Whitehead's, defined as "concrete facts of relatedness" under the "Categories of Existence" in *Process and Reality,* corrected ed. by David Ray Griffin and Donald W. Sherburne (New York: Free Press, 1978 [1929]), 22. Sherburne concisely says that "prehensions are the vehicles by which one actual entity becomes objectified in another" in *A Key to Whitehead's "Process and Reality"* (Chicago: University of Chicago Press, 1966), 235.

57. Hartshorne, "Four Principles of Method—with Applications," in *Monist,* 43 (January 1933): 40–72.

58. See Whitehead, *Process and Reality,* 65–66 [102].

59. Unfortunately the envelope in which Hartshorne's letter of May 8, 1939, was sent has not been preserved, so there is no way to know what the "unusual message" was.

60. See note above for Brightman's letter to Hartshorne, December 10, 1934.

61. Brightman refers to his book *A Philosophy of Religion* (New York: Prentice-Hall, 1940).

62. Professor Hartshorne particularly regrets the gender exclusivity of this book title (see the note on this at the end of the Introduction). Upon being asked in June 1996 what he would call the book if he could retitle it today, he answered, "Our Vision of God."

63. Reprinted from the *Journal of Religion,* 22 (January 1942): 96–99.

64. It is true that the University of Chicago was founded with Rockefeller money and, at John D. Rockefeller's insistence, as an explicitly Christian institution, particularly Baptist and evangelical. See George M. Marsden, *The Soul of the American University* (Oxford: Oxford University Press, 1994), 236ff. But that is not why Brightman calls it a "modern citadel" of Type I theology. What Brightman is alluding to is the neo-Thomistic worldview so forcefully advocated by Robert Maynard Hutchins (1899–1977), who took over as Chicago's president two years after Hartshorne took up his position—one wonders whether Hartshorne would have been hired to

teach there if Hutchins had been president in 1927. Even though Hutchins was at best only a lukewarm supporter of Christianity, he was nevertheless a true "friend of the forms." See Hutchins, *The Higher Learning in America* (New Haven: Yale University Press, 1936).

65. Brightman refers to Theodor Haering (1848–1928), *Hegel: Sein Wollen und sein Werk* (Leipzig: Tuebner, 1929).

66. Gersonides was a Jewish philosopher of the fourteenth century whom Hartshorne believes is wrongly neglected. See *Man's Vision of God, and the Logic of Theism* (Chicago and New York: Willett, Clark, 1941), 5.

67. This is a shortened version of Brightman's refutation of pantheism in *The Problem of God,* 115f.

68. At the top of this letter, Hartshorne typed on a different typewriter or with a new ribbon: "This letter got mislaid. I am sending it without change, except for a few lines. March 29, 1942." Indicated below are the parts of the letter that were added March 29, 1942. They are easily distinguished in the original letter by the darkness of the type itself.

69. Henry Nelson Wieman (1884–1975) preceded Hartshorne at Harvard, and he was for many years Hartshorne's colleague at the University of Chicago. He was a force in naturalistic process philosophy and theology throughout the early and middle parts of the century. See *Man's Vision of God,* 209–211.

70. See David Hume, *Dialogues Concerning Natural Religion* (written before 1761, published 1779), ed. Henry D. Aiken (New York: Hafner, 1948), esp. part 7, 47–51; Immanuel Kant, *Critique of Pure Reason* (1781, 2d ed. 1787), trans. N. Kemp Smith (New York: St. Martin's, 1965), 518–524.

71. Hartshorne, "A Philosophy of Democratic Defense," in *Science, Philosophy and Religion: Second Symposium* (New York: Conference on Science, Philosophy and Religion in Their Relation to the Democratic Way of Life, 1942), 130–172. Hartshorne also has "Commentary on 'Democracy and the Rights of Man'" in this same volume, 292.

Two years later, at the fourth symposium of the same group, Hartshorne and Brightman participated in the same session, at which Brightman presented his paper "Philosophical Ideas and Enduring Peace," and Hartshorne was among the respondents, along with Charles W. Morris, F. S. C. Northrop, Paul Weiss, and others. See *Approaches to World Peace: Fourth Symposium,* L. Bryson et al. (New York: Conference on Science Philosophy and Religion, 1944), 542–571. This work of Brightman's is crucial for understanding the debate between Hartshorne and Brightman over pacifism in this correspondence. See the interpretive essay by Mark Y. A. Davies in Appendix 4 for a fuller discussion.

72. This final sentence was added March 29, 1942. It is difficult to be certain to which of his writings Hartshorne refers here, but a pamphlet on this topic, based on a radio discussion, was published with Edwin Aubrey and Bernard Loomer (Chicago: University of Chicago Round Table, 1944). It is also possible that the pamphlet of which he speaks was never finished or never published.

73. See Whitehead's discussion of the role of experience in speculative philosophy in *Process and Reality,* 3–4.

74. Brightman wrote in the margin at this point, "Known as men know?"

75. This final paragraph was added March 29, 1942.

76. Nels Ferré (1908–1971), "Christianity and Compromise," in *Fellowship,* 8 (April 1942): 53–55. See also "The Non-Conformist Conscience" in *Christian Century,* 58 (April 30, 1941): 586–587.

77. Kant never uses the word *"Gedankenexperimente,"* but he discusses the structure, use, and justification of what might be termed thought experiments in philosophy in *The Critique of Pure Reason,* 22–26 (B xvi–xxiv).

78. Hartshorne adds the following here in the margin: "Of course math is often said to have none, but I think this may be an excess of caution. Self-evident does not mean beyond doubt, as Spiegelberg points out." Herbert Spiegelberg (1904–1990) states this in many places, but it seems most likely, given the date of this letter, that Hartshorne is thinking of Spiegelberg's article "Phenomenology of Direct Evidence," in *Philosophy and Phenomenological Research*, 2 (June 1942): 427–456.

79. These are Hartshorne's abbreviations for "absolute perfection," or "unsurpassable in conception or possibility even by itself," and "relative perfection," or "unsurpassable except by itself." See *Man's Vision of God*, 7ff.

80. In the view of many, Hartshorne's most important contribution to twentieth-century religious scholarship is the work he did on St. Anselm and the ontological argument, even though it did not come fully to fruition until some twenty years after he wrote this letter. Of particular note are the monographs: *The Logic of Perfection* (LaSalle, Ill.: Open Court, 1962) and *Anselm's Discovery: A Re-examination of the Ontological Proof for God's Existence* (LaSalle, Ill.: Open Court, 1965). Also of interest, as a briefer course in Hartshorne's interpretation of this argument, are his introduction and introduction to the second edition of St. Anselm, *Basic Writings,* trans. S. N. Deane (LaSalle, Ill.: Open Court, 1962), 3–46.

81. Brightman wrote in the margin at this point: "Then the belief is not in God as it is in me."

82. See Hartshorne's fuller discussion of his "neo-Fechnerian" view of activity and passivity, which is central to his view of human freedom, in *Man's Vision of God*, 291ff. Hartshorne bases his use of Fechner on the latter's work *Zend Avesta* (1851), which has never been fully translated into English. However, Hartshorne and William L. Reese did translate some significant passages from this work for their joint volume *Philosophers Speak of God* (Chicago: University of Chicago Press, 1953), 243–254; commentary follows on 254–257. These excerpts contain precisely the discussion of God's will to which Hartshorne refers in this letter. See also the sections from *Zend Avesta* in *Religion of a Scientist: Selections from Fechner,* ed. and trans. Walter Lowrie (New York: Pantheon Books, 1946), esp. 222ff. Hartshorne reviewed this volume in the *Journal of Religion,* 27 (April 1947): 126–128. Here Hartshorne summarizes concisely Fechner's position on the "will" of God and the presence of the "involuntary"—or as Brightman would say, "the Given"—in God. Hartshorne's essay "Lotze, Fechner, Cournot, and Other Nineteenth-Century Forerunners of Process Metaphysics," in *Insights and Oversights of Great Thinkers: An Evaluation of Western Philosophy* (Albany, N.Y.: State University of New York Press, 1983), 246–252, contributes to this discussion as well.

83. Hartshorne is referring to DeWitt H. Parker (1885–1949) and probably has in mind Parker's book *Experience and Substance* (Ann Arbor: University of Michigan Press, 1941), chs. 10–11. Hartshorne had written a review of this book about a year before he wrote this letter. See *Christian Century* 48 (July 2, 1941): 864; see also *Philosophical Review,* 51 (September 1942): 523–526.

84. Hartshorne refers here to Albert W. Palmer (1879–1945), who was president of the Chicago Theological Seminary. Palmer published many practical tracts and books on ministry; his important writings on pacifism in the *Christian Century,* which Hartshorne read at this time, include "Call a World Economic Conference!" 55 (November 9, 1938): 1368–1369; "What Should the Church Do Now?" 55 (December 21, 1938): 1573–1575; "A Christian Fourteen Points," 56 (September 13, 1939): 1101–1103; "A Road Away from War," 57 (June 19, 1940) 793–795; with Dwight J. Bradley, "America and the War," 57 (August 21, 1940): 1025–1027; "If America Is Drawn into the War, Can You, as a Christian, Participate in It or Support It? Sixth in a Series of Ten Answers," 58 (January 8, 1941): 51–53.

85. Hartshorne refers to John Hanes Holmes (1879–1964), who was a well-known minister of the Community Church of New York and chair of the American Civil Liberties Union. He wrote *New Wars for Old, Being a Statement of Radical Pacifism in Terms of Force Versus Non-Resistance, with Special Reference to Facts and Problems of the Great War* (New York: Dodd, Mead, 1916) and *Patriotism Is Not Enough* (New York: Greenburg, 1925). In the period surrounding this letter, Holmes had published some highly visible articles in the *Christian Century,* including "A Pacifist Minister to His Brethren," 56 (November 8, 1939): 1374–1377; "If American Is Drawn into the War, Can You, as a Christian, Participate in It or Support It? Second in a Series of Ten Answers," 57 (December 11, 1940): 1546ff.

86. Hartshorne most likely refers here to Robert S. Hartman, also known as Robert Schirokauer (1910–1973), whose pacifist convictions led him to flee Germany on the eve of Hitler's rise to power in 1932. At the time Hartshorne made this remark, Hartman was a vocal graduate student at Northwestern University. Hartman already had an impressive chain of accomplishments and was an outspoken pacifist before he decided to pursue philosophy as a vocation. His important writings on pacifism may be found in *Critique of War,* ed. Robert Ginsberg (Chicago: University of Chicago Press, 1970).

87. Hartshorne refers to Eduard Heimann (1889–1967), who came to the United States to teach at the New School for Social Research when Hitler rose to power in 1933. He was the author of *Communism, Fascism or Democracy?* (New York: Norton, 1938), to which Hartshorne refers here. Later he wrote *Freedom and Order: Lessons of the War* (New York: Scribner's, 1947); see p. 148 of *The Divine Relativity.* Heimann and Hartshorne were colleagues when Hartshorne was a visiting scholar at the New School during the 1941–1942 academic year.

88. Hartshorne typed "good and wise" between the words "most" and "men" but then marked through it in proofreading the letter, leaving it quite legible.

89. Assuming Hartshorne is still referring here to Ferré's article and not to a personal conversation or letter, the closest Ferré ever comes to saying this is: "He [the Christian] conforms as far as he can, for instance, in the constructive use of force issued on behalf of the people for the common welfare—that is, under judicial processes and not by a 'closed society' against other peoples," in "Christianity and Compromise," 54.

90. Hartshorne probably refers to a conversation with Ferré here, since the former seems not to have said this in print.

91. Hartshorne adds the following side note here: "The most peaceful and prosperous of all centuries resulted, with only local wars not very close together as wars go (1814–1914)."

92. Hartshorne adds the following side note here: "Policing = in interest of people generally."

93. See George Berkeley, "A Treatise Concerning the Principles of Human Knowledge," pars. 145ff. In *Principles, Dialogues and Philosophical Correspondence,* ed. Colin Murray Turbayne (Indianapolis: Bobbs-Merrill, 1965), 94ff.

94. See Spinoza, *Ethics,* part I, definition 6. In *The Ethics and Selected Letters,* trans. Samuel Shirley, ed. Seymour Feldman (Indianapolis: Hackett, 1982), 31.

95. Hartshorne refers to Fechner's "hundred pages of the chapter on 'God and the World' in *Zend-Avesta,*" in Hartshorne's review of *Religion of a Scientist: Selections from Fechner,* 127. Hartshorne was disappointed when this volume contained only six pages from that chapter. Hartshorne did later translate substantial parts of this chapter in *Philosophers Speak of God,* 243ff.

96. See Borden Parker Bowne (1847–1910), *Theism* (New York: American Book Co., 1902), 202; *Personalism* (New York: Houghton Mifflin, 1908), 96, 125–126, 279; *Introduction to Psychological Theory* (New York: Harper and Bros., 1887), 132–133; and *Theory of Thought and Knowledge* (New York: Harper and Bros., 1897), 10.

97. Brightman wrote "*True* only about personality" at this point in the margin.

98. Brightman circled the words "mind as whole" and wrote "good" in the margin at this point.

99. Hartshorne typed "which are highly dogmatic and without rational context to my sense of such matters," but then typed *x*'s over this comment, leaving it still legible upon close scrutiny, and said instead, "though I may easily have forgotten something here."

100. Originally Hartshorne typed "I'll give you a dollar for every place you have stated a carefully conceived reason for this," but he typed *x*'s over this, leaving it still fairly legible, and changed it to "Is there a carefully conceived reason against this?"

101. Brightman wrote "Belief as propositions" in the margin at this point.

102. Hartshorne's initial formulation of this sentence was "**an act of** believing *within* must be **an act of** believing *by* . . . ," but he scratched out "an act of" in both cases with a pencil.

103. C. S. Peirce, *Collected Papers*, ed. C. Hartshorne and P. Weiss (Cambridge, Mass.: Harvard University Press, 1931–1932), vol. 1, par. 274. Cf. vol. 2, par. 29.

104. See Fechner's discussion of the relation between psychology and philosophy in *Elements of Psychophysics*, vol. 1, trans. H. E. Adler, ed. D. H. Howes and E. G. Boring (New York: Holt, Rhinehart and Winston, 1966), 7ff. See also Fechner's chapter in *Philosopher's Speak of God*, 243ff.

105. See William James's chapter 4, "Concerning Fechner," in *A Pluralistic Universe* (New York: Longman's, Green, 1909), esp. 155ff.

106. Bernardino Varisco (1850–1933), author of *Know Thyself*, trans. G. Salvadori (London: Allen and Unwin, 1915). See *Philosophers Speak of God*, 271–272.

107. Brightman wrote "Ep. monism vs. Ep. dualism" in the margin at this point. One would assume that "Ep." stands for "epistemological."

108. Brightman wrote "Ep. dualism" in the margin at this point.

109. See Bergson's discussion of these two types of memory in *Matter and Memory*, trans. N. M. Paul and W. S. Palmer (New York: Zone Books, 1988 [1896]), 72–90; 150ff.

110. Brightman wrote "Right" in the margin at this point.

111. The meaning of the word "plus" in this sentence is technical and is clearer as "surplus." It means whatever the whole has, *as* a whole, which cannot be derived from the mere collecting of its parts as such.

112. In proofreading, Hartshorne added an asterisk after "difficulties" and wrote in the top margin "*This by no means applies to your whole treatment of philos., but only some parts of it."

113. Hartshorne refers to his essay "Mind and Body: Organic Sympathy," which is chapter 12 of *Beyond Humanism: Essays in the Philosophy of Nature* (Lincoln: University of Nebraska Press, 1968 [1937]) , 194–210.

114. Hartshorne at first typed "ultimate" after the word "as," but then he scratched over it with a pencil and substituted the phrase beginning with "explanatory. . . ."

115. Hartshorne wrote "After June 16th" before the address, indicating that it was the address to which Brightman should reply after June 16.

116. Brightman wrote in the margin at this point: "I.e., in the best possible way, fitted to the object—past, future, others—"

117. Brightman wrote in the margin at this point "Perfect of its kind. Memory."

118. Brightman wrote "Diff. from present exp." in the margin at this point.

119. See note accompanying Hartshorne's letter of November 9, 1942.

120. In proofreading, Hartshorne placed an asterisk at this point in the text and wrote this in the margins: "*We are mainly fighting over words, like 'in.' You mean by 'not in but known by' about what I mean by 'in (or part), though with its own self-activity as part.'"

121. Brightman underlined the words "always a unity of knowing and known" and wrote "never!" beneath it.

122. See Fechner, "The Highest Universal Law and Its Relations to Freedom: Reasons for the Existence of God," in *Philosophers Speak of God*, 245–246 (par. 317). See James, "Theism and Monism," in *Philosophers Speak of God*, 343–344 (par. 497).

123. See Brightman's letter of January 31, 1943.

124. At this point Hartshorne typed "must they also enact the very same acts?" and typed *x*'s over this, leaving it legible.

125. Brightman wrote "I find no other persons within me" at this point in the margin.

126. See Brightman's letter above of January 31, 1943.

127. Brightman wrote "Nature" in the margin at this point.

128. In 1943 Hartshorne typed "God" here, but in 1995 he changed it to "deity" in proofreading the correspondence.

129. In Hartshorne's 1995 reading of the letters, he indicated that this was an allusion to Whittier. Further research turned up a relevant line from John Greenleaf Whittier's poem "Eternal Goodness." The entire stanza is:

> I know not where His islands lift
> Their fronded palms in air;
> I only know I cannot drift
> Beyond His love and care.

See *The Complete Poetical Works of John Greenleaf Whittier* (New York: Houghton Mifflin, 1892), 442.

130. See Hartshorne's letter of June 5, 1943.

131. See Hartshorne's letter of July 31, 1937.

132. Mary Whiton Calkins (1863–1930) was an American philosopher and psychologist who taught at Wellesley from 1891 until her retirement. Her most important work in philosophy is *Persistent Problems of Philosophy* (New York: Macmillan, 1907), which went through five editions during her lifetime, the last being published in 1925.

133. There is no date on this letter, but its contents along with Brightman's letter of September 5, 1943, establish its date as September 1, 1943. Robert Gillies also came to this conclusion in "The Brightman-Hartshorne Correspondence, 1934–1944," in *Process Studies*, 17 (Spring 1988): 9–18 (see 17).

134. Albert C. Knudson (1878–1951) does not seem to have said this in print, but since Brightman was in daily contact with Knudson for many years at Boston University, it seems probable that he refers to something Knudson said in personal conversation.

135. Hegel, *Phänomenologie des Geistes* (Frankfurt am Main: Suhrkamp, 1986), 24. "The True Is the Whole," in *The Phenomenology of Spirit*, par. 20.

136. Contrary to what this sentence seems to suggest, no theory of "telepathic knowledge" ever played an important role in Brightman's epistemology. He associates the term with Ward's (and Lotze's) theory of "*rapport*," but he does mean by "telepathy" what is normally meant by the term in popular parlance, namely "transmission of thought from mind to mind without a physical medium," in *A Philosophy of Religion*, 538. Brightman only mentions telepathy as a possible source of knowledge in the same book (359). It comes up again in *Person and Reality* (109), where Brightman reaffirms it as a possible source of knowledge, making approving references to Ward, to Whitehead's use of the term in *Process and Reality*, to C. J. Ducasse's work on clairvoyance, and to J. B. Rhine's well-known work on extra sensory perception—but again the idea is not developed.

137. Brightman, "A Christian View of Nature," in *Christian Bases of World Order*, ed. Ralph E. Diffendorfer (Nashville: Abingdon-Cokesbury, 1943).

138. See David Hume's exploration of personal identity in *A Treatise of Human Nature,* ed. L. A. Selby-Bigge (Oxford: Clarendon Press, 1888), 251ff (book 1, part 4, sec. 6).

139. Hartshorne refers to his own article "A Mathematical Analysis of Theism," in *Review of Religion,* 8 (November 1943): 20–38.

140. Edgar A. Singer, Jr. (1873–1955), "Thoughts on a Translation of Schelling's *Weltalter:* A Review Article," in *Review of Religion,* 8 (November 1943): 39–54.

141. In all likelihood Hartshorne refers to *An Encyclopedia of Religion,* ed. Vergilius Ferm (New York: Philosophical Library, 1945), to which Hartshorne contributed some thirty-five articles, including the articles on pantheism (557–558) and panentheism (557). This collection appeared the year after this letter was written, although perhaps its final title had not been decided when Hartshorne wrote this, and there is no record of Hartshorne ever contributing to a book called "The Dictionary of Theology." Brightman also contributed forty articles to Ferm's encyclopedia and lent his editorial advice on the project.

142. Hartshorne, "The Formal Validity and Real Significance of the Ontological Argument," *Philosophical Review,* 53 (May 1944): 225–245.

143. Hartshorne is thanking Brightman for referring to him in Brightman's chapter in *The Philosophy of Bertrand Russell,* Library of Living Philosophers, vol. 5, ed. Paul A. Schilpp (Evanston, Ill.: Northwestern University Press, 1944), 549. Hartshorne returned the kindness in his review of the book in the *Journal of Religion,* 25 (October 1945): 280–284, defending Brightman's view of God and his criticism of Russell (281–282).

Appendix 1: Brightman's Review of *The Divine Relativity*

Reprinted from "Philosophy and Religion," in *United States Quarterly Book List,* 4 (December 1948): 431–432.

1. This review is followed by a biographical blurb on Hartshorne that is almost entirely inaccurate. There is no particular reason to believe that Brightman wrote the blurb, since he would have known very well that it was inaccurate. It is probably the work of the editors of the *United States Quarterly Book List* and is thus omitted here.

Appendix 2: Brightman's Theory of the Given and His Idea of God

1. *Person and Reality,* ed. Peter Bertocci, J. E. Newhall, and R. S. Brightman (New York: Ronald, 1958).

2. *Journal of Religion,* 12 (October 1932): 545–555.

Appendix 3: Interview with Hartshorne

This interview was taped at KOCU-TV on December 1, 1993, but it was never broadcast.

Appendix 4: God, Process, and Persons—Charles Hartshorne and Personalism

First published as "God, Process, and Persons: Charles Hartshorne," in *Process Studies,* 27 (Fall–Winter 1998): 175–199.

1. Dewey's pragmatism is reconcilable with personalism at least in the domain of education. See Auxier, "Is There Room for God in Education?" *Public Affairs Quarterly,* 9 (January 1995): 1–13.

2. Whitehead, *Religion in the Making* (Cambridge: Cambridge University Press, 1926): "Thus religious experience cannot be taken as contributing to metaphysics any direct evidence for a personal God in any sense transcendent or creative" (74). Cf. 66.

3. Hartshorne definitely thought of Brightman as a process philosopher, largely on the basis of Brightman's "A Temporalist View of God" in *Journal of Religion,* 12 (October 1932): 545–555, which Hartshorne cites with some frequency in his writing from the 1930s through

the 1950s. See Hartshorne's statements about whom he holds to be the true process idealists in "A Reply to My Critics," *The Philosophy of Charles Hartshorne,* ed. Lewis E. Hahn (LaSalle, Ill.: Open Court, 1991), 712–713.

4. McMurrin, "Hartshorne's Critique of Classical Metaphysics and Theology," in *The Philosophy of Charles Hartshorne,* 435–436.

5. See Hartshorne, *Philosophy and Psychology of Sensation* (Chicago: University of Chicago Press, 1934), 101. This passage is quoted below in full.

6. See, for example, Hartshorne, *The Divine Relativity* (New Haven: Yale University Press, 1948), 77; Brightman, *The Problem of God* (New York: Abingdon, 1930), 113; also, perhaps the clearest explanation of Brightman's notion of passivity is in *Personality and Religion* (New York: Abingdon, 1934), 82ff. In the correspondence (June 5, 1943) Hartshorne says:

> Maybe it is time to list some of the things we do agree upon. They are considerable.
>
> 1) God knows all things perfectly, including all our acts.
> 2) What we do, our acts, are done by us not by God.
> 3) Would you also say that in so far as we are active God is passive, that he suffers what we do?

Robert Gillies also notes these passages as important in "The Brightman-Hartshorne Correspondence, 1934–1944," 16. See the editors' Introduction to this book.

7. See Brightman, "Do We Have Knowledge-by-Acquaintance of the Self?" in the *Journal of Philosophy,* 41 (December 1944): 694–696: "Reflection leads us to the conclusion that the given is always a datum self. That is, it is a conscious experience, connected by memory and anticipation with past and future 'datum selves,' as well as being connected by causal interaction with its environment" (695).

8. See, for example, Hartshorne, *The Divine Relativity,* 59; and Brightman, *The Problem of God,* 116.

9. For example, one may think of Hartshorne's well-known doctrine from *The Divine Relativity* that we can know and love ourselves only because God knows and loves us (see 16–17). In Brightman's case one may see the same mode of thought at work in his account of unconscious purposes in *Person and Reality,* ed. P. Bertocci, J. E. Newhall, and R. S. Brightman (New York: Ronald, 1958). There he suggests that our tendency to call purposes unconscious is a misleading way of speaking, since they are in fact *God's* conscious purposes (see 207–209). This will become an important issue later in this essay.

10. Brightman is very cautious about using analogies in speaking about God, particularly if they involve spatializations of the relations. Here he follows a criticism that Bowne often made of "picture-thinking." See especially Brightman's letter of October 31, 1942, and our accompanying note concerning Bowne.

Hartshorne is much bolder about the use of analogy. See *The Divine Relativity,* 30–40; *Man's Vision of God,* 174–211; and his letters to Brightman of November 9, 1942, and June 5, 1943. In the latter, Hartshorne responds to Brightman's charge of "picture thinking" as follows:

> I think the debate about analogy is a misunderstanding between us. My point was an analogy between our minds and the divine. You don't avoid such analogy. The very word "mind" means it. We are agreeing here I imagine. We both seek that in our experience to which certain features in God's experience can be thought

analogous. For surely they are not identical with features of our experience. In other words analogy means generalization here.

This statement seems to settle the matter in the correspondence, and Hartshorne refocuses the issue upon disagreements about how to describe human experience, rather than its analogousness to divine experience.

11. A subject of considerable debate between Hartshorne and Brightman in the last years of the correspondence is whether Hartshorne is or is not a pantheist. Hartshorne certainly *claims* he is not a pantheist, and he complains that Brightman does not understand or appreciate the difference between pantheism and pan*en*theism. Gillies has treated this aspect of the debate as well as it can be in "The Brightman-Hartshorne Correspondence: 1934–1944," 14–15. I would add to Gillies's research the following passage by Hartshorne that describes his relation to pantheism, published shortly after having it out with Brightman over this issue:

> It will perhaps appear that our argument defines a "pantheistic" not a theistic position. But we have not identified God or perfect being with the totality of things in any sense which prevents him from being personal and free with respect to them; for he is the *flexibly* self-identical totality, which is so radically independent of its parts (and they, in another way, of it) that it will be *itself*, no matter how they, as contingent and more or less free beings, develop. . . . This view should be called "panentheism" not pantheism. Many [read Brightman and secondarily Whitehead] actually define "pantheism" as the doctrine that God is impersonal; but they also intend it to mean that God is the whole. Now this double definition neatly begs the question whether or not the whole is personal.

"The Formal Validity and Real Significance of the Ontological Argument," 241–242. One cannot possibly understand the full reason why Hartshorne includes this passage in the article unless one has read the correspondence. This passage is also the reason that the article interested Brightman enough to "respond promptly" with his final preserved letter on May 19, 1944.

12. For Brightman the term "monad" seems almost interchangeable with the "datum self"—which not only human beings have, but also God. He did not really think of monads as little bits of stuff of which the universe is made, and he was not a panpsychist. It may be the case that while Hartshorne works within the three "levels of being" set out earlier, Brightman really has only two—the datum self and God. If that is the case, then including the monadic as a separate level in this paper already favors Hartshorne's view. However, Brightman was quite willing to speak about "monads," and he never explicitly identifies them with the datum self. It is unclear whether they constitute a different level of being, but at the least, the vocabulary is not inappropriate.

Also, in at least two instances, Brightman mentions in print that he thought there may be "sub-human persons," and this suggests that perhaps he is at least open to discussing what I have been calling the "monadic level." See Brightman, "Philosophical Ideas and Enduring Peace," in *Approaches to World Peace: Fourth Symposium*, ed. L. Bryson et al. (New York: Conference on Science, Philosophy and Religion, 1944), 545, 570. Hartshorne gives a brief commentary on this paper by Brightman on page 557.

For Hartshorne, the term "monad" really means occasion of experience, and these must have a material aspect. They are also infused with a tiny portion of consciousness, or feeling of feeling. The needed material aspect, or, more properly, sensible aspect, is what makes feeling of feeling, or mutual immanence, possible as the basic relation of all actual entities. Even God must have a body for Hartshorne, i.e., the universe. But Hartshorne, as his career progressed, became less and less willing to use the term "monad," and he accepted Fechner's distinction between the two types of panpsychism (or "psychicalism," as Hartshorne came to prefer): the "monadic," which he associates with Leibniz and rejects, and the "synechological," which he associates with Fechner's view and is willing to accept with some qualifications. See Hartshorne, *Insights and Oversights of Great Thinkers* (Albany: State University of New York Press, 1983), 248–249.

One thing is certain: both Brightman and Hartshorne reject the Spinozistic version of pantheism.

13. According to the bibliography compiled by Jannette E. Newhall in *Philosophical Forum*, 12 (1954): 27. Also, Albert C. Knudson, a far more established personalist than Hartshorne, not only contributed liberally to the same volume, but even wrote the general article on "God" immediately preceding Hartshorne's article on "God, as personal." Ferm had two more established personalists to choose from and had the benefit of their editorial advice, yet he still asked Hartshorne to write the single article most near and dear to the personalist position.

14. See Ferm's "Editor's Preface," in *Encyclopedia of Religion* (New York: Philosophical Library, 1945), vii.

15. See Ferm, *Encylopedia of Religion*, 302–303.

16. Interview for KOCU Television, Oklahoma City; December 1, 1993. See Appendix 3.

17. Hartshorne, *The Divine Relativity*, 142–143. Cf. 39–40, 88–89.

18. For example, Hartshorne's statement in his letter to Brightman of January 22, 1942: ". . . in God's immediacy is everything, everything actual as such, everything potential also as such."

19. Hartshorne, *Philosophy and Psychology of Sensation*, 101.

20. See Brightman's letter of May 12, 1939.

21. See Brightman, "A Temporalist View of God," 555.

22. See Hartshorne, *Man's Vision of God*, 289.

23. See Brightman's challenge to Hartshorne in his review of *Man's Vision of God* above. As mentioned earlier, this is a shortened version of Brightman's refutation of pantheism in *The Problem of God*, 115f., and this point is adapted by him from Borden Parker Bowne's statement in *Theory of Thought and Knowledge* (New York: Harper and Bros., 1897), 55. See Hartshorne's response to this in his letter of January 22, 1942.

24. See especially *Person and Reality*, 22ff., where Brightman explicitly rejects Kant's approach as nonempirical and then characterizes his own method, using James's phrase, as "radical empiricism" that "will assume no source of information about the real, other than the experience of conscious persons". He calls this "personalistic method" and emphasizes that "the term 'personalistic' is not used to anticipate the outcome of the use of the method, but to insist on the duty of the metaphysician to include all the data provided by personal consciousness" (23). Also see the defense of his method in *Personality and Religion*, 86–97.

25. Cf. Brightman, *Person and Reality*, 35ff.

26. Brightman, "A Temporalist View of God," 544–545.

27. For example, in Brightman's article "The Self, Given and Implied—A Discussion," *Journal of Philosophy*, 31 (May 10, 1934): 263–268, he actually says that "'The Innocence of the Given' treats of the fundamental epistemological situation, which is just as truly the fundamental metaphysical situation" (263).

28. Brightman, letter of May 12, 1939.

29. The phrase "the innocence of the given" and its meaning Brightman takes from an essay by Donald C. Williams, "The Innocence of the Given," in *Journal of Philosophy*, 30 (November 9, 1933): 617–628. Brightman responded to this article (cited above) early the next

cause it acknowledges the fact of immediate experience. It is not the whole truth about any experience except the first, and perhaps even the first was too complex to be entirely innocent." *Person and Reality,* 47–48. There can be little question that Brightman is backing away from his earlier commitment to the innocence of the given. He must do this in order to avoid solipsism.

39. See Hartshorne, *The Divine Relativity,* 60ff.

40. See Brightman's letter of January 1, 1939.

41. See Brightman's discussion of the "illuminating absent" in *Person and Reality,* 34–88.

42. Hartshorne, "The Structure of Givenness," in *Philosophical Forum,* 18 (1960–1961): 22–39. This essay was reprinted under the title "Brightman's Theory of the Given and His Idea of God," in Hartshorne's *Creativity in American Philosophy* (New York: Paragon House, 1984), 196–204.

43. Hartshorne, letter of July 19, 1935.

44. Brightman, letter of July 12, 1943.

45. Hartshorne, letter of July 19, 1935.

46. In many ways this point calls to mind Descartes's criterion of clarity and distinctness of ideas as the measure of their certainty—as well as Hume's "force and vivacity" of simple impressions that enable us to distinguish present perception from memory. Epistemology seems to have progressed little in the past four hundred years.

47. Hartshorne's letter of September 1, 1943. Cf. Gillies, "The Brightman-Hartshorne Correspondence," 17.

48. Hartshorne, letter of July 19, 1935.

49. Interview for KOCU Television, Oklahoma City; December 1, 1993. See Appendix 3.

50. Hartshorne expends a great deal of effort in clarifying this difficulty later in *Creative Synthesis and Philosophic Method* (Lanham, Md.: University Press of America, 1983), originally published 1970. See esp. 241. on the matter of "literal participation."

51. Hartshorne, *Creative Synthesis and Philosophic Method,* 65.

52. Hartshorne, letter of July 31, 1937.

53. Brightman, letter of January 1, 1939.

54. Brightman, letter of May 12, 1939.

55. See Brightman's review of Hartshorne's *Man's Vision of God* in *Journal of Religion,* 22 (January 1942): 97 (reprinted above).

56. Hartshorne seems to recognize that this reduction has taken place when he says, "I assert a duality in experience, and you and Wieman seem, though I am never sure about this, to assert a *monistic* view from the standpoint of modality, of contingency and necessity" (letter of January 22, 1942). It is interesting that Brightman should insist so ardently upon his own dualism and Hartshorne's monism and then be charged with monism by Hartshorne in the same sentence in which Hartshorne is declaring his own commitment to duality, if not dualism. Gillies oversimplifies this in the conclusion to his article on the correspondence; see 18.

57. Hartshorne, "Some Causes of My Intellectual Growth," in *The Philosophy of Charles Hartshorne,* 18.

58. See Hartshorne's letter of January 22, 1942.

59. Ibid.

60. Brightman says in the letter of January 1, 1939: "I am not able to persuade myself that my participation in the life of another self is literally immanence in that other self."

61. Brightman, letter of May 12, 1939.

62. Hartshorne, *Man's Vision of God,* 73–74. Hartshorne puts this succinctly in the letter

year; and Williams replied in the same issue on 268–269. It is interesting that Williams's response makes substantially the same criticism of Brightman as Hartshorne makes. In answer
to Brightman's view "that immediate experience is a part or a product of what is customarily
called a self or person," Williams replies that this is "rather the apex than the foundation of a
philosophy, and not properly described as 'an experienced fact' nor its acceptance as 'radically
empirical'" (268). In a phrase, Williams is pointing out that Brightman's deepest commitments are metaphysical and nonempirical. Cf. Brightman, "Do We Have Knowledge-by-Acquaintance of the Self?" 694–696.

30. Brightman is not unaware of this problem. Even before the correspondence began
he formulated this exact criticism of himself and attempted to answer it in *Personality and Re-*
ligion, 86–97. There he gives a fairly unsatisfactory account of how a strict empiricist may
slowly build a reliable case on the basis of how both *reason* and *value* as given in experience
point beyond our experience and lead us through three stages of knowledge—other selves are
known first, then nature, and finally the personal God. It is quite possible that Hartshorne's
criticisms in the correspondence led Brightman to see the partial inadequacy of this kind of
defense. After the correspondence Brightman even begins to sound like a mystic whose confidence in *reason* is exhausted. See *The Spiritual Life* (New York: Abingdon-Cokesbury,
1947), esp. 135–137. However, he still has not abandoned his confidence in the idea that value
points beyond itself to a reality greater than is given in experience.

Brightman's three stages in *Personality and Religion* are reminiscent of Descartes's attempt in the *Meditations* to restore our knowledge of the world on the basis of the *cogito*, but
there the order is self, God, other minds, and finally nature. It seems fair to say that Descartes
did more for skepticism than for knowledge by attempting to escape solipsism through reason. Brightman may have reenacted the same process, and with similar effect.

31. Brightman, letter of January 31, 1943.

32. Brightman emphasizes the social character of human persons, but not as much as
does Hartshorne. For example, Brightman puts explicit limitations on the sociality of personhood in *Personality and Religion*, 144–148.

33. See Brightman, *Person and Reality*, 206ff.

34. Brightman, *Person and Reality*, 206–207. The influence of Kant's natural teleology
in the *Critique of Judgment* should be noted here.

35. Ibid., 207.

36. Brightman seems to recognize that this is a stretch for him, for when he asks the
same question of himself after his correspondence with Hartshorne has ceased, Brightman
expresses epistemological diffidence, counterbalanced only by a peculiar attitude of scriptur-
al faith:

> A human purpose is not necessarily also a divine purpose. How then can we
> tell when the purposes of our life are in harmony with the purposes of God? A per-
> sonalistic philosophy of life does not offer us absolute knowledge; . . . we discover
> divine purpose in so far as our human purposes are ruled by the New Testament
> principles of *logos* and *agape*—reason and love.

Nature and Values (New York: Abingdon-Cokesbury, 1945), 159.

37. Brightman, *Person and Reality*, 56n.

38. Brightman makes the needed qualification of "the innocence of the given" to accommodate this change of view, saying "the innocence of 'the given' . . . does not mean that the
given is always or in all respects innocent. . . . The present as given is innocent. Every present
can be viewed in its innocence, but the point of view of innocence is important chiefly be-

of July 31, 1937: "Personalism apparently accepts a conception of causality not illustrated in experience in order to transcend experience."

63. Hartshorne, letter of January 30, 1939.

64. Brightman, letter of May 12, 1939.

65. Hartshorne, letter of January 30, 1939.

66. Brightman, letter of December 10, 1934.

67. Brightman himself seems to concur in this judgment to some degree in that he recognizes in Hartshorne's *The Divine Relativity* that "the idea of God as personal is retained and even enlarged." See Brightman's review in "Philosophy and Religion," *United States Quarterly Book List,* 4 (1948): 431–432.

68. Hartshorne, letter of June 5, 1943.

69. The author thanks Tom Buford and the Personalist Discussion Group for inviting him to speak on the correspondence before their annual session at the 1995 Eastern Division meeting of the American Philosophical Association. Without the invitation this essay would not have been written, and it has contributed a great deal to helping clarify the author's thoughts about the correspondence—which has in turn improved the editing work. The author also acknowledges the cooperation of Margaret Goosetray of the special collections division of the Mugar Library at Boston University and the generous comments on this paper made by my former colleagues Toby Sarrge and Mark Y. A. Davies.

Appendix 5: The Pacifism Debate in the Correspondence

First published as "Pacifism Debate in the Hartshorne-Brightman Correspondence," in *Process Studies,* 27 (Fall–Winter 1998): 200–214.

1. Reprinted above between the excepts from *Man's Vision of God* (following Brightman's letter of May 12, 1939) and Hartshorne's letter of January 22, 1942.

2. Hartshorne, *Man's Vision of God and the Logic of Theism,* (Chicago and New York: Willett, Clark, 1941), 167. The complete argument is also reprinted above in the midst of the correspondence, between Brightman's letter of May 12, 1939, and Brightman's review of *Man's Vision of God.*

3. Ibid., 168.

4. Ibid., 165.

5. Ibid., 168.

6. Ibid., 168, 173.

7. Ibid., 173.

8. Ibid.

9. Ibid., 168.

10. Brightman, review of *Man's Vision of God,* 98.

11. Hartshorne, letter of January 22, 1942, edited and sent March 29, 1942. The last sentence quoted was added on March 29, 1942. Hartshorne refers in this passage to his essay "A Philosophy of Democratic Defense," in *Science, Philosophy, and Religion: Second Symposium* (New York: Conference on Science, Philosophy, and Religion in Their Relation to the Democratic Way of Life, 1942), 130–172.

12. Brightman, letter of September 18, 1942. The article referenced in this passage is Nels Ferré, "Christianity and Compromise," *Fellowship,* 8 (April 1942): 53–55.

13. Hartshorne, letter of September 23, 1942.

14. Ibid.

15. Hartshorne, letter of September 23, 1942. See the note accompanying this letter above for information on Eduard Heimann.

16. Ibid. The reader should note that the words "good and wise" were stricken with a pen mark before Hartshorne mailed the letter.

17. Ibid.

18. Ibid.

19. Brightman, letter of September 25, 1942.

20. Charles Hartshorne, "How Christians Should Think about the Peace," a radio discussion by Edwin Aubrey, Charles Hartshorne, and Bernard Loomer. Pamphlet. *University of Chicago Round Table* (April 9, 1944): 6.

21. Charles Hartshorne, "A Philosophy of Democratic Defense," in *Science, Philosophy, and Religion: Second Symposium*, 133.

22. Ibid., 139.

23. Charles Hartshorne, comment on "Philosophical Ideas and Enduring Peace," by Edgar S. Brightman, in *Approaches to World Peace, Fourth Symposium*, ed. Lyman Bryson, Louis Finkelstein, and Robert M. MacIver (New York: Harper & Bros., 1944), 557.

24. Hartshorne, "How Christians Should Think about the Peace," 12.

25. Charles Hartshorne, *Beyond Humanism: Essays in the New Philosophy of Nature* (Chicago and New York: Willett, Clark, 1937), 26–27.

26. Edgar S. Brightman, "Philosophical Ideas and Enduring Peace," in *Approaches to World Peace, Fourth Symposium*, ed. Lyman Bryson, Louis Finkelstein, and Robert M. MacIver, (New York: Harper & Bros., 1944), 544.

27. Ibid.

28. Ibid.

29. Ibid.

30. Ibid., 546–553.

31. Ibid., 548.

32. Ibid., 553.

33. Edgar S. Brightman, *Moral Laws* (New York: Abingdon, 1933), 45.

34. Ibid., 125.

35. Ibid., 142.

36. Ibid., 154.

37. Ibid., 156.

38. Edgar S. Brightman, "The Best Possible World," in *Journal of Bible & Religion*, 11 (February 1943): 8.

39. Ibid., 14–15.

40. Brightman, *Moral Laws*, 223.

41. Brightman, "The Best Possible World," 10.

42. Ibid., 15.

43. Cf. Randall C. Morris, *Process Philosophy and Political Ideology: The Social and Political Thought of Alfred North Whitehead and Charles Hartshorne*, (Albany: State University of New York Press, 1991), 167.

44. Hartshorne, comment on "Philosophical Ideas and Enduring Peace," 557.

45. Edgar S. Brightman, "The Philosophy of World Community," in *World Order*, ed. F. Ernest. Johnson (New York and London: Harper & Bros., 1945), 23.

46. Martin Luther King, Jr., *Stride toward Freedom: The Montgomery Story* (New York: Harper & Row, 1958), 98.

47. For an excellent account of the influence of the moral laws on King's thought, see Walter G. Muelder, "Martin Luther King, Jr. and the Moral Law," Lecture given at Morehouse College, 1983; Special Collections, Boston University School of Theology Library, Boston, Mass.

48. John J. Ansbro elaborates on this point in his *Martin Luther King, Jr.: The Making of a Mind* (Maryknoll, N.Y.: Orbis Books, 1982), see especially chaps. 4. and 6.

Appendix 6: Immediacy and Purpose in Brightman's Philosophy

1. Brightman, *A Philosophy of Ideals* (New York: Henry Holt, 1928), 13–19, italics added.

2. Brightman quotes with favor Hegel's assertion in the *Science of Logic* that "there is nothing in Heaven, Nature, Spirit, or anywhere which does not contain immediacy as well as mediacy" (*Person and Reality*, 45). For a discussion of mediation and immediacy in Hegel's *Phenomenology of Spirit*, see Auxier, "The Return of the Initiate: Hegel on Bread and Wine," in the *Owl of Minerva*, 22 (Spring 1991): 191–208. Here the issue of mediation is treated by means of the example of Hegel's treatment of the relation between spirit and life in the Eucharist and the Eleusinian Mysteries, but it is as good an approach as any to defending the thesis that desire (*Begierde*) is mediation for Hegel. This is nothing like Brightman's view and is really closer to Diotima's speech in Plato's *Symposium* (201d-212b) than to anything distinctively modern.

3. Lotze, *Logic: In Three Books; of Thought, of Investigation, of Knowledge,* trans. Bernard Bosanquet, 2d ed. (Oxford: Clarendon Press, 1888), II: 104–105 (278).

4. See Lotze, *Logic,* II: 79, 83, 103ff.

5. See Brightman, *Person and Reality,* 38. Here Brightman explicitly cites Lotze favorably in setting out his notion of "fact." It is common for Brightman to cite Lotze and Bowne in the same sentence, crediting them jointly with an idea. This is appropriate since Bowne was Lotze's student and dedicated the first edition of his *Metaphysics: A Study of First Principles* (New York: Harper & Bros., 1892) to Lotze. But Bowne also said that for him, "Leibnitz furnishes the starting-point, Herbart supplies the method, and the conclusions reached are essentially those of Lotze. I have reached them, for the most part, by strictly independent reflection; but, so far as their character is concerned, there would be no great misrepresentation in calling them Lotzian" (vii). This was all cut out of the revised edition of *Metaphysics*. But it explains Brightman's pattern or habit of citing things as he does. The question of what he got directly from Bowne and what he took from his own reading of Lotze would not be worth pursuing, at least regarding "immediacy." The point is that he writes like Lotze does even more than he writes like Bowne does.

6. See G. M. A. Grube, *Plato's Thought* (Boston: Beacon, 1958 [1935]), 19, 34–35, 39–42, 239.

7. Descartes, *The Philosophical Writings of Descartes,* ed. and trans. John Cottingham et al., vol. 2 (Cambridge: Cambridge University Press, 1984), 122–124 (reply to Hobbes's Second Objection).

8. See Crispin Sartwell, *Obscenity, Anarchy, Reality* (Albany: State University of New York Press, 1996), 134–135. Sartwell argues that what here is called (c) is the *only* kind of immediacy that is not just the bare abstractions and worthless inventions of philosophers who wish to turn their backs on reality, and he condemns things such as "ideals" wholesale, since in saying that something that is not *ought* to be, one says by implication that what *is* ought not to be. Although this as a false dichotomy, there is a message in it that *ought* to be heeded, even if that means one is telling the world that *is* (the one in which no one pays much attention to Sartwell's shrill rhetoric) that it ought not to be.

9. Although he does not always do so, Brightman does sometimes use the term "metaphysical" in the ways that it is used here. See for example, *Person and Reality*, 272, as well as the quote from *A Philosophy of Ideals* above: "A mere physical or metaphysical. . . ."

10. See Brightman, *Person and Reality,* 61.

11. Ibid.

12. Ibid., 27.

13. See Auxier, "Return of the Initiate," 200–208, for an account of how language is related to immediacy by means of desire for Hegel.

14. This importance of this notion of "problem" becomes clear when one notes that it is the central idea in Brightman's next two books, *The Problem of God* (New York: Abingdon, 1930) and *The Finding of God* (New York: Abingdon, 1931).

15. Brightman, *Person and Reality*, 272. This passage occurs in the portion of the book reconstructed by the editors from Brightman's notes. What the editors did in this part of the book was to take passages from Brightman's other books that dealt with the same subjects his notes and outlines mentioned and then alter the grammar as little as possible in weaving them into a continuous treatment of the subject at hand. Thus the extended quote with the blood analogy is from Brightman's article "Immediacy?" in *Idealismus*, 1, no. 1 (1934): 97. *Idealismus* was a journal that Brightman helped to launch by contributing this significant article to the initial issue (87–101).

16. See Brightman, *Person and Reality*, 58.

17. Ibid., 40–41. Here Brightman makes it clear that time is a mediator in the unanalyzed shining present. It is also a category of all possible realms of being (see 103–104), but this is a postanalytical proposition about time—the results of an investigation, not the starting place, to recall the distinction Brightman borrowed from Loewenberg, cited earlier.

18. See Brightman, *Person and Reality*, 267.

19. Ibid., 142, 261; Brightman regards Royce's account of a time-span in *The World and the Individual* to be a still closer analogy to his idea of the "shining present."

20. Ibid., 44, 99.

21. Ibid., 142; the Whitehead quote is from *Process and Reality* (New York: Macmillan, 1929), 95. See also *Person and Reality*, 111.

22. Brightman, *Person and Reality*, 61.

23. Ibid., 36.

24. Ibid., 61.

25. Ibid., 50.

26. Ibid., 261–262.

27. José Ortega y Gasset, *History as a System*, trans. Helene Weyl (New York: Norton, 1961), 217.

28. In distinguishing the temporality of the shining present from its duration, Brightman states, "There is no objection to saying that the shining present is temporal. The present is surely present; and however fragmentary it is, it contains a real duration—a present-past-future 'time-span' grasped in one whole experience," *Person and Reality*, 40.

29. Ibid., 53. At this point Brightman places a note to Royce, Whitehead, and Bergson that praises Royce's notion of a "time-span" and stating Bergson's *durée réelle* is close to it but less analyzed. He criticizes Whitehead for too much ambiguity on the topic of duration.

30. Ibid., 122.

31. Ibid., 125–126.

32. Ibid., 47–48.

33. Ibid., 48. The statement about there being a "first" experience may be problematic, since Brightman holds God to be thoroughly temporal and time to have had no beginning (see *Person and Reality*, 133). Granted, time could be bigger than God, but Brightman begs off of giving a complete account of God on points such as this (see *Person and Reality*, 309),

so it is hard to know where one stands, aside from admitting that not all of God's memory, feeling, and purposes are available to us.

34. Ibid., 263.

35. See Martin Heidegger, "What Is Metaphysics?" in *Basic Writings*, revised and expanded ed. by David Farrell Krell (San Francisco: HarperCollins, 1993), 103.

36. Brightman, *Person and Reality*, 272. See note 16 above for an explanation of how the editors crafted this section of the book from earlier publications. The extended quote with the blood analogy is from Brightman's article "Immediacy?" 97.

37. For Brightman's admission that his account of the shining present may not be adequate, see *Person and Reality*, 46, where he admits that the term "shining present" is abstract and figurative and that the phenomenon he wishes to describe evades all attempts to describe it.

38. Brightman, *Nature and Values* (New York: Abingdon-Cokesbury, 1945).

39. Brightman, *Person and Reality*, 262–263.

40. Ibid., 263, italics added.

41. See the section "The Past as a Test Case" in Auxier, "God, Process and Persons: Charles Hartshorne and Personalism," above.

42. Brightman, *Person and Reality*, 123.

43. Ibid.

44. Ibid., 124.

45. The reader will find a thorough account of this feature of Bowne's method, called "the Bowne move" in Auxier, "Bowne on Time, Evolution and History," forthcoming in the *Journal of Speculative Philosophy.*

46. Brightman, *Person and Reality*, 124.

47. Ibid., 117ff. See also 322–331.

48. The issue of the growth of human knowledge by means of scientific method has not been discussed herein, but the same metaphysical considerations that make possible a moral meaning in human life are those that ground the possibility of the growth of knowledge for Brightman. As a result the preceeding discussion can and should be used to provide the basis for understanding Brightman's formal epistemology.

49. Brightman, *Person and Reality*, 124–125.

Index